ABBEY ROAD

Also by David Hepworth

1971: Never a Dull Moment

Uncommon People: The Rise and Fall of the Rock Stars

Nothing is Real: The Beatles Were Underrated and Other Sweeping Statements About Pop

A Fabulous Creation

The Rock & Roll A Level

Overpaid, Oversexed and Over There: How a Few Skinny Brits with Bad Teeth Rocked America

ABBEY ROAD

THE INSIDE STORY OF THE WORLD'S MOST FAMOUS RECORDING STUDIO

DAVID HEPWORTH

WITH A FOREWORD BY
PAUL McCARTNEY

PEGASUS BOOKS
NEW YORK LONDON

ABBEY ROAD

Pegasus Books, Ltd.
148 West 37th Street, 13th Floor
New York, NY 10018

First Pegasus Books cloth edition August 2023

ISBN: 978-1-63936-431-2

10 9 8 7 6 5 4 3 2 1

Printed in the United States of America
Distributed by Simon & Schuster
www.pegasusbooks.com

To Sam

For the music makers and the dreamers of dreams.
For the movers and shakers of the world, forever,
it seems.

(Inspired by *Ode*, by Arthur O'Shaughnessy)

Contents

Foreword

I remember the first time walking into Abbey Road sixty years ago, it was such a scary session with George Martin there as the presiding 'grown-up'. Then thinking about how much we grew from doing the first album in a day to spending weeks and weeks in the studio . . . To think of how many great memories and creative moments that happened there, it's very hard to pick one out. But I do always remember recording the orchestra on 'A Day In The Life' – that was pretty special.

You know, I try to resist going, 'Wow, this is where it all happened . . .', but it really is trippy. When I visit, it makes me want to just sit and think, *Ah, there's John doing 'Girl' . . .*, etc. The stars really aligned for us at Abbey Road in terms of the creative stuff we brought, the musical knowledge and direction George Martin brought, and the technical side of things with some incredible engineers who were inventing new ways to record, and then also some incredible gear. It's the only studio I've ever known in the world where you have one grand piano, one super grand, one medium grand . . . everything, just there in the studio for normal use. Long before and long after the Beatles some of the best music in the world was born in those rooms, and they are still carrying on as one of the best studios in the world. Long live Abbey Road!

Paul McCartney

Intro:
THE LONG AND WINDING ROAD

They come from all over the world.

They ascend in gaggles via the pleasingly period escalator from the tube station at St John's Wood. They ask locals for directions. These people have issued the same instructions so many times they point in the right direction without following the gesture with their eyes. Rounding the corner of Grove End Road these pilgrims in skinny jeans, who may have found their way here from Murmansk, Manchester or Mobile, Alabama, find it hard to suppress a Christmas morning smile on finding themselves suddenly inside a picture with which they have been familiar since they can remember, looking up and down this particular road and gazing dreamily at this very particular pedestrian crossing.

London has many such crossings – known locally as 'zebras' – but this one is unique. It's the only one in the land which is listed as a site of outstanding historical interest. As such it may not be repositioned by so much as a foot in either direction without discussions at the highest level and in all probability questions in the House of

Commons. It is also the only zebra people queue up to cross, hoping that they and their companions might be magically isolated and captured in the same way those original four mates were all those years ago. The crossing is also, to the acute frustration of corporate bean counters keen to look at every possible way in which musical history might be 'monetized', one destination of historical interest in London that remains free.

London is not short of historical attractions. Londoners are used to seeing reluctant processions of adolescents being ushered in organized parties through the baleful portals of the Tower of London or beneath the improving colonnade of the National Gallery. The difference with this site of cultural and historical interest is that these young people have come under their own steam and of their own volition, in groups of two and three, and since there are not even any signs to indicate what they have come looking for, this may even have involved some effort. No guide book has sent them here. No teacher has prodded them in this particular direction. They come because they want to, and they come without the expectation of actually seeing anything more spectacular than what they do see as they round Grove End Road.

The house itself, a solid Victorian family villa which has been steadily extended over the years to accommodate the changing shape of the business that is carried on behind its facade, is of no great distinction. The two iron gates which separate its small car park from the road outside are heavy enough to discourage anyone minded to just drop in and check out the place. If they pressed their case further they would be greeted by signs sternly pointing out that photography of any kind is not permitted within the building. In the basement of the address next door, which houses some of the studios' considerable back office functions, is a gift shop where tourists can purchase T-shirts, tea mugs or a leather 'ticket to ride' card holder for their travel card. A considerable number of the younger visitors feel the need to add their message of devotion to the thousands of others which cover the low wall outside. Every month Westminster Council, keen to placate those local taxpayers who feel that graffiti, even of the sort seeking to assert a spiritual connection between the late John Lennon and Pedro from Argentina, lowers the tone of the neighbourhood, sends a team of painters to whitewash the wall and the scribbling starts all over again on a clean sheet.

It would not be accurate to say these scribblers have been drawn here by nostalgia. Most of the people who take this journey are far too young to remember Britpop, let alone the Beatles. They have been brought up in an altogether different world. In the sense that they conduct much of their lives online they're also what we call digital natives, children of the iPhone, who have grown up with the idea that a few clicks on their hand-held device can conjure any entertainment experience. All the music they consume has been assembled by a person or persons using some form of computer and can be accessed in the same way. Where and when it originated seems neither here nor there. Yet they know some remarkable things have taken place where they are now standing. Furthermore they come to this particular London pavement, like pilgrims of long ago, drawn by the opportunity to momentarily genuflect and re-enact something which occurred in the same few feet in a few minutes during a lunch hour over fifty years earlier. They're additionally attracted by the idea that this crossing sits outside a very special place where things occurred which could only be done in a place of this kind. Religions have been based on flimsier foundations.

They can see in their mind's eye John, Ringo, Paul and George crossing that street in an easterly direction on that August morning in 1969. Were they of a William Blake turn of mind they might even close their eyes and picture the choir invisible whose feet have also walked across that same road in the ninety years since the studio opened: Edward Elgar, Paul Robeson, George Bernard Shaw, Steven Spielberg, Yehudi Menuhin, Bette Davis, Peter Sellers, Ravi Shankar, Gracie Fields, Syd Barrett, Judy Garland, Ella Fitzgerald, Glenn Miller, Sophia Loren, Luciano Pavarotti, Eartha Kitt, Al Bowlly, Noël Coward, Liam Gallagher, Amy Winehouse, John Barry, Kate Bush, Kanye West and Jacqueline du Pré.

Not all the musicians who did their work here over the years are accorded quite the same bold-face reverence – this has also been the *atelier* of Pinky and Perky, Ken Dodd, Russ Conway, Ken 'Snake-hips' Johnson, Freddie and the Dreamers, the Temperance Seven, Bucks Fizz, Reg Dwight, the Mike Sammes Singers, Mrs Mills, and Manuel and the Music of the Mountains – but the building and the people who worked in it took that work every bit as seriously.

The mainly young people outside on the crossing have never actually been inside a recording studio and in all probability never will, but they have nonetheless absorbed some sketchy idea of what is supposed to go on in a recording studio. This idea may have been assembled from dimly remembered scenes in ancient movies, the kind in which the 'recording' light would go on and an ulcerated executive would reach for the talkback through a pall of smoke and then bark something like 'Go, fellas. Take one!' At this the band of youngsters on the other side of the glass would try all kinds of things which didn't quite make it – as we can see from the concerned faces in the control room – before finally one youngster would try another thing, possibly something which nobody had tried before, and this time when they listened to it over the playback the kids and the grown-ups exchanged that look, that very special look which can only indicate fame and money. These are the magic moments which studios are in the business of facilitating.

Of course such a superficial view passes over the drudgery, the personal friction and the wrestling with recalcitrant equipment with which all such processes are beset, but there is nonetheless more than a kernel of truth in it. That truth is that what's going on behind the doors of a studio like Abbey Road – and as we shall see there never was a studio like Abbey Road and there certainly never will be again – is the attempt to create something which is greater than the sum of the parts involved. It's attempting to ignite a spark which was not there when the musicians arrived at the studio. It's attempting to make something happen which could never have happened had they remained at home and phoned it in. It's the further urge to capture that something and polish it in such a way that people will want to listen to the resulting record again and again and again, and again fifty years later. This is the essential business going on behind the doors of Abbey Road, the doors through which you may not enter. What's been going on there for over ninety years has called for skills that are musical, chemical, mechanical, technical, interpersonal, logistical, managerial and, romantics might be tempted to add, close to magic.

What follows is for the people who believe in the magic.

1

In the pioneering days, Fred Gaisberg (centre) needed singers who could project sufficiently to make an impression on the heavy recording equipment in his Covent Garden studio.

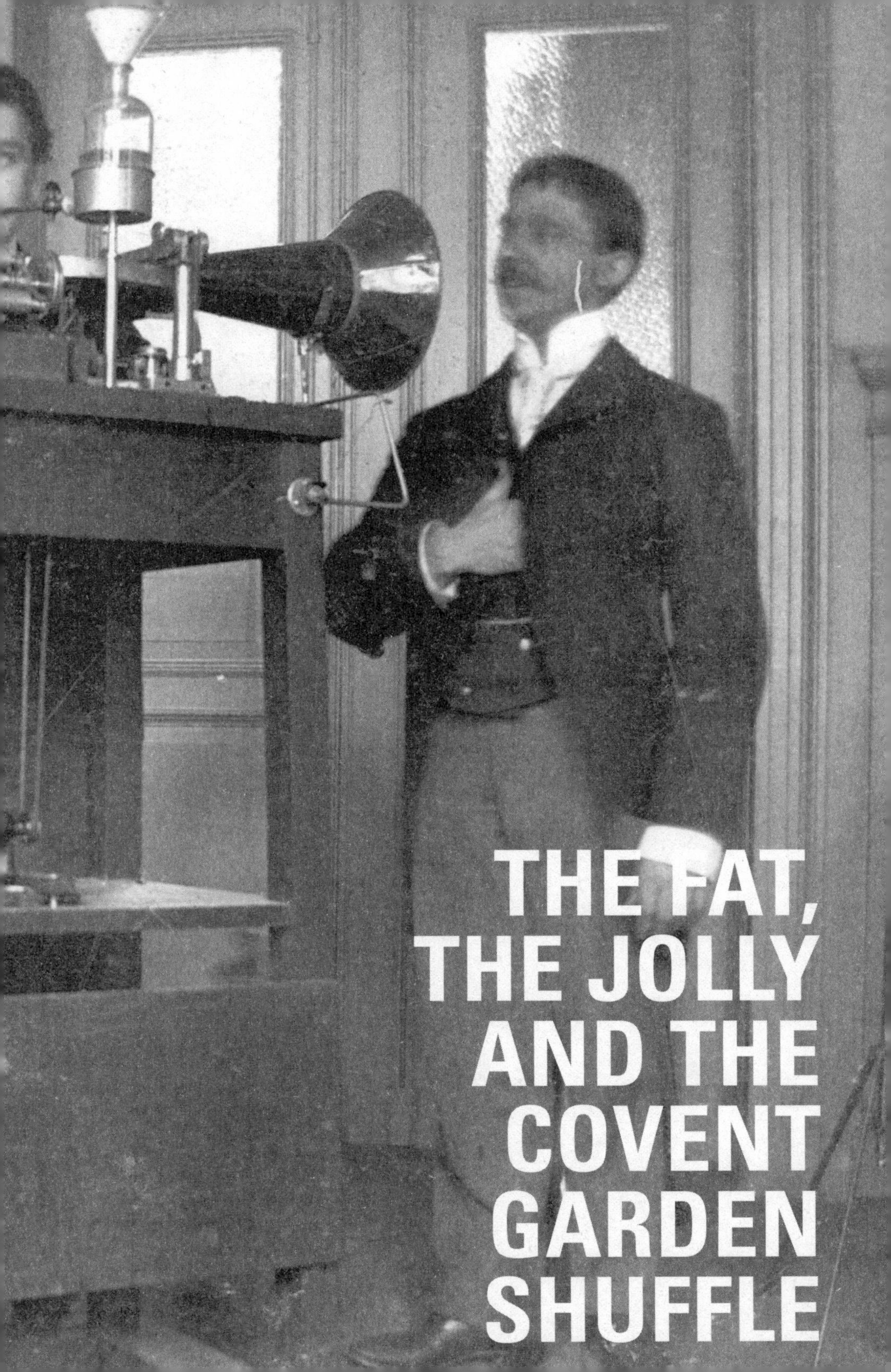

THE FAT, THE JOLLY AND THE COVENT GARDEN SHUFFLE

In 1898, when the first recording studio was opened in London, the majority of people went through their entire lives without expecting ever to hear the sound of their own voice. Nowadays, on the other hand, the whole business of recording is so commonplace that small children grow up expecting every noteworthy moment to be endlessly replayed.

The early phonograph, which was the first form of record player, was not initially for entertainment at all. It was marketed as a talking rather than a singing machine. Its backers saw it primarily as a business tool into which bosses could dictate and from which typists could transcribe. Even when it branched out from business to artistic use nobody thought of investing in a dedicated place where an artist might go to record. It was far more likely that the recording equipment would have to go to the subject, no matter how much trouble might be involved. In the late nineteenth and early twentieth centuries opera was as much of a force in music as hip hop is today and the big stars were similarly keen on exacting the tribute they felt they were due from any new technology that demanded their cooperation. Thus the tenor Francesco Tamagno, for instance, would only agree to record for the Gramophone Company, one of the new ventures which would eventually be absorbed into EMI when it formed in 1931, if they sold his records at a pound each and gave him his own label. Even when they acquiesced and handed him a £2,000 advance he still insisted their engineer haul his heavy recording equipment to his Ligurian home high above Ospedaletti where the recordings would actually be made.

These recordings were a success, which is probably what encouraged the Australian soprano Nellie Melba to allow the Gramophone Company to release recordings she had already made for her own purposes. To outdo Tamagno she insisted these be sold for a guinea each, which was a shilling more expensive than his. Ears were pricking up across the world of opera upon hearing of this strange new revenue stream. It piqued the interest of the Italian diva Adelina Patti, then living in retirement in a castle in Wales. After fully two years of negotiations, she allowed that she might just be prepared to give the record-buying public a taste of the genius they had only read about if the record company shipped all their kit to her distant fastness in Powys and just hung about until she felt like singing. When she finally came before the equipment it was clear that at sixty-two her golden days were gone.

The first proper recording studio in London was set up in the smoking room of the old Coburn Hotel on Maiden Lane in Covent Garden in 1898. This was just off the Strand, Europe's cab-choked Great White Way, which at the time had more theatres than any other street in London. Here the night air still reeked of burnt cork and limelight. Here Bram Stoker had dreamed up Dracula while totting up the nightly receipts at the Lyceum. Here Gilbert and Sullivan, in their pomp in the 1880s, unveiled their every new masterpiece at the Savoy Theatre, the first public building in the world to be lit entirely by electricity. Theatreland was its own world with its own rules. A few days before Christmas in 1897 the actor William Terriss was murdered while entering the stage door of the Adelphi Theatre on Maiden Lane. His murderer had only recently been consigned to Broadmoor when the twenty-five-year-old Fred

Gaisberg arrived from the United States to supervise recordings for the Gramophone Company at 31 Maiden Lane.

Born in Washington DC to a German immigrant family, Fred had a grounding in music and a passionate interest in the technology which promised to capture it. Having impressed Emil Berliner, the American inventor of the gramophone record which supplanted Edison's cylinder, with his knack for persuading people to submit to being recorded, he was dispatched to London to help Berliner's English partners drum up interest among potential investors. The new company brought him from the US because he had the potential to be a one-man record industry. In his new role at Maiden Lane he had to be. Fred had to find the talent and also operate technology which was anything but plug-and-play. At the time the last word in sophisticated equipment in this regard was a recording machine placed on a high stand from which would project a long thin trumpet into which the singer was invited to pour his or her heart. This worked on entirely mechanical principles. Because, according to Gaisberg, the diaphragm which captured the performance was not very sensitive, it needed a certain kind of performer to make the kind of record that people would pay for. Recording at the time was 90 per cent projection, much as it was in the unamplified world of the music hall. One of the reasons the tenor Enrico Caruso became the first superstar recording artist (he made almost half a million pounds from recordings in his lifetime) was that he had a voice strong enough to be heard above the surface noise which was an inescapable fact of recording life.

Because one of the main challenges in those early days was persuading performers to come in and give recording a try, Gaisberg had to be ready to do further duty as accompanist. On one occasion in 1902 when a long-wooed artist turned up unexpectedly alone, Fred had to start the recording machine and then immediately dash to the piano to accompany the famous droll on a recording of one of his most popular tunes, 'Mrs Kelly'. Because he was also a champion clog dancer they hoisted him on to a table to record his distinctive solo. It proved to be the artist's last session. The legendary Dan Leno, arguably the inventor of the English comic tradition, died two years later in 1904.

The emergence of a recorded music business depended on two things. The first was the recording machinery that captured the sound in the studio. The second was the music carrier that delivered the recording into the home. Carriers had moved on from the cylinder to the relatively sensitive machinery of Berliner's gramophone. However, it was still the case that to make a successful record required the kind of back-stalls belter who could project sufficiently to loosen the mouldings in the dress circle, articulate with piercing clarity so that the audience could follow the dense plot of a comic song, and deliver a climax sufficiently jarring to rouse even the somnolent stage-door Johnnies who might have dined too well prior to taking their seats.

Gaisberg often found these very qualities directly across Maiden Lane in London's oldest restaurant, Rules, which was founded in 1798, then as now a place with a special appeal to theatricals. One of the first to cross the road was Burt Shepard, an experienced entertainer popular on both sides of the Atlantic thanks to his mastery of such crowd-pleasing favourites as the tear-stained Irish ballad, the stirring negro spiritual, the ever-popular yodel and his 'Laughing Song', which never failed to fill the stage with flags. With Burt as his Judas goat, Fred would entice other music-hall brethren into the studios, often with as much thought to their own amusement as to the benefit of posterity. In this way Fred was granted the rare privilege of capturing voices which would otherwise have escaped entirely; it's thanks to him that we have them still, like the last transmissions from a dying planet on which nobody had grown up with the expectation of ever being able to hear anything twice. It is in this way that the likes of Gus Elen, Albert Chevalier, Marie Lloyd and Vesta Tilley came to be memorialized, albeit through a fog, on records bearing the distinctive label of His Master's Voice.

A tougher sell than the over-lunched stars of the business of show were the heavily corseted battle-axes of grand opera. These divas who filled the finest venues all over the world took some persuading that a recording studio of any kind was a fit and proper place on which to set their expensively shod feet. When the French soprano Emma Calvé, who originated the title role in Bizet's *Carmen*, was first delivered to Maiden Lane by carriage and four in 1902 she initially refused to alight, claiming she had arrived at a place that looked more like a thieves' den than the kind of premises suitable for an artiste of her standing. It was only when somebody emerged from the building with the 100 guineas she was being paid for six records that she managed to overcome her fear. Furthermore, like many of her kind, once she was inside the studio she wasn't entirely clear what kind of performance she was expected to deliver, having to be discouraged from breaking into dancing while singing as she did on stage.

This was a world before radio when the only music the overwhelming majority of people had ever heard was live or via the barrel organ. Musicians had never had the opportunity to hear themselves and they weren't always sure they wished to. The story goes that the German pianist Hans von Bülow was persuaded to record a Chopin mazurka during a visit to the Edison factory in New Jersey. When he put the pipes to his ears to hear the playback the shock of hearing his own performance caused him to faint. The singers who were the musicians most keenly sought by the record companies were attracted by the money they could make but were also understandably nervous of the fact that by allowing themselves to be recorded they might be putting their voices up for judgement in a way they had never been before.

It was a simpler business to adapt solo singers to the limitations of the recording medium than it was to record full orchestral works. In the early days, when the performance of an entire orchestra would have to be directed towards one recording horn, there were whole areas of the orchestral spectrum which had to be dispensed with altogether for fear they would prove either too loud or too soft for the recording machinery. Certain instruments had special instructions. French horn players would have their backs to the conductor, following his instructions in a wing mirror mounted on their instruments. Timpani and double basses would be left at home altogether, and it was cheaper to pay one superstar for his services than to have all the members of a symphony orchestra hanging around for the three days it would take to record even a drastically abbreviated *Nutcracker* suite. There were whole areas of the canon that were simply not worth the trouble of recording.

This changed following the First World War with the advent of electrical recording. The very first experiment came on Armistice Day 1920, with a recording of the dedication of the tomb of the Unknown Soldier at Westminster Abbey. This engineering breakthrough had been made by two people working for the Columbia Graphophone Company, which would soon be merged with the Gramophone Company to make EMI. At that stage microphones were not much better than telephone mouthpieces. By 1925 nine hundred male singers could be ranged below a single microphone on stage at the Metropolitan Opera House in New York for a recording of 'Adeste Fideles', which became a huge success. The sales literature called it the most thrilling sound ever heard on a phonograph record. Suddenly there was a sense of space, of power, of drama, and even a hint that a record might be better than a live performance.

The subsequent growth of electrical recording in the decade that followed meant that musicians no longer had to huddle together in small rooms in order to produce enough volume to make an impression on the recording diaphragm of the old acoustic process. They could spread out in bigger rooms, which meant that recordings could capture some of the ambient sound that seemed to lend recorded music its drama. It was time for studios as spacious and impressive as those being built by the film companies. It was time for a corporate headquarters which announced the fact that this was a respectable business. Maybe it was finally time for a temple of recording into which even the grandest diva would be happy to set foot.

2

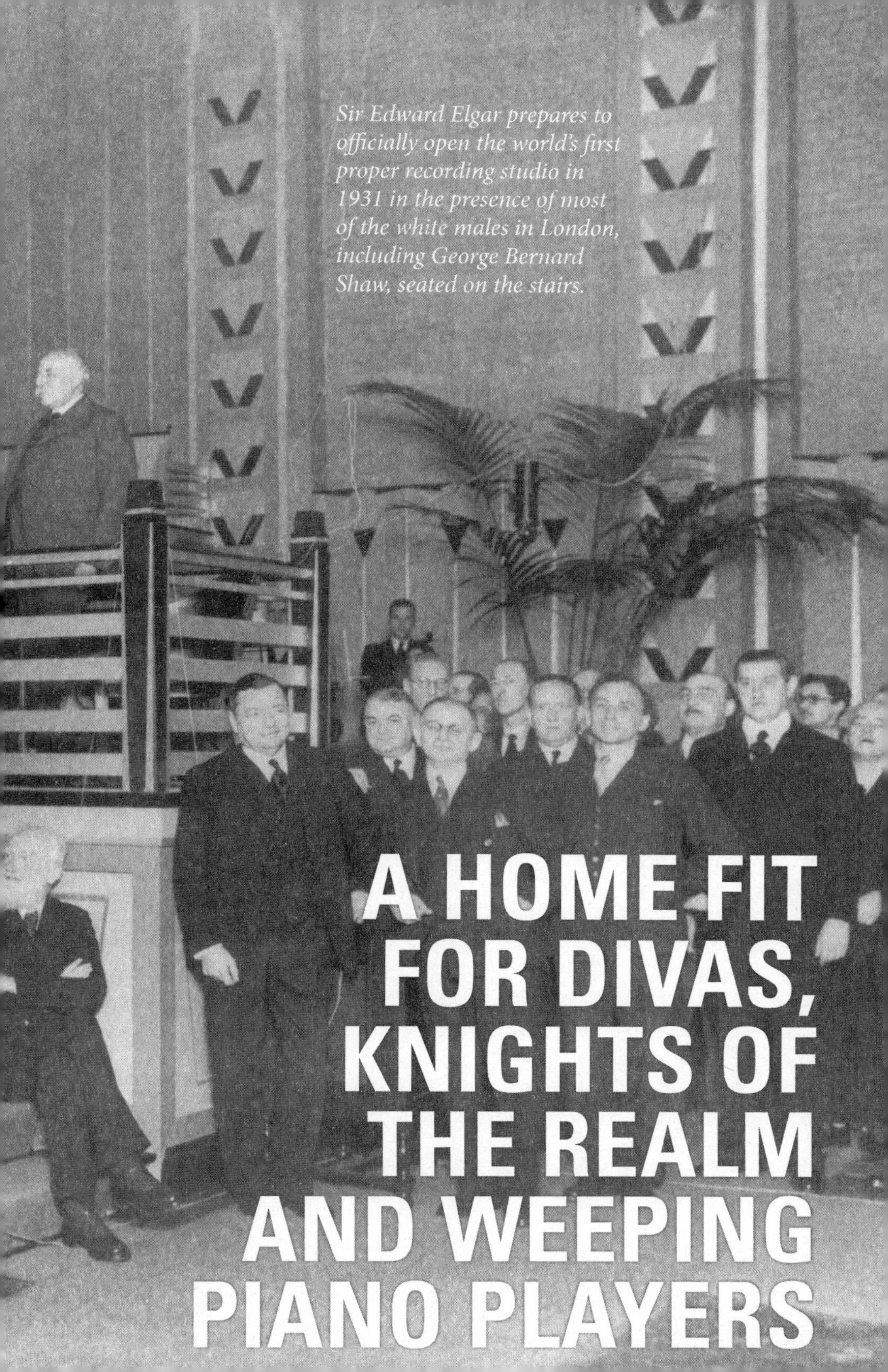

Sir Edward Elgar prepares to officially open the world's first proper recording studio in 1931 in the presence of most of the white males in London, including George Bernard Shaw, seated on the stairs.

A HOME FIT FOR DIVAS, KNIGHTS OF THE REALM AND WEEPING PIANO PLAYERS

In the year 1929, when property people working for the Gramophone Company first set eyes on the large house at No. 3 Abbey Road, St John's Wood, it was by no means clear that it was worth a company investing in a building dedicated to recording. The introduction of radio to America in 1922 had made the gramophone seem like yesterday's papers as far as the mass market was concerned. Nor was it by any means obvious that the exposure gained by radio play was in the interests of record companies. Following a court case in 1934 when the two major English companies, EMI and Decca, disputed with a Bristol coffee shop which had had the temerity to entertain its customers with gramophone records, it was agreed that the rights holder's permission was required to play records in public. In the same year in the United States a singer called Bing Crosby argued in court that he offered 'personal, original and individual interpretations' and thus his records were clearly marked 'not licensed for radio broadcast'. However, even in the face of such commercial headwinds the new company, which clearly took every word in its new name seriously, felt a music factory was no less important than the record factory it had recently built just outside London at Hayes.

One of the aspects of the wind-up gramophone that had recommended itself to the market was the fact that it was portable. It could be taken on picnics. It could even be taken to war. Indeed one 1915 model was carried to the Western Front so often it was known as the Trench Decca. Since it cost £8 at a time when a private soldier's pay was a shilling a day it was more popular with officers than men. Even during the post-war boom the market for records had yet to settle down into predictable patterns. One of the first exceptional sellers was a recording of 'O For The Wings Of A Dove' sung by a fifteen-year-old choirboy from West Ham. Released by HMV in 1927 it sold six hundred and fifty thousand copies in six months. Demand was so high it was said that six presses had to work night and day to keep up with it. Eventually they pressed so many that the master disc could no longer be used and a second recording had to be made in 1928, by which time the boy soprano was old enough for military service. The new company realized it could not legislate for such freak sales events and had to stick to its core mission, which was recording the classical repertoire for the first and, as far as anyone knew, only time.

Before the opening of the new studio full orchestras could only be recorded in rented concert halls in the West End. The development of the new electrical recording process meant that there was an increasing need to control every element of the recording environment and have the musicians come to the equipment rather than the other way round. In the early 1930s St John's Wood, which was known as the haunt of 'whores and artists', was where many musicians made their homes. In the Victorian era the area had been known as the place where gentlemen kept their mistresses. Holman Hunt's Pre-Raphaelite masterpiece *The Awakening Conscience*, in which a swell dallies with his unstayed plaything before returning to his office, was painted in one such House of Convenience. Although the company had already built two small studios as part of its Hayes factory there was clearly something to be said for a recording studio that was closer to the venues and hotels of the West End. Thanks to the transport links that went through St John's

Wood, musicians of the 1930s could provide their services and be back to their proper work as quickly and efficiently as the City philanderers of earlier decades. And thanks to the fact that from the street it gave the appearance of being a handsome family home of impeccable respectability even the grandest dames of the opera would not fear to mount its steps.

What they found when they visited after it opened in 1931 was that what presented itself as a villa from the outside was, when you entered, a sound laboratory, an office complex and a concert hall. Before the advent of electrical recording there was very little need for a studio large enough to accommodate an orchestra. Mechanical recording could just about capture the highest and lowest frequencies. Anything in the middle – anything concerned with tone, flavour, harmony or texture – it simply couldn't deal with. The best mechanical recording could offer was a pencil sketch of whatever was placed in front of what the poet Philip Larkin called its 'huge remembering pre-electric horn', and the fewer musicians involved the better. With electrical recording, where one or more microphones could be advantageously positioned and musicians no longer had to huddle together and blare to be heard, recording was beginning to approach something like colour. Recording sessions done the mechanical way were remembered as being claustrophobic and sweaty. They were claustrophobic because the musicians always had to crowd round the horn. They were sweaty because everybody was justifiably terrified of making a mistake.

When Fred Gaisberg had first heard the results of electrical recording, in a locked room in Russell Square, he was shocked to be able to hear sibilants for the first time. He immediately realized the old way was as dead as corsetry. Gaisberg's generation of recording maestros, whose skills had encompassed the musical as well as the mechanical, would soon be supplanted by a younger generation trained in the management of this new force called electricity. These new men became known as balance engineers because for the first time they were able to balance the inputs coming in from the studio floor, so that singers could be heard without having to assert themselves above the musicians. Where stars of the mechanical era had been belters like Al Jolson, the new technology suddenly made possible the rise of crooners like Bing Crosby, who sang into the shell-like of the swooning damsel with whom they were sharing a notional swing. This wasn't immediately apparent to the powers that be at the new studio, who were primarily keen on being able to make recordings that reflected the full spectrum of a symphony orchestra. They didn't realize that the electrical microphone had made a new sort of music possible, a form which would come to be called pop.

The plan to invest in the only dedicated recording centre in the world sought to take advantage of these exciting technical advances. Inevitably the most vigorous resistance came from inside the tent. The editor of *The Gramophone* magazine, launched in 1923 for classical pedants of the most horn-rimmed variety, begged for relief from the apparently dazzling brightness of the new electrical recordings. Fred Gaisberg was against this kind of investment in such an uncertain economic climate and insisted he would keep his office at Hayes. But even the venerable Fred could not compete with the energy of the idea's main sponsor, Trevor Osmond Williams, who was head of the international artistes department, and in vain was it muttered that the Abbey Road house had been chosen because it was only ten minutes away from the latter's smart flat. If this was an arrangement he looked forward to, he was not to see it come to fruition. He died in Vienna in July 1930 while the builders were still working on the site.

The plot at No. 3 had been chosen because it had at its rear a garden big enough in which to mount a game of association football, or build a studio big enough to accommodate two hundred and fifty musicians and a thousand audience members. Because the builders working to the plan of Wallis, Gilbert and Partners were pioneers they were inevitably out there with neither map nor compass and had very little best practice to call on. Their initial plans, which envisaged tiny control rooms with just enough space for a wax recording machine and a small control panel, would soon have to be torn up. Within a month of the opening they had to remove a quarter of the thickness of the material they had placed on the ceiling to reduce reverberation. None of this is surprising because the beast they were building – a massive recording studio – was something nobody had constructed before. Once they had built it they weren't entirely sure what was the best way to use it.

It took two years to convert the original property, which planning regulations stipulated had to retain the same appearance from the outside, into one of the most technologically advanced facilities in London. The press release from EMI billed it as 'London's Latest Wonder' and boasted that its three studios with their four and a half miles of electric cable were what was needed to accommodate the different varieties of music they would be called upon to record. The living quarters which had been used by the home's previous occupants were repurposed as offices, reception areas and 'retiring rooms'. Some original features were retained; senior staff were particularly pleased if they found that an old fireplace gave their office the atmosphere of a gentleman's study.

When Sir Edward Elgar opened the studio on 12 November 1931 by conducting 'Land Of Hope And Glory' in Studio One for the newsreel cameras of Pathé, he and the orchestra were on a stage at one end of the room, apparently ready to give a performance rather than make a recording. The assembled dignitaries, who included all the top brass of EMI and George Bernard Shaw, watched in respectful silence as the great man's valet relieved him of his heavy winter coat, he ascended the podium, and began with the modest injunction to the gentlemen – for be assured there were no women in his orchestra – to 'play this as though you had never heard it before'. Like all musical artistes, Sir Edward liked the idea of being seen to be at the cutting edge and recognized as the one chosen to represent the musical community at this very significant event. He also liked the attention. In response to Fred Gaisberg's request that he allow himself to be filmed by the Pathé cameras he gave his assent but jokingly added that if he was required to speak he would of course put in an invoice.

The PR announcements that accompanied the grand opening sought to assure that the new facility would afford the highest standards that might be expected of a concert hall, including 'waiting and retiring rooms for artistes'. In fact it seemed that they had taken every possible step to conceal from the performers the building's true purpose. There was no playback in the studio. That took place in another suite of rooms set aside for listening. Everybody turned up dressed as though for the concert stage, which is where the early recordings had been made. That was Studio One. At the other end of the scale was Studio Three, where recordings of solo singers or small ensembles would be made.

Extravagant displays of temperament were not invented with the Marshall stack. The tweedy maestros of the classical world who were the studio's main clients in the thirties had their rock star moments too. The Italian maestro Arturo Toscanini flounced from Studio One in June 1935, claiming to be unhappy with the acoustics, getting in his car and being driven off, leaving a few hundred pounds' worth of orchestra to pack their fiddles and get in the bus queue. Austrian violinist Fritz Kreisler would turn up with a special device for measuring the humidity of the room and, having measured, would choose his fiddle accordingly. A good deal of the ten years before the war it took Artur Schnabel to record Beethoven's

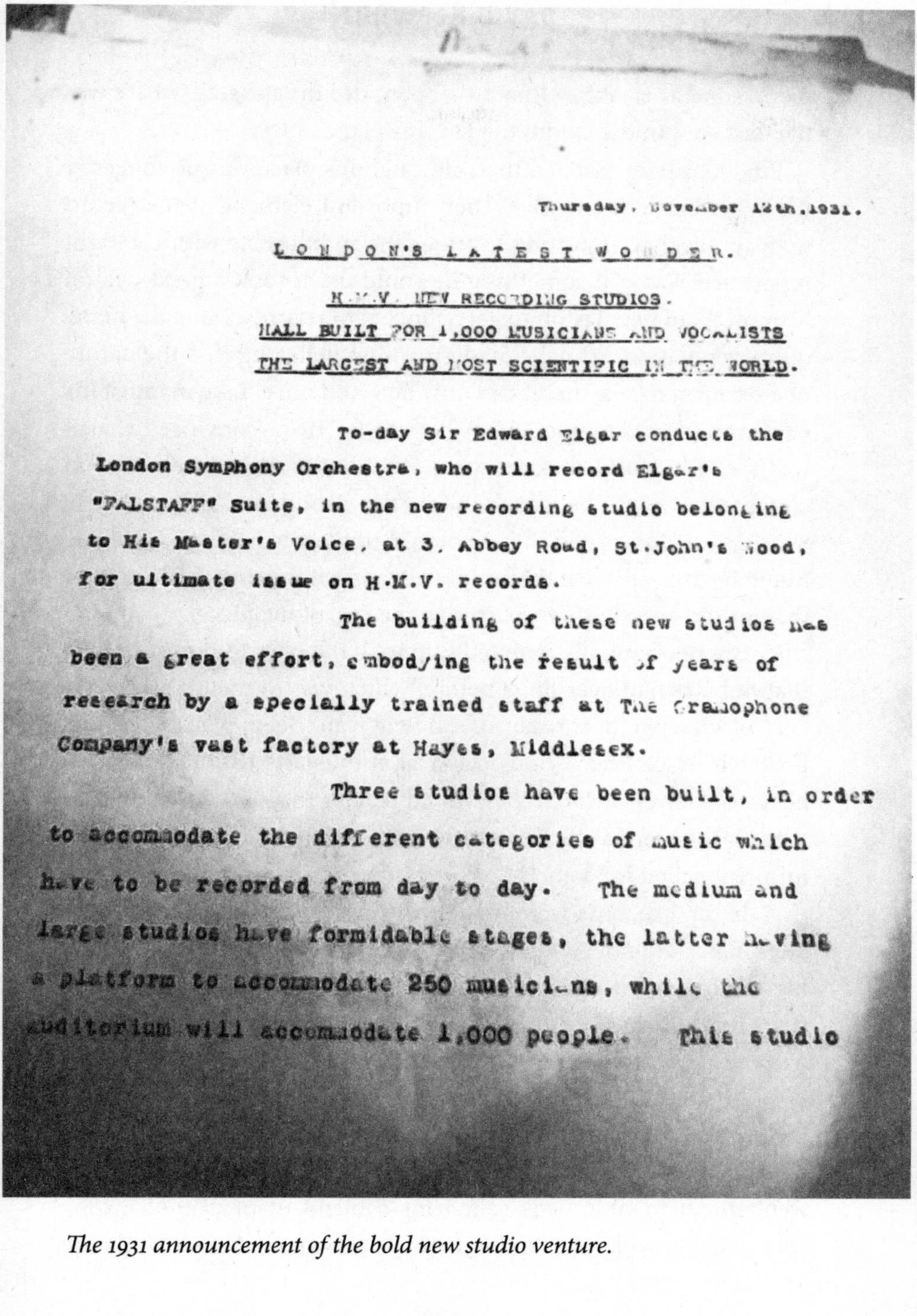

Thursday, November 12th, 1931.

LONDON'S LATEST WONDER.

H.M.V. NEW RECORDING STUDIOS.

HALL BUILT FOR 1,000 MUSICIANS AND VOCALISTS

THE LARGEST AND MOST SCIENTIFIC IN THE WORLD.

To-day Sir Edward Elgar conducts the London Symphony Orchestra, who will record Elgar's "FALSTAFF" Suite, in the new recording studio belonging to His Master's Voice, at 3, Abbey Road, St. John's Wood, for ultimate issue on H.M.V. records.

The building of these new studios has been a great effort, embodying the result of years of research by a specially trained staff at The Gramophone Company's vast factory at Hayes, Middlesex.

Three studios have been built, in order to accommodate the different categories of music which have to be recorded from day to day. The medium and large studios have formidable stages, the latter having a platform to accommodate 250 musicians, while the auditorium will accommodate 1,000 people. This studio

The 1931 announcement of the bold new studio venture.

piano sonatas at Abbey Road was spent deciding exactly where was the best spot in the studio to place his piano.

Fred Gaisberg realized that, although his place was no longer at the recording console, the other important element of the record man's craft, that of putting together the right artists with the right repertoire, was still something he could do. It took a great deal of his powers of persuasion to get Schnabel to record at all. Like many of his generation Schnabel had grown up believing that the nature of a performance is that it can only be given once. Like many of his background and temperament he was far from convinced that it was a good idea to make records at all because there was a good chance they might be listened to by the wrong kind of people. He was further concerned that he would not know how those people might be dressed, what they might be doing at the time, and whether they would even bother to listen to the end of the piece.

Gaisberg eventually tempted him with the offer to do something that nobody had ever done before, which was to record all thirty-two of the piano sonatas of Ludwig van Beethoven. This was financed by getting serious classical enthusiasts to join the Beethoven Society, via which they would receive the works as and when they were recorded by this most rigorous of musicians. This commitment called for a good deal of patience from the subscribers, in that the first records were made in 1932 and the last recordings of the sonatas did not go out until five years later. The effort of recording all thirty-two took a great deal more out of Schnabel. At one stage he came out of the studio into the street and began weeping from the sheer effort it had cost him.

Nobody yet thought of themselves as a recording artist. Performing on the concert platform was a walk in the park when set against a major recording project in the days before tape, when recordings went direct to disc. This called for a blend of precision, inspiration and dog work which musicians had never known before. And since no musician had ever attempted the Beethoven sonatas before, Schnabel couldn't be expected to know what he was letting himself in for. Because a 78 rpm disc could only accommodate, at most, four minutes a side, he first had to work out for each piece suitable junctures at which recording could be stopped – meaning that one movement of a sonata might have to be broken as many as three times. Then there were the sheer technical demands of playing such exacting music accurately and with the precise degree of emphasis. (Earlier on in his career, when a piano roll company had told him they had sixteen different weights of 'touch' on a key, he is said to have replied, 'I have seventeen.') There would be the inevitable technical breakdowns and pauses to replace the wax on to which the music was being inscribed, at the beginning of each of which the people in the control room would look to him to provide a faultless take.

Schnabel wrote to his wife explaining why he was finding the experience so draining. In four minutes, he explained, two thousand or more keys would be hit. 'If two of them are unsatisfactory you have to repeat all of the two thousand. In the repeat the first faulty notes are corrected but two others are not satisfactory and so you must play all two thousand again. You do it ten times, always with a sword of Damocles over your head. Finally you give up and twenty bad notes are left in it. I am physically and mentally too weak for this process and was close to a breakdown.'

The recording studio lured the musician with the promise of immortality while torturing him with a level of scrutiny that was entirely new. An intellectual like Schnabel wasn't Dan Leno. He didn't need the reassurance of the hot breath of the multitudes upon him as he performed, but even he sought a form of forgiveness which the studio didn't appear to offer. Fred Gaisberg, who was present throughout the twenty sessions a year it took to get the thirty-two sonatas satisfactorily recorded over those five years, knew that it was sometimes a good idea to take the performer's mind off the job in hand. When there was a break in the proceedings he would come out of the Recorder's Box (as they called the control room) smiling and doing everything in his power to lighten the mood, up to and including his imitation of Charlie Chaplin's famous walk. His niece Isabella, who was studying the piano, had the demanding duty of turning the pages for each sonata. Schnabel, like all musicians, loved an audience even if that audience was singular.

Gaisberg was hugely attracted by the big projects and he reached round the world to make them happen. He was also a believer in star power. It was at his instigation, also in 1932, that the sixteen-year-old American violin virtuoso Yehudi Menuhin was brought to Abbey Road to record Elgar's Violin Concerto under the baton of England's greatest composer, then in his seventy-fifth year. The boy genius was picked up at Dover by Rolls-Royce and conveyed to Grosvenor House, where he was barred from the dining room if he didn't put on long trousers. When he and the composer got together a couple of days before the session to agree on an interpretation, the boy hadn't even got to the second theme when Elgar announced that it would all be fine and since it was a lovely day he was off to the races. When they came together in Studio One after the weekend, the session proved equally congenial. The venerable knight turned up like an Edwardian country gentleman who, by rights, should have had hounds at his heels and conducted the orchestra with the authority that comes from having your name on the score, as Menuhin brought to life what he called the 'passionate innocence' of the English with an assurance which belied his head boy appearance. In his memoirs, Menuhin recalled how impressed he was by Elgar's lightness of touch when dealing with the orchestra. In an English studio, he noted, what seemed to count was invisible authority. 'This taught me something about England,' he wrote. 'That authority must present itself unobtrusively, even humbly. It is an exercise of authority developed through handling dogs, horses and regiments.'

The recording of the Violin Concerto was accomplished in a day and a half, which was quick considering that it was having to be recorded in fragments. Any extended piece such as this would eventually be published as an 'album' of 78s in a wallet and therefore would have to be recorded as such. There was no such thing as editing. As the performance was happening the signal from the microphone was being permanently inscribed into a wax master disc from which the stampers that were used to manufacture the record would eventually be made. If there was a fluff or a mistake there was no way it could be edited out. The musicians simply had to stop, throw away the old disc, send for another one and start again. This made it an expensive as well as time-consuming business. Musicians who couldn't get it right first time would not be asked again. Electrical recordings may have improved the quality, but they hadn't made the process any more forgiving or any easier on the artists. It would be a long time before any musician would regard going into the studio as an enjoyable experience.

The Russian composer Sergei Prokofiev was very excited to be allowed to make his first recording in June 1932 at Abbey Road but found the experience far more of a grind than he'd expected. He had to do two run-throughs of his Piano Concerto No. 3 with the orchestra, purely in order to get the proper balance between the two. As soon as you played one of the discs back to find out which balance was acceptable, the disc was of no further use. By the time they got to do the real take they were starting to regret that they hadn't kept the earlier ones. In his diary he wrote: 'The first recording came out well, only the second clarinet played some wrong notes. We did it again; the clarinet played the right notes, but my playing was worse. It went on like this for three hours. It was very interesting work but I was glad when it was over, because I was worn out with concentrating.'

In the middle of all this he had to pause to receive a celebrity visitor, the Duke of Kent, who was visiting the studios at the time. Prokofiev was slightly put out because this meant he had to restore the braces, waistcoat and jacket of which he had divested himself in order to be more comfortable in the hot studio. The Duke, who had already done a tour, did not stay long. The conductor thought he might have been frightened by the violent character of the music. It was thought he might want to go back to the smaller studio, where he had been witnessing an actress making a voice recording.

Within a few years of the studios' opening it seemed that No. 3 Abbey Road had already become one of the most cosmopolitan places in London. In 1934 Igor Stravinsky conducted his own dance cantata *Les Noces* in Studio One. Here in 1936 Pablo Casals made the first ever recording of Bach's cello suites, at a time when many people still believed they couldn't be performed as written. Indeed before the place had even been opened by Sir Edward the facilities had been used by artists from all corners of the world. Talented musicians flocked to London to train and to make their names. One such was the dazzling syncopated pianist Raie Da Costa. She came from a Portuguese-Jewish background in South Africa and had ventured to London in 1925 as a nineteen-year-old to make it as a concert pianist. The competition there was too fierce and she had switched to hot music, being billed as 'The Parlophone Girl – Dance Pianiste Supreme'. While she hadn't been able to match the discipline of her peers when training to be a classical player she could outdo most of them when it came to improvisation. She recorded three tunes in Studio Three on 18 September 1931, two months before the studios' official opening, including a medley based on the operetta *Viktoria and Her Hussar*, which had opened in London the evening before. She was never to achieve the success as a recording artist which her skills demanded. In the summer of 1934 she was appearing at a hotel in Hove when she suffered a sudden attack of appendicitis and died. She was only twenty-eight.

Paul Robeson, who was living in London at the time in a rented flat on a road just off Abbey Road while playing Othello opposite Peggy Ashcroft in the West End, was actually the first artist to officially record there, on 17 September 1931. On this day he cut four songs in the smallest of the three studios, the most memorable of which was Hoagy Carmichael's 'Rockin' Chair'. This song, which had been written a couple of years before, summons up a picture of an elderly black man enjoying his retirement in the Deep South, a part of the world with which the sophisticated urbanite Robeson was no more familiar than the musical director that day, Ray Noble, who came from Brighton.

Just a few days before the Christmas of 1931 Robeson returned to the studio and made one of the most striking records ever laid down at Abbey Road. It was a song by Lew Brown and Ray Henderson, who also wrote 'Life Is Just A Bowl Of Cherries' and 'Button Up Your Overcoat'. In the long-running Broadway revue *George White's Scandals* it had been one of the hits of 1931, sung by the baritone Everett Marshall in blackface, which was not unusual at the time. It's a song apparently resigned to the fact that it is the fate of the black man to labour for the white man and to sing when he's weary, sing when he's blue, sing because that's what he taught the white man to do. The song is called 'That's Why Darkies Were Born'. This is not a title you can imagine anyone introducing today, even after the most elaborate disclaimer. It is however a great song, and only those privy to what was going on in the minds of Brown and Henderson when they wrote it or of Paul Robeson when he chose to record it can write it off as racist. Robeson's delivery has some of that swallowed anger of 'Remember My Forgotten Man', the song about unemployed veterans which memorably provided the bass note of the film *Gold Diggers of 1933*.

What makes it one of the first great Abbey Road records, and in a sense marks the beginning of the age of records, is that it has an air of uniqueness about it. This arises from the coming together of one particular artist with one particular song on one particular medium, the 78 rpm record, at one particular moment. For a start this is clearly no longer just any white performer in blackface. This is Paul Robeson. Here is a song about slavery sung by a man whose father had been born a slave, a man who had reached a level of worldly distinction that clearly mocks the superficial message of the song. You could record the song again differently but it is impossible to imagine making it any better. There had always been performers. There had always been songs. But here, suddenly, you had a record. A few moments in time inscribed into wax. That record was more than the sum of the two parts that had gone into its making. The record was, as Bing Crosby's lawyers were soon to argue, 'personal, original and individual'. This is where the record business begins.

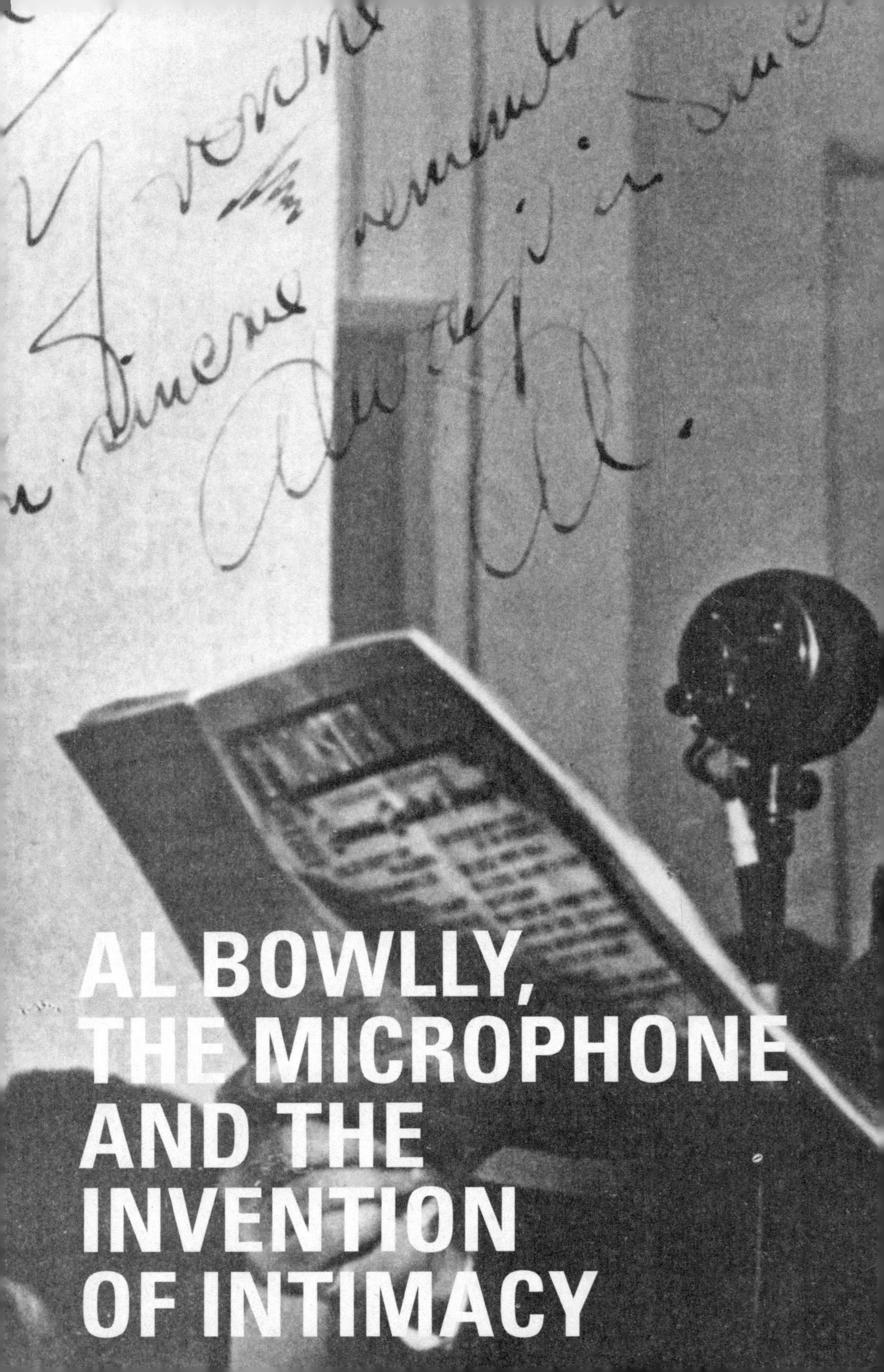

AL BOWLLY, THE MICROPHONE AND THE INVENTION OF INTIMACY

3

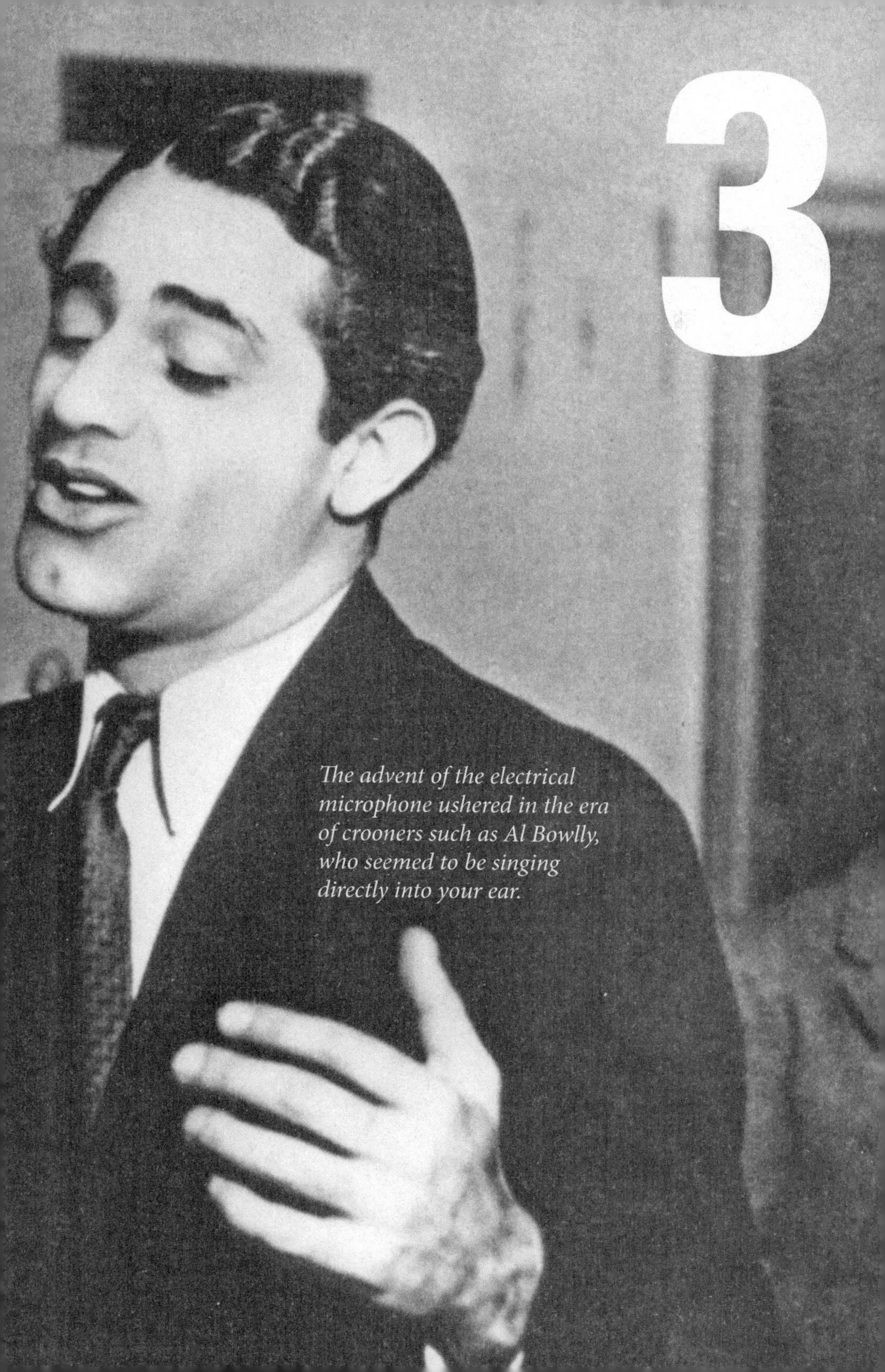

The advent of the electrical microphone ushered in the era of crooners such as Al Bowlly, who seemed to be singing directly into your ear.

The name of the company was Electrical and Musical Industries. This laid every bit as much stress on the firm's commitment to technology as on its interest in keeping the nation entertained. It was this image which enabled it to attract the brightest and best mechanical and electrical engineers. One such was Alan Blumlein, an Englishman with a German-Jewish background whose first and most pressing job was to design and build EMI's own patented disc cutter, thereby freeing the company from the obligation to pay royalties to an American patent holder. For much of the life of EMI, equipment like this, like so much of the machinery involved in making records, could not be purchased off the shelf and was often actually built at the EMI factory in Hayes.

Blumlein had a particularly restless curiosity which led him to innovations far ahead of their time. Watching a cinema film with his wife and noting that the sound didn't emanate from the part of the screen where the action took place, he set out to remedy this deficiency. In 1934 he took his invention into Studio One at Abbey Road to record Sir Thomas Beecham rehearsing Mozart's Jupiter Symphony with the London Philharmonic. This turned out to be the first stereo recording made on these shores. By 1935 he had produced the film *Trains at Hayes Station* where the sound followed the engines across the screen. He referred to his system as 'binaural'. In time the world would come to know it as 'stereo sound'. Anyone born between the release of the Beatles' *Revolver* and the attack on the Twin Towers would continue to refer to their domestic means of music reproduction as 'the stereo', regardless of whether it was or not.

Blumlein didn't live to see his creation achieve its potential. With the approach of war he contributed to EMI's work on developing the radar required to track enemy aircraft. On 7 June 1942 he was in a Halifax bomber which was testing his system over the Welsh borders when an engine malfunction brought the plane down, killing all on board. He was thirty-eight.

The studios at Abbey Road depended on a steady supply of new technology from engineers like Blumlein. It had opened its doors in the same year the moving coil microphone had been invented. This innovation, in which a small induction coil moved in response to the vibrations of the voice to produce a varying electrical current, offered a significant improvement in the nature and subtlety of the musical sounds which could be captured. Most importantly, it seemed to bring music closer.

In the cavernous space of Studio One the advent of the electrical microphone had made it possible to capture the full spectrum of sounds produced by a symphony orchestra. Recording technology could now keep up with the way the music was played in the concert hall. The orchestra no longer had to compromise the sound it made for the benefit of this new medium. They could spread out in Studio One's broad acres and let rip, if that was called for. The announcement of the new studios made a lot of the fact that as many as six microphones could be used in one studio and that each one would have a separate control. This ability to manipulate the inputs put new power in the hands of the engineers and radically changed the way recorded music sounded and felt.

However, the place where the moving coil microphone was to make most difference was in the part of the studio complex where the classically trained rarely ventured. This lay on the other side of an invisible line of demarcation which would be an issue for the studio for the remainder of the century.

There is a widespread misconception that music is a unifying force. The closer one draws to music and musicians the less this seems to be the case and the more obvious is the evidence pointing to the contrary. Much of this was apparent in the early days of the EMI technical department, as the grand new facility in Abbey Road was then known elsewhere in the company. Here under one very extensive roof could be found every day a wide variety of musicians working on a wide variety of music, some of which the musicians from other backgrounds would barely regard as music at all. This tension between what was thought of as 'proper music' and what was thought of as 'the rest' would be a fact of life in the studio for decades.

Studio One was where the orchestras were recorded. Here was where the knights and barons of classical music held sway. Studio Three, being the smallest room, was ideal for soloists and ensembles such as string quartets. Studio Two was suited to dance bands. These might have as many as twenty members who inevitably brought a lot of kit with them. Studio Two was consequently regarded by the classical players, who viewed themselves as being engaged in the building's proper business, as some kind of speakeasy. Studios One, Two and Three were referred to within the company respectively as the HMV, Parlophone and Columbia studios to indicate the kind of work that tended to be done there. By the time Studio Two had been open for two years it was also known by the people who worked in the building but rarely went beyond its door as the Pop Studio.

The dominant form of pop music during the years between the wars was jazz. Jazz hadn't yet reached its chin-stroking years. At the time it was predominantly played by young people and it was overwhelmingly created with dancing in mind. A few of the American originators, stars such as Duke Ellington and Louis Armstrong, visited London to play but this was in exceptional circumstances. On both sides of the Atlantic the respective musicians' unions did everything in their power to keep the other side's dance bands off their turf for fear of losing out on employment opportunities. Every Atlantic crossing had to be done on a strict exchange basis, to the extent that if a British band was broadcasting to the United States, an American band of equivalent size would have to be paid to sit in another studio, twiddling its thumbs on full pay for the duration of the broadcast.

The overwhelming majority of musicians in these jazz bands had no thought of ever being recorded. They relied on live work. In America, Prohibition gave musicians lots of places to play. In Britain, the revolution in cinemas wrought by the advent of the talkies in 1927 meant that they could no longer rely on work in pit orchestras. Since only the best were good enough to play dance music for the patrons of the smart hotels, a lot of them were out of work. They would never be asked to record. Only a handful would ever be equal to the demands of playing accurately under the pressure of the red light in a recording studio like EMI's. Musicians were far more likely to become well known by turning up regularly on the radio than by having a hit record. The BBC dominated radio in the UK, but it was restricted in the number of gramophone records it could play in a week by agreements with the Musicians' Union and the record companies and by its own conservatism. The majority of radio programmes would feature orchestras, dance bands or organists. (The latter instrument was so popular that in 1937 a massive Compton organ was taken from a cinema in Birmingham and installed in Studio One, where it was used by Fats Waller during a session in 1938.) In the period between the wars *A Programme of Gramophone Records* was such a novelty that it was billed in the *Radio Times* in precisely those terms. In the early days of the BBC the announcers were compelled to state the full details of any record played, together with its full catalogue number. Following a 1935 agreement the BBC could only broadcast fourteen hours of recorded music a week. Even as late as 1948 both the union and the record companies were arguing that gramophone records were primarily recorded for private use and as such their public performance had to be restricted.

What went on in Studio Two was already very different from what went on down the hall. While the classical people might seek fidelity to an original performance, the pop people were beginning to think more about effect. They weren't trying to reproduce what they did on stage so much as make something that would appeal to the people who listened to records, most of whom had never heard a high-calibre dance band in full effect. In Studio Two they didn't care how many compromises they made as long as they came up with something that was popular. They didn't fully realize it at the time but they were already making music that would be transformed by technology.

For a start, the microphone meant that singing was suddenly more important than it had been. In the days when the singers with dance bands pitched their songs to the back of the room by using a megaphone they had to put up with all manner of indignities, up to and including hyper-critical patrons who tried to pitch coins into the horn just as they had raised it to their mouth to sing. In this era, singing was a part-time job. Even in the world of musicians it was not regarded as a proper job for a man. As soon as they had provided their 'vocal refrain', which usually came halfway through the tune, they took up the instrument which was their true work and resumed their place on the bandstand. On the label of a record the singers would rarely be mentioned. They were anything but the stars of the show.

This changed with the microphone. In America, the person who changed it was a singer with the Paul Whiteman Orchestra by the name of Crosby, who was very soon known on every continent by the euphonious monosyllable Bing. He couldn't have recorded without the new microphone because his soft baritone would have left no trace. The microphone, on the other hand, as all of us who've had the smallest experience of public speaking are acutely aware, made his voice sound not only bigger and louder but also more important. With its aid, Bing was suddenly, powerfully, gently God-like. At the same time, by opening up the full spectrum of colours and textures which lived in his unique instrument, the microphone made it possible for him to exhibit a range of voices and different personalities. When he sang 'Where The Blue Of The Night Meets The Gold Of The Day' he could be meltingly romantic, when he set about 'Ol' Man River' he could be deeply stirring, and when he took on 'I'm An Old Cowhand (From The Rio Grande)' he could make you believe that his greatest gift was for sending himself up. The microphone made Bing sound like a person, like your friend or boyfriend, in a way that was never available to Caruso. The electrical microphone brought him close enough to make listeners feel that they knew him. Frank Sinatra, who never sought to hide the fact that he learned everything from Crosby, used to say that the only instrument he played was the microphone. Its invention was to recorded music what the close-up was to cinema. The microphone made stars. Its role in transforming the importance of the singer in the band was celebrated in every new publicity image, where the vocalist was often pictured cradling this magical new electrical device, which was soon bracketed in the public mind with romance itself.

This new style of romantic singing, pioneered by Crosby, was referred to, often with calculated disrespect, as 'crooning' to distinguish it from the kind of proper singing that real, barrel-chested men went in for. A generation of young men who aspired to croon, it was said, would be no match for a German reoccupation of the Rhineland. However, what the men might have thought didn't matter. In the course of the 1930s millions of young women joined the workforce to take up clean jobs like typist, telephonist or shop assistant, and they were in the market for new forms of entertainment. They went to the cinema at least once a week and prided themselves on keeping up with the latest tunes and dances. The croon was a form of music which had great appeal to female listeners. In most cases it was directly addressed to them. Crooning marked the beginning of recorded music's pursuit of the mirage of sexual conquest through the medium of sound. It shaped pop music in ways we still live with today. Lenny Kaye, punk scholar and guitarist with Patti Smith, wrote an entire book about the American crooner Russ Columbo in which he suggested that what truly mattered in crooning was the 'oo' sound to be found in words like swoon, spoon, woo, soothe, tune, soon, moon and, inevitably, June.

Crooning was clearly the low, quivering sound of surrender and as such was the kind of thing the British would expect the Yanks to be good at. But nowhere was it made better than in Studio Two in St John's Wood. That's because nobody did it better than Al Bowlly, who was the first one to take advantage of the moving coil microphone and hence became the first heart throb of British music.

Al Bowlly's life reads like a Patrick Hamilton novel. His father was Greek, his mother Lebanese, and they met on a ship en route from America to Australia. Their son was born in Mozambique, in 1898, and they moved to South Africa when he was a baby. After leaving school, Al became a singing barber, accompanying himself on the guitar, until he was discovered by South Africa's top band leader. He worked his way to Europe via gigs in Mombasa, Singapore (where he played the Raffles hotel), and then the Grand Hotel, Calcutta, where he somehow had a sideline as a jockey. When a big orchestra turned up he offered his services as a singer and banjoist.

What he really wanted to do was work in London. Hearing that Fred Elizalde, a Spanish band leader, had a residency at the Savoy he put his services forward by sending him a record he had made in Germany. The song was the same 'Muddy Waters' that Bing had first recorded with Paul Whiteman. It got him the job, and he came to London.

Thus Bowlly embarked on the life of the professional dance band musician of the day, a life which was unrelenting if you were in work and as tough as anyone else's when you weren't. Days were spent rehearsing or recording, nights were spent entertaining the quality from the bandstand at the Ritz, the Savoy or the Monseigneur in Piccadilly. Every Tuesday you went to the Musicians' Union headquarters in Archer Street to pick up your money and to stand in the street swapping gossip and leads for work with other musicians. You would think this would have kept anyone out of mischief, but Al had that reckless disregard for the sensible option which has marked out the musician down the ages. Even with that busy schedule he found time to make a most unsuitable marriage in December 1931, splitting up with his wife two weeks later.

Al Bowlly turned up for hundreds of recording dates at Abbey Road, either as a guitarist or a singer or both, and most of the time he was unbilled. He was at one time or another part of the following ensembles: Len Fillis and his Novelty Orchestra, Nat Gonella and his Trumpet, Roy Fox 'The Whispering Cornetist' and his Band, the Phantom Players, the Durium Dance Band, Alfredo's Band, Rolando and his Blue Salon Orchestra, the Savoy Hotel Orpheans, Billy Hill and his Boys, the Aldwych Players and, most notably, the New Mayfair Dance Orchestra. What had initially brought him to St John's Wood was the HMV label's need for a singer who could knock out songs in Afrikaans for the South African market. This led to his meeting with band leader Ray Noble, a shrewd man of many talents who realized that he had blundered into London's answer to Bing Crosby. The recordings Bowlly made for HMV with Noble's band went under the name of the New Mayfair Dance Orchestra. Under that name they existed in the studio to supply the UK market with a reliable stream of British versions of the latest hits from Broadway and everywhere else. As a live performer Al graduated from the role of strummer and occasional singer with Lew Stone's band to star of the show. Al was the one whose entrance into proceedings the ladies would hotly anticipate. He reached some sort of climax on 11 September 1933 when he appeared at the Holborn Empire as a solo artist, accompanied only by a piano. This was a rare elevation for a dance band singer, not least because the only other act on the bill that night was Louis Armstrong. Al Bowlly was Britain's first pop star.

Even in America they recognized the fact that the recordings coming out of St John's Wood on the HMV label, many of which were released on RCA in the United States, demonstrated a superior command of dynamics. One example is 'Midnight, The Stars And You', which Al recorded at Abbey Road with Ray Noble on 16 February 1934. There are three elements in the record: the muted horns of the ensemble, a pianist who seems to be playing for his own amusement, and Bowlly, who oozes belatedly into proceedings like a Wodehouse butler. The listener's attention is gently directed around those three elements, none of which seem in any kind of hurry to grab the attention. There's an entirely new kind of experience on offer here. It's the experience of a record. All records are moments, but the great records offer moments to which we wish to return. Fifty years after its moment, 'Midnight, The Stars And You' was picked by Stanley Kubrick as the perfect illustration of the refuge that listeners had sought in music during the harsh winters of the 1930s for his film *The Shining*. A great record, such as they were starting to make in Studio Two, has something which a song alone doesn't have. It has an atmosphere, it has a mood, it has many of the qualities of a dream.

With the microphone in the hands of a singer like Al Bowlly came the invention of intimacy. Suddenly, for the first time in the short history of recorded music, here was something that live music could never do. With the new ability to control the inputs, recording music successfully involved something more than fidelity to the original performance. It suggested that the record could even offer, in certain cases, something better than live music, something more mysterious, more narcotic, something which, over repeated listens, got under the listener's skin.

The records Al Bowlly made with Ray Noble at Abbey Road between its opening in 1931 and their departure for the United States in 1934 – and he did hundreds – took this experience beyond the Monseigneur, where Bowlly sang for men who owned their own tails while less affluent customers looked down from the balcony and enjoyed the spectacle. There were also, thanks to the invention of radio, millions of others listening out there in the dark, at the far end of unmade roads. These people rolled back the carpet in living rooms from Stockton-on-Tees to Southwold, actually put on their best clothes, and took whatever partner they could find. The appeal of the dance records of the time went beyond their tunefulness and the dazzling polish of the arrangements. It derived mainly from the fact that it was only when in the act of dancing that any of the listeners stood a chance of grabbing a handful of another human being. It is a fact of life that we have lost touch with since the sixties, when dancing was reinvented as a non-contact sport. Dancing was how you were most likely to meet your life partner. Small wonder people invested so much in it. And Al wasn't just singing to the people who were lucky enough to have a partner, particularly during the prolonged man shortage of the 1930s. There was also a longing in his records, songs like 'Love Is The Sweetest Thing', 'The Very Thought Of You' and 'Dinner For One Please, James', which spoke every bit as powerfully to the wallflowers.

Al Bowlly went to America with Ray Noble and opened the Rainbow Room restaurant atop the Rockefeller Center – a 'Look, Ma, top of the world!' moment, if ever there was one. He came back to Britain in time for the war. He had stayed away too long. He was too old to be called up but did some entertaining of the troops before teaming up with another slacker of Greek extraction called Jimmy Messene, billing themselves as the 'Radio Stars with Two Guitars'.

Playing live during the London Blitz could be a very hazardous business. Al had recorded at Abbey Road with the legendary Ken 'Snakehips' Johnson, a band leader from the Caribbean who was resident at the Café de Paris. On 8 March 1941 there was a particularly bad air raid over London but Johnson was determined to make the gig. His band had already struck up his theme tune as he entered the club, decked out in white tie and tails, as you might expect of a band leader. At that precise moment a 50kg high-explosive bomb dropped on the club, killing Johnson and thirty-three others. They laid their bodies out in the snow. Eyewitnesses recalled how in their evening dress they looked like dolls.

It's said that Bowlly was in the area at the time but retained a child-like belief that some Lord of the Crooners would shield him from harm. Therefore he carried on playing his shows with Messene. Their last recording date at Abbey Road was 2 April 1941, when they cut an Irving Berlin song about Hitler called 'When That Man Is Dead And Gone'. However, it would turn out that Al was dead and gone before that man. Two weeks after the recording Al returned to his flat in St James rather than stay the night after a show in High Wycombe. He didn't set much store on sirens. He was sitting up in bed nursing an ailing throat when a Luftwaffe parachute mine descended slowly on Duke Street, detonating directly opposite his window. When they found him, the explosion had blown the bedroom door off its hinges but had in no way disfigured Al, which would have been some comfort to his band of female admirers. At the time his career was in the doldrums. His last hit, which he had made at Abbey Road in 1940, was 'It's A Lovely Day Tomorrow'.

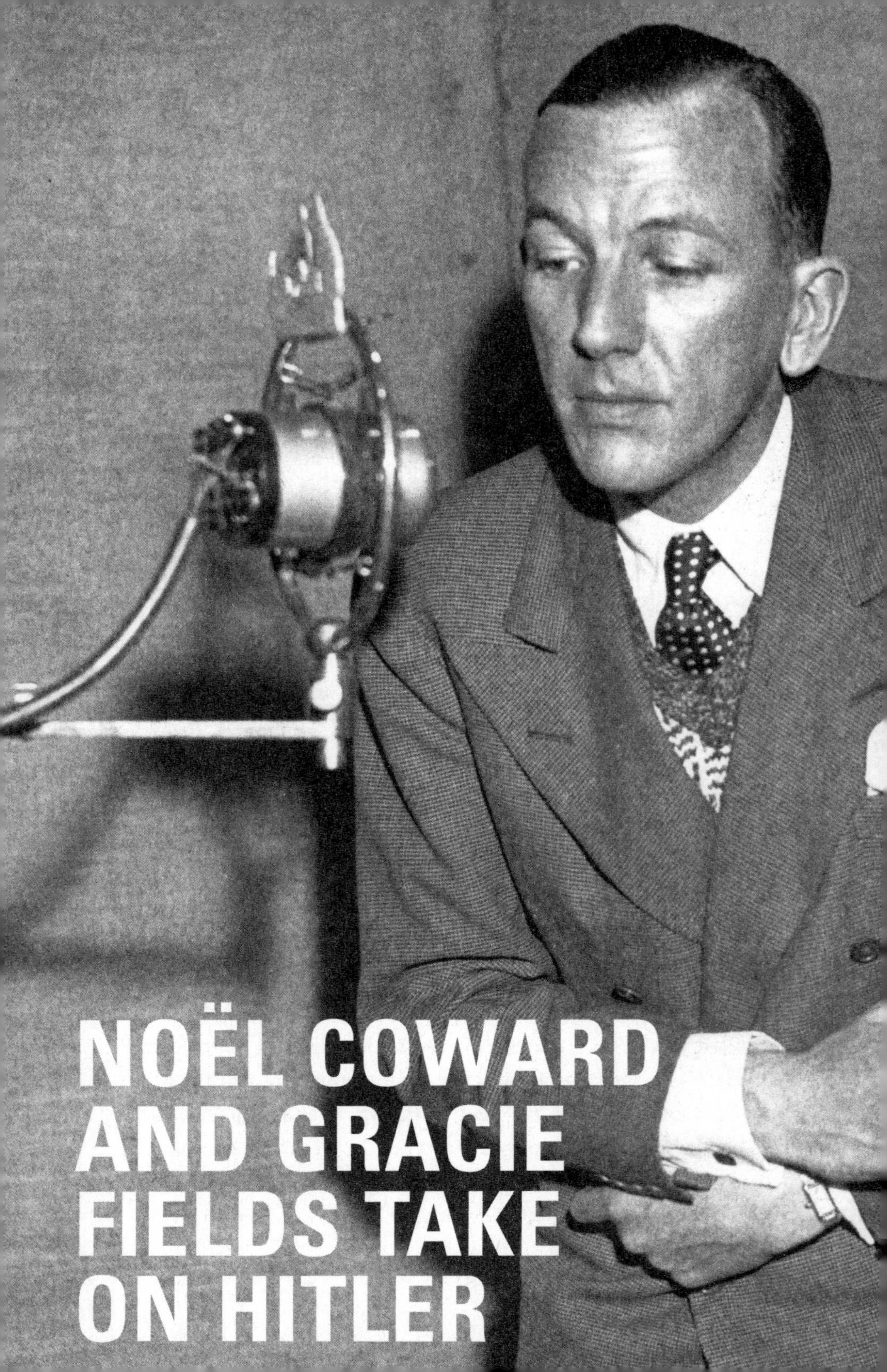

NOËL COWARD AND GRACIE FIELDS TAKE ON HITLER

4

Noël Coward records the London cast of Conversation Piece at Abbey Road in 1934. His co-star Yvonne Printemps spoke no English, learning the script and songs phonetically.

The Second World War was declared on radio and it was conducted the same way. Radio as a medium delivered company, comfort and reassurance, which were particularly valued as the skies above grew darker. Nothing could deliver those qualities more powerfully than the voice of your favourite singer coming through the mesh of the wireless in the corner of your very own parlour. The kind of records beginning to find favour at the time were starting to be known as 'personality records', indicating that the identity of the singer mattered more than ever. The job of a recording studio was now to deliver as affecting a version as possible of whatever it was that people liked about their favourite personality singers.

The war placed the music business on rations. Many of the staff at Abbey Road were redeployed to Hayes, where the company was doing work with military applications. Those who remained were working on music which was to be used to entertain the troops and in most cases was never commercially released. Hundreds of dance band musicians found themselves in the forces. Petrol was in short supply and there wasn't enough to press up the same number of records. The saving grace for a handful of performers, as well as the musicians and technicians who served them in the studio, was that the delicate flower which is morale was known to respond to music. Thus began the only five-year period in modern times when His

Majesty's Government was, to all intents and purposes, in charge of what reached the ears of the listening public.

The case for classical music when it came to summoning up the blood did not seem to need making. Thanks to Hitler's Nuremberg Laws, reception at Abbey Road was full of distinguished musicians who had decided to make London their home. In his native Austria, tenor Richard Tauber was known for his monocle and for being the true voice of the Germanic repertoire. In May 1938, just weeks after Hitler had annexed his homeland, Richard was at Abbey Road giving equal attention to 'Mother Machree' and 'The Rose Of Tralee'.

Where dance music was concerned, the BBC, still a young organization but showing an early flair for indulging in agonies of conscience, was at first not sure the foxtrot or the palais glide oughtn't to be put away until ploughshares were no longer being beaten into swords. Happily the argument prevailed that just as the sound of Elgar stiffened the sinews, so the velvety music of singers such as Leslie Hutchinson – better known simply as Hutch – had a stiffening effect on other vital organs and therefore should continue to flow free. But everything had to be justified on the grounds of how well it helped the war effort. There was no time for musical frivolity. By 1941 the BBC had dedicated itself to achieving 'victory through harmony' via programmes like *Music While You Work*, at the time an entirely unprecedented idea.

Thanks to the by now symbiotic relationship between music and radio, this was the first war in which music could be used as a weapon, and the best way to wield that weapon was to place it in the hands of a star. The stars made by the war were stars for life. Thus came the finest hour of Vera Lynn, previously an also-ran but soon to achieve immortality as the Forces' Sweetheart. This was also the moment when there was unlimited appetite for the creamy cosiness of Flanagan and Allen. It was the only time in British history when audiences sang along without a scintilla of self-consciousness, coming together around music simply to make themselves feel better. It was a time when even a sybarite like Noël Coward could come to the aid of the national party.

Coward had been Britain's most prolific composer of original popular songs during the decades following the First World War. He returned to what he called in his diary 'the HMV studio' at regular intervals to record them. Many were written to be sung by characters invented for his shows but were fated in time to be eclipsed by the versions he recorded at Abbey Road. His theatrical productions may have made Coward rich but it was the slightly pained delivery he affected for the records he made in St John's Wood that allowed his music to endure. His performances of his most celebrated compositions, such as 'Mrs Worthington' and 'The Stately Homes Of England', seemed all the more exhilarating for being apparently wrung from him in a state of high dudgeon, and all the more dazzling for managing to pack in quite so much plot.

Sometimes there was so much plot there was barely room for any music. 'I Went To A Marvellous Party', which he recorded at Abbey Road in July 1941, was inspired by his being invited to what he thought was a beach party but turned out to be a hundred guests in their finery expecting him to put on a show. What makes the 'Marvellous Party' recording, in which his regular pianist the American Carroll Gibbons keeps him company, so unique is the manner of its beginning, with the microphone seeming to discover him midway through laughingly relating how he turned out to be there before snapping into focus with 'quite for no reason I'm here for the season'. It's one of the first uses of what is essentially a filmic device in the context of a record. The 'Marvellous Party' dilemma was a recurring theme in Coward's life and art. Was he invited to the house party or entertaining it? Even when he had a meeting with Churchill at the beginning of the war to offer his services as a spy the Prime Minister wouldn't let him leave without playing 'Mad Dogs And Englishmen'. Twice.

At the outbreak of war Coward rashly swore that he would set aside his frivolous art until victory was won. When bombs were raining down on London nightly and there were too many funerals to attend there was surely no place for a song like 'The Stately Homes Of England'. He soon changed his mind, realizing that if everyone else was doing their bit, this was apparently the precise bit he of all people should be doing. After all, he was the finest musical exponent of the Charters and Caldicott view of international relations, according to which invading Poland is one thing but threatening the Trent Bridge Test is frankly a bit thick – a pose that appeals greatly to the English view of themselves as an insular people, slow to stir. In July 1941, when Britain stood alone against Hitler, Coward was writing and recording songs which sought to stiffen the national backbone while lampooning the uselessness of the people at the top. 'Could You Please Oblige Us With A Bren Gun?' is a plea to equip the Home Guard with something other than broomsticks and shovels. Others, such as 'London Pride', which came along the same month and was recorded with a full orchestra, sentimentally celebrated the city's ability to endure in a way that would have drawn tears from a Warren Street spiv.

Coward saw as much of the Blitz as anyone, albeit from a nicer table, recording in his diary in April 1941 how his drinks at the Savoy had been marked by a few bombs which fell nearby during dinner. He was relieved to note that while a door blew in and the wall 'bulged a bit' the orchestra went on playing and the diners kept on dining. He also recorded how he 'wished the whole of America could really see and understand it'. Since he was one of the few English musicians whose records were likely to be heard by the sort of powerful Americans who influenced public policy, Churchill had clearly been correct when he advised him that if he wished to do his patriotic duty he should forget any idea of being a spy and stick to the piano. There were times when Coward fell foul of the tendency of His Majesty's press to search out the wrong end of the stick and grasp it firmly, such as in 1943 when he had to take great pains to point out that 'Don't Let's Be Beastly To The Germans' was in fact a joke, but he contributed as much to the home front as anyone without exposing himself to the hazards of entertaining the troops in person – hazards which would have had less to do with stray munitions than speculations about his sexuality arising from the cheap seats.

Speaking of which, on 20 September 1932 Coward had been in Studio Two with an orchestra conducted by Ray Noble, performing his own versions of songs from his latest revue, *Words and Music*. They recorded all afternoon and were particularly pleased with 'Mad Dogs And Englishmen'. At the end of the session he sat at the piano and played the love song from *Words and Music*. In the actual show each verse is sung by a different woman mooning over the remote figure of a matinee idol. As sung this day by its creator, 'Mad About The Boy' became something so different it was later discarded. This was allegedly on the grounds that the vocal was 'too weak' but more probably because the very idea of a man singing about and sounding as though he was in love with a boy would have been too much for anyone to process. It was only in 2003 that the recording surfaced and was released into a world where male performers were suddenly queueing up to perform it. 'Mad About The Boy' is now Coward's highest-earning song.

When it came to the important business of maintaining morale on the home front, personality seemed to be at least as important as musicianship and many different kinds of personalities would be pressed into service. Some, like Coward, were perceived by the public as belonging to the officer class, while others, such as Gracie Fields and George Formby, were seen as sharing the travails of the common folk. Since both performers were born into show business stock this was an illusion, one bolstered by a succession of gramophone records designed to underline their public persona. People referred to them unselfconsciously as 'our Gracie' and 'our George', as though to stress a bond that could not possibly just have been invented by the entertainment business.

Gracie Fields had been one of Britain's most popular recording stars in the years between the wars, which was remarkable since the majority of her material was dedicated to promoting the small corner of England which is Lancashire. No British musical performer before or since has managed to combine nationwide popularity with such laser focus on a part of the country which most of her fans had never visited and would never visit. Even when she wasn't as anthropological as in songs like 'In A Little Lancashire Town' and 'Mary Ellen's Hot Pot Party', the subliminal message of everything she did, from 'Sally' to 'Turn 'Erbert's Face To The Wall, Mother', was that first the spectre of want that had stalked the previous decade and now this bloke Adolf Hitler would eventually be vanquished by the grit, the elbow grease and the almost supernatural savvy of the folk of Lancashire and, at a push, a few places a short bus ride away. Fields played this role of the Diva of the Cobbles for so long and so persuasively that even we who grew up after the war believed that she had actually been a mill girl, when the truth is she was on the halls at the age of twelve and was as familiar with mill work as Britney Spears.

The moment war was declared Gracie was dispatched, like a tactical weapon, in the direction of the nearest barracks (which happened to be in Chelsea) with the mobile recording unit from Abbey Road to make the first of a number of recordings which would be billed as *Gracie With The Troops*. While the prospect of facing a room full of khaki might have made Noël Coward blench, it put Gracie in her element. She turned out to be one of that handful of entertainers whom war could be said to suit. The main feature of these recordings, which she made on home territory and in France with the ill-fated British Expeditionary Force, who were soon to endure Dunkirk, was not actually Gracie so much as the sound of a barrack room full of homesick, frightened men, joining in readily with 'Sing As We Go' or 'There'll Always Be An England'. That's why people wanted to hear these records. It gave the troops comfort to be singing along with our Gracie and it gave their loved ones at home comfort to think that their own boy might be among the choir invisible in a camp that the label would only concede was 'somewhere in England'.

Gracie's songs of hearth and home became newly powerful once the war broke out and people feared for that very hearth and their actual home. She was so much about home that she would even focus on its constituent elements. Having done well with 'The Lovely Aspidistra In The Old Flower Pot' in 1930, she returned to the subject in 'The Biggest Aspidistra In The World', which she recorded in Studio Two in 1938, and furthermore re-recorded in the unlikely surroundings of Los Angeles in 1941. She had relocated there for the duration to avoid her husband, an Italian, being interned on the Isle of Man as an enemy alien. This re-recording underlined to what extent the mundane comforts of English life had had to be weaponized during the war since it contained disobliging remarks about the Führer, which got a lot of play. This led to a German magazine stating that as 'Gracie Fields has earned for England the equivalent of a hundred new Spitfires, she is judged a war industry, and should therefore be treated accordingly'.

Gracie was the queen of the personality records. Although she could sing anything, from opera through devotional songs and torch ballads to music-hall belters, all of which she recorded at one time or another at Abbey Road, the thing that made her a star was the personality she projected and the way she was seen to represent something in the English character, something which might see it prevail. The Depression had made Gracie Fields a star. The war made her a legend.

George Formby, the other personality singer to come out of the studios in the 1930s, could not sing just anything. However, nobody made a narrower range go further. Formby had taken his act from his father, who had modelled it on an old Lancashire stereotype of the put-upon male who enjoys no prestige but somehow can always put one over on the toffs, and it delivered him a successful film career as well as a musical one. Come the war, he was even more in his element. Whereas Gracie might require an orchestra to entertain the troops, George needed only the ukulele. He accompanied himself on this most unassuming instrument while singing songs celebrating the possibilities for voyeurism in the window cleaner's trade or the simple joys of walking down the promenade with 'My Little Stick Of Blackpool Rock' ('it may be sticky but I never complain / it's nice to have a nibble every now and again'). The lyrical content of a remarkable proportion of his songs would have him horse-whipped through the digital square of today. He was ever in trouble with the Dance Music Standards Committee, who regularly took him to task over his lyrics. This was a classic British moral panic in a kettle. On one side a mass audience who weren't offended; on the other a small group of educated people who thought they ought to be; in the middle a performer milking it for all the profile it was worth.

Seen in a different light Formby could be considered one of the more politically engaged performers of the time. He recorded a song in 1941 called 'Thanks Mr Roosevelt', which expressed the nation's gratitude for lend-lease 'for helping us to carry on'. The fact that the song was played by the BBC was marked in the *New York Times* in January 1941 opposite a news story in which America's aviator hero Charles Lindbergh was quoted as saying 'aid to Britain is useless'. Pop music could evidently drop a word in an ear that might be closed to diplomacy. Formby kept up a furious pace during the war, starring in a string of morale-boosting films, performing for ENSA within the sound of shellfire, playing three shows a day on an eight-week tour of North Africa and winning the Order of Lenin, which is more than most ukulele-wielders can claim. He knew how to get the public on side. When Sabbath-observance campaigners criticized him for doing his weekly radio show on a Sunday he said he would only stop when British soldiers stopped dying on the same day.

After June 1944, when Allied troops still had only a toehold on mainland Europe, the emphasis shifted from maintaining morale on the home front to boosting that of the army in the field. To this end the American band leader Glenn Miller was flown to Britain with his fifty-piece Army Air Force Band to broadcast to the Allied troops via a special forces radio station, play a number of live dates, and to record some songs at Abbey Road. Their visit had been identified as a priority by Allied Supreme Commander Eisenhower. Miller was a lot keener to make this visit than his band, who were disturbed by the fact that their manifest unfitness for combat had been waived for the visit, and further discomfited when they arrived in London to find the city being peppered by daily attacks from Hitler's 'vengeance weapons'. The recordings at Abbey Road were for inclusion in a programme to be beamed into Germany, aimed at serving soldiers and prisoners of war, to make the point that 'Uncle Sam' had their best interests at heart. Miller talked to Ilse Weinberger, who translated his thoughts into German. The editor of the *Melody Maker* was on hand to approve the way 'the Major' used a pencil or a cigarette to conduct the band and how he managed to dominate the proceedings with military dignity, only unbending in the presence of star singer Dinah Shore, who arrived wearing military uniform and a pair of boots she had procured from an unusually small paratrooper. Then Sergeant Ray McKinley sang 'Is You Is Or Is You Ain't My Baby?' The last of these recordings was on 6 November 1944. It was to be Miller's final time in a studio. On 15 December he boarded a small plane on the outskirts of Bedford. The plan was to fly to Paris and for his band to follow him in due course. The plane took off and was never heard from again.

The records of Glenn Miller are, however, another story entirely. They have been playing ever since, largely because he disappeared in the way he did. Like the wartime recordings of Flanagan and Allen, Gracie Fields, George Formby, Henry Hall, Gertrude Lawrence and Noël Coward, which between them sketch a cross-section of English society in musical terms the way the Master did in dramatic terms in his play *This Happy Breed*, the undimmed power of the sentiment that rises from their grooves helps account for the fact that even those of us who were born long after the war still feel as though we lived through it. Every time we hear them it confirms our feeling that in the embrace of those benign, occasionally preposterous, always cosy recordings which helped deliver our grandparents from evil, we too may feel safe.

5

George Martin joined Abbey Road at the birth of the tape era and was the first to come to the realization that recording was just the beginning of the process.

GEORGE MARTIN, TAPE AND THE SMELL OF MONEY

Most Germans never set eyes on Hitler, either in the flesh or on film, but thanks to the German audio industry and the invention of the tape recorder, his voice reverberated in every parlour in the Reich. With the end of the war, what had been theirs became ours. The conquest of Germany revealed the fact that even the most advanced Allied audio people were way behind the Axis. In the wake of the Allied armies occupying Germany came a handful of boffins keen to learn why German broadcasts of classical music seemed to have so little surface noise. They could surely only be live. The major revelation was that these performances had been recorded not on discs, as they would have been in the UK and the USA, but on magnetic tape running on a Magnetophon recorder from the German equivalent of EMI, which was AEG.

The American specialists got first look at the machine and took it home to the West Coast, where it was first tried out on a Bing Crosby radio show. In 1946 a deputation of British sound people went to Berlin to discover the secrets of technology the Germans had considered so commonplace they hadn't bothered making them classified. In that deputation was an engineer from Abbey Road called E. W. Berth-Jones, who had the opportunity to inspect captured enemy equipment, including magnetic tape that had been used in code-breaking. Upon his return the people at Hayes started developing the BTR or British tape recorder, which would soon be the most important piece of technology in every EMI studio.

The first version of this, a beast weighing almost 600lb, was used initially to back up the wax discs on which recordings had been made rather than as the primary recording tool. EMI was by nature a belt-and-braces organization. Anything new had to undergo a prolonged testing period before being put to daily use. Even the exciting new omnidirectional microphones which they bought from the German company Neumann and the Austrian AKG had to be tested for two entire years before being cleared for use in St John's Wood. New mixing desks and recorders for the studio had to come out of the Central Research Lab at Hayes. In 1955 the company started its own record engineering development department out of which came a series of consoles with the REDD prefix. On their fact-finding trips to Germany in the 1950s EMI's engineers noticed that the German arm of EMI had already acquired a multi-track tape machine. They could have acquired one for London. But that would never do. Instead they ordered REDD to build their own.

Tape transformed everything. Not only was the sound quality far better than with the direct-to-disc method; far more significant was the fact that with tape it was now possible, for the first time, to edit what had been recorded. This meant that the performance in the studio was no longer the final act of the recording process. It was simply another stage. Tape opened up a whole new world of post-production. With tape you could record longer performances, do multiple takes and compare them, take sections out of this tape and splice it into a second tape, and then make adjustments to the final recording in the process of transferring it to the master disc from which the records would be manufactured. And since the only people who had the skills to perform all this magic were the studio technicians, the performers, intuiting the fact that this new machinery had the capability to conceal or expose their occasional shortcomings, began to view them with new respect. In the wake of tape came cutting rooms, with specialist engineers able to control how the performance got from the tape to the lacquers from which the actual discs would be manufactured.

As all this was going on the American record companies RCA and Columbia combined their expertise in 1948 to invent the microgroove long-playing record, which offered the chance to own a symphony on one indestructible record playing at 33⅓ revolutions per minute rather than on ten brittle shellac discs playing at 78. EMI were not going to be distracted by any shiny new thing. It took four years before they felt bold enough to issue their own long-playing records. Even when EMI finally decided to dip a toe into the manufacture and distribution of seven-inch 45 rpm records it was with a classical rather than a pop record. However, elsewhere in the organization there were some signs that Tin Pan Alley was beginning to infiltrate. With the arrival in 1948 of two new record men there grew a new commercial sensibility, a determination to get into position for the new world that was bound to arrive when fun came off the ration book and they could start manufacturing records in quantity again, with the clear imperative that a successful studio must be a hit factory as well as a conservatory. One was called Norman and the other was called Wally, as yeoman-like a pair of names as Central Casting could ever come up with.

Wally Ridley was brought in as recording manager for the HMV label with a brief to wean it away from its traditional reliance on the classical catalogue. Wally was all hail-fellow-well-met. His background was in the kind of music publishing where you have to sit down at the piano and demonstrate the company's wares. He was broader than Broadway. He had an office to the left of reception so he could observe the comings and goings. Wally wasn't one to let anyone look down on him. He had done a lot in radio and therefore was all about casting and coaching. In his hands the personality side of the repertoire developed. They say Wally was the man who taught Alma Cogan to sing with a giggle in her voice. He was certainly the man who in 1958 saw the sheet music for an overripe American ballad called 'Mad Passionate Love' and decided it would be a hit in Britain if it was done by comic actor Bernard Bresslaw, who specialized in intellectually challenged softies. In another life Wally had discovered and trained Vera Lynn, of whom he liked to boast that she sings slow, then slower, then even slower than that. Wally was show business to his boots and not one to dally with critical acclaim. He it was who in 1954 insisted on taking an edgy young comedian called Max Bygraves and making him sing a song called 'Gilly Gilly Ossenfeffer'. When Max's wife asked 'What does it mean?' he told her it meant it was a hit song. They recorded it in Studio One with a group of kids and Wally recalled he almost choked up, not because he was swayed by their angelic voices but because he realized there was no way this was not going to be a major hit. Like every record man who came after him, he could smell hits the way others could smell money.

While Wally Ridley was in charge of the fortunes of HMV, his greatest competition came from the other new boy, Norman Newell, who was responsible for Columbia. Norman was a graduate of Tin Pan Alley who loved a show tune and knew how to deal with stars. He was the first person to record teenage sweetheart Petula Clark with 'Put Your Shoes On, Lucy' in 1949. He hit big with *siffleur* Ronnie Ronalde, whose 1949 recording of 'In A Monastery Garden' bears the curious credit 'sung by Ronnie Ronalde' when what he clearly does is whistle. Norman did records with Rosemary Squires, the Beverley Sisters, Shirley Bassey and pretty much anyone who owned their own evening gloves. He would bring in the cast of London productions of hit musicals like *The Boyfriend* and record them in the studio, always on a Sunday, which was when the theatres were dark and the Abbey Road staff were allowed to wear sports jackets and flannels instead of suits. Norman was also a songwriter and began the tradition of slipping one of his own compositions on to the B-side of a certain hit, thus securing the kind of bonus his EMI masters were not going to provide via his pay packet.

As a consequence of business tangles which reached back decades, arrangements with RCA and Columbia in the United States meant that HMV released the former's records in the UK and Columbia did the latter's. The arrangements with both companies ended after the war, as both set their sights on establishing UK-based operations. This meant that Norman suddenly had to come up with a supply of home-grown records to do battle on the newly established singles chart. It was through one arrangement with RCA, which would end in 1957, that they first came into contact with the new fad for electrified hillbilly music, which came into vogue in the United States in 1956 in the shape of Elvis Presley. The first thing that struck the people at Abbey Road about 'Heartbreak Hotel', which was sent to them from the US to be remastered for release in the UK, was the amount of echo. Staff above a certain age felt certain this had to be the result of some kind of equipment malfunction. The younger ones understood that this was not a mistake. Instead it was a different kind of good. Whereas the people working in classical music wanted to record music, the people in pop increasingly wanted to record sounds.

When Wally and Norman came to Abbey Road, Britain had just one television channel and no talent shows. Had there been talent shows, they would probably have been the first to be asked to sit in judgement. Judgement was their wheelhouse. They were talent scouts. These were men who had peddled sheet music. Now they were selling records. They had the kind of minds the new post-war record business would need, mental chambers in which were housed delicate machinery capable of assessing the most unlikely wannabe at their door and instantly working out how, with the right piece of material, the support of this radio producer and the introduction of that gimmick, they might be able to climb to the top of the best-sellers.

At the time Norman and Wally were called recording managers but in time they would be known as artists and repertoire (A&R) men. Their job was to find the material and put it together with the people who could sing it. The material all came from the professional songsmiths who worked for the publishers in Denmark Street. The singers came from the agents. It wasn't until many years later that they started to deal with singers who wrote their own songs. Neither Wally nor Norman ever touched a fader or spliced a tape in their entire careers but it was nonetheless their job to make a record happen.

In those post-war years, when you could have gathered all the people who could make a record a hit around a table in Quaglino's, the leading names of British pop read like a poster for a variety show. Every name was followed by its own 'bill matter'. Alma Cogan was the Girl with the Giggle in Her Voice, Eddie Calvert the Man with the Golden Trumpet, Frankie Vaughan Mr Moonlight and Michael Holliday the British Bing Crosby. Nobody used their real names and Abbey Road was where they were issued with their new ones. When Norman Newell happened upon the handsome piano pounder whose gimmick was that he appeared to be the only person in fifties Britain who, despite smoking eighty untipped cigarettes a day, still had straight white teeth, he realized he would never get anywhere with the name Trevor Stanford and therefore decided that he would henceforth be known as Russ Conway, under which name he topped the charts with 'Side Saddle' and similar relentlessly cheerful fare, all of which he played on the tack piano Abbey Road wheeled out when they wished to suggest loose morals.

Pop music as we understand it today was not invented in Britain until the year 1952, when the first British singles chart was launched in the *New Musical Express*. Here, where art met commerce in a simple easy-to-read format, is where the great game of uppers, downers and hanging-arounders began. In its early years the charts were dominated by Americans such as Doris Day, Perry Como, Slim Whitman, Frankie Laine and Frank Sinatra. They had the best songs, they had the golden voices, and they enjoyed the incalculable advantage of being American. The same thing seemed to apply to what came next. When Wally Ridley was first sent 'Heartbreak Hotel' by RCA in the United States, together with a note saying 'you won't understand a word of it', he put it out even though RCA were right and he didn't. The fact that it went to number two in the singles chart didn't seem to compensate for the fact that most of his peers in the music industry felt he should be horse-whipped for flying in the face of taste, decency and musical form. He decided there was no point looking for British rock and roll talent because this was not a language we spoke, and it would take us years to catch up; in any case, he had just recorded Malcolm Vaughan doing 'St Therese Of The Roses' and that had sold a quarter of a million without frightening a single horse.

The one place where home-grown seemed to be best was in comedy. Here two things counted: the first was the ability to bring all the tools of the studio to bear in order instantly to summon the genre that was being pastiched; the second was a sensibility that was distinctly British. EMI was to have a lot of success working this seam at a time when their efforts at pop music were second-best to the Americans. One of the first comedy records to taste chart success was 'The Cowpuncher's Cantata', a Max Bygraves spoof of the kind of Western music which was such a staple of British radio in the cowboy-obsessed fifties. The years have not been kind to either singer or song. What makes it noteworthy is that the person charged with bringing it home was a young man who was good at dealing with musicians and had recently arrived at Abbey Road as number two at the Parlophone label. His name was George Martin.

Parlophone was a Cinderella label within the EMI compound and there were many times in the fifties when its continued existence was in question. George Martin was similarly a misfit on the Abbey Road staff. He could read and write music but he wasn't a Tin Pan Alley man. Although he was excited about what could be done with records he wasn't to be found discussing impedance in the canteen. His time in the services had given him an officer's polish but his background was other ranks. Although he liked music well enough, what he really loved were records.

In that decade Britain wasn't conspicuously overstocked with outstanding musical talent. What there was often lost its way during National Service. It did, however, thanks to BBC radio, have the best comic talent. At this time the likes of Tony Hancock, Sid James, Kenneth Williams, Spike Milligan and Peter Sellers were household names, and comedy records were big. The Sunday lunchtime request shows which were appointment listening for every family in the country regularly featured the likes of humorist Gerard Hoffnung speaking to the Oxford Union and even 'Mock Mozart' by Peter Ustinov. This last was George Martin's first venture into humour. It wasn't his last. Sensing that comedy was a route to securing the future of Parlophone and his continued employment, he sought out promising shows to record. On one of these safaris he found Michael Flanders and Donald Swann, a Fry and Laurie forerunner, performing in a revue called *At the Drop of a Hat*, and decided to record them live. The show then transferred to the West End, with the result that songs such as 'A Transport Of Delight', 'The Gnu Song' and 'The Hippopotamus' became turntable hits and the LP, a format which EMI had been rather late to, was also a success. In one bit from the show Flanders pokes fun at this new tribe of hi-fi fans who are trying to get the sound of an orchestra in their living room. Personally, he reflects, he couldn't imagine anything worse.

In 1959's *Songs For Swingin' Sellers*, George Martin employed the full resources of EMI Studios to create something beyond the reach of the traditional comedy album, which had tended to rely on volleys of audience laughter to mark the whereabouts of the funny bits. This record was different. Each track on *Songs For Swingin' Sellers* sets the listener down in a fresh part of its comic universe – from the Mayfair flat where Major Rafe Ralph schools would-be rock idol Clint Thigh ('How many times have I told you? The hole points away from you!') to the gated London garden ('private without being insulated if you know what I mean') wherein a French gigolo flirts with widow Irene Handl – and each sketch required no introduction beyond the soundscape provided by music and distant effects. Much of it was fashioned in the studio. 'Shadows On The Grass' was brilliantly improvised on the basis of Handl's original idea. Sellers sings 'I Haven't Told Her, She Hasn't Told Me' in silly-ass guise, accompanying himself on ukulele mainly because he fancies it. The actual form of the LP, a medium which was only ten years old at the time, is spoofed throughout. The opening track 'You Keep Me Swingin'', which is supposed to be Sellers doing Frank Sinatra, is in fact British balladeer Matt Monro performing under the name Fred Flange. Martin had initially brought Monro in to provide a guide for Sellers. Sellers, rightly, realized he couldn't do any better. In the run-up to Christmas 1959, *Songs For Swingin' Sellers* reached number three on the LP charts, which placed it one place below *Cliff Sings* and half a dozen above Russ Conway's *Family Favourites*, further products of the same studio. *Songs For Swingin' Sellers*, which has rarely been out of the catalogue since, remains a masterpiece which used the studio to build pictures in sound ten years before Martin's illustrious later clients got round to doing the same thing.

Not all the comedy records that George Martin oversaw for Parlophone at the time deserve to be quite so fondly remembered, but they all demonstrated an attention to detail and a respect for the strange dignity of show business which you would be unlikely to find anywhere other than the BBC. Parlophone had another thing in common with the BBC: George Martin assumed that the performers knew best. However, he also knew he had to be ready to step in on occasion to save those performers from the consequences of their actions. In 1961 a super-session of sorts took place in Studio Two when George brought Sellers and Spike Milligan together with up-and-comers Peter Cook and Jonathan Miller, newly famous thanks to *Beyond the Fringe*, to record a parody of the recent hit film *The Bridge on the River Kwai*. In order to reproduce the sound of some unfortunate having his head chopped off George had to send out, at Sellers' insistence, for a cabbage to be gruesomely bisected on microphone. Only when the recording, which was planned for an entire LP, was completed did somebody in the legal department make the fundamental error of asking the film's producers if they had any objection. They did. Therefore it fell to George Martin and the studio's specialist tape editors to comb through the entire finished recording, painstakingly excising the opening consonant from every single use of the word 'Kwai' until it was reborn as the rather less resonant 'Bridge On The River Wye'.

It would not be the last time the engineers at Abbey Road laboured far into the night to save the bacon of performers who had clocked off and were out enjoying themselves. In the new world of tape no record could be considered finished until the final cut had been made; and the person who did that was now called the producer.

6

Cliff Richard recorded his first album 'live' at Abbey Road in 1959 in front of an audience made crazy by free sandwiches and orange squash.

CLIFF, THE RS 124 AND THE QUEST FOR ROUGH

The first rock and roll records came from America. More specifically they came from independent labels like Sun in Memphis or Specialty in Los Angeles and were often made in studios where there was no accepted way of doing things, no technical department imposing standards of sound quality, and therefore accidents tended to be embraced rather than erased. In fact the first rock and roll record, Jackie Brenston's 'Rocket "88"', which was made in 1951, had a distorted guitar sound on it because a speaker cone had been damaged when the amplifier came off the roof of the car that was conveying the band to the studio. The lyrics of Little Richard's 'Tutti Frutti' had been hastily written over the chassis of a dirty song at the end of a frantic session in New Orleans. Elvis Presley had happened on the magic groove of 'That's All Right' after months of trying in the Sun studio, causing producer Sam Phillips to exclaim 'That's a pop song now' over the talkback. Phillips didn't know what he wanted but as a regional indie he knew his only chance of being heard amid the hubbub was to make a record such as people hadn't heard before, and if it sounded strange so much the better.

It was lively in a new way. Here, all of a sudden, was music which appeared to challenge the accepted wisdom that music should ideally soothe the savage breast. Here was music which seemed to positively embrace the rough rather than the smooth. Here was music that preferred raising a ruckus to knitting up the ravelled sleeve of care. To ears accustomed to the creamy, cardigan sound of Perry Como or Doris Day such records could often sound like mistakes. To technicians at the EMI studios, whose very title 'balance engineer' was designed to stress the fact that their role was to impose order on chaos, this music sounded unbalanced, sometimes deliberately so. Furthermore, some of it was clearly being made by people who were new to the whole business of being musicians. To hear some of their adherents talk you might even think the fragile hold they had on their professional skills was part of what fans seemed to like about it. They didn't quite know how to respond. Some of the productions which came out of the EMI studios in the late fifties when they were trying to come up with their own versions of American hits using local talent suggested that the people in charge didn't have the foggiest notion exactly where the sweet spot of the originals lay.

The experience of Larry Page, who went on to become a successful manager but in 1957 was being set before the public as 'Larry Page the Teenage Rage' (to conceal the fact that at the time he was working as a packer at EMI's factory in Hayes), was par for the course in an Abbey Road where too many producers seemed to be trying to tame the manners of American music in order to come up with records which might be acceptable to the producers of *The Billy Cotton Band Show*. 'The record producers had the idea that if you went in with a big orchestra, a few doo-wops and a few backing singers you had a rock and roll record, but you didn't,' he recalled. 'They told me they had found the right song and the original would never be released here. I did "That'll Be The Day" with the Geoff Love Orchestra and the Rita Williams Singers and it had no feeling and it was a silly arrangement. As soon as we hit the market the Buddy Holly original was released and went to number one.'

EMI did better with skiffle, which was a genuinely British twist on American vernacular music. George Martin produced hits with the Vipers Skiffle Group, which provided some competition for king of the genre Lonnie Donegan, who recorded for the smaller British label Pye. Vipers sessions offered some foretaste of the coming erosion of formality. They often took place late at night, with the band walking in from Soho after finishing at the 2i's Coffee Bar, and they insisted that a bottle of Scotch be on hand at all times. On one occasion when their bass player didn't turn up George Martin went next door and borrowed Jack Collier, a former stalwart of Geraldo's orchestra, to fill in. According to John Pilgrim of the Vipers, Jack steeled himself for this new experience of vamping a song called 'I Was Born 10,000 Years Ago' by mixing strong ale with a bottle of whisky.

The people at the helms of EMI's three labels HMV, Columbia and Parlophone, who were responsible for keeping the company competitive with its great UK rival Decca, viewed this rock and roll from the other side of the Atlantic with suspicion if not outright alarm. While they were happy to concede that rock and roll was here, they were not convinced that it was here to stay. The bulk of EMI's talent were stars who had made their bones before the war, who occupied a place in the British public's affections and were regulars on prime-time TV. There seemed no reason this happy state of affairs should not continue. The younger employees joining the organization in the early 1950s were still schooled in the old ways. Young George Martin continued to be dispatched to Scotland with a mobile recording unit complete with disc-cutting lathe to literally cut twenty sides with Scottish country dance maestro Jimmy Shand, a strong seller among Scots at home and in exile. Not only did this save the expense of bringing all the musicians down to London and paying for their accommodation, it also meant their work need no longer be conducted according to the studio clocks.

For the staff there was often much to be said for recording on location. One of the first duties of Ken Townsend, who had joined the company on the same day as George Martin, was to visit Blackpool with the company's mobile recording equipment. One of EMI's biggest-selling recording artists at that time was Reginald Dixon, whose instrument, the mighty Wurlitzer of the ballroom of Blackpool Tower, was anything but mobile. To young Ken fell the dizzying responsibility of ascending from the bowels of the building alongside Reg, holding the microphone as the great man rose into view, grinning triumphantly as he played his signature tune, 'Oh I Do Like To Be Beside The Seaside'. In those days the company's relationships with its artists were much like that of a long-established department store of impeccable respectability with its Captain Peacocks. When Reginald was marking fifty years with the company, EMI threw a little party for him and he drove down from Blackpool for the occasion, towing his caravan in order to have a place to stay. Different times.

Of course any man called Reginald was unlikely to survive the changes that were taking place in mass entertainment as Britain came off its war footing and embraced the consumer society. The seven-inch 45, which had been launched by EMI in 1952 and was to overtake the 78 by 1959, quickly transformed the record market into a young person's market. These young people, suddenly known for the first time as teenagers, were the ones who crowded the record shops of the country on a Saturday morning. They were the ones putting money into coffee bar jukeboxes; they were the ones making the running. And young people appeared to demand records by other young people. In fact they seemed less bothered about musical distinction, more about having somebody to identify with. Wally Ridley had already been given the hard word by his counterpart at RCA in New York, where they were a couple of years ahead. The pop people, he said, have taken over. No sense fighting it. It's not that the people at Abbey Road weren't trying. In 1958 Norman Newell had a number one hit with sixteen-year-old Laurie London and his version of 'He's Got The Whole World In His Hands', which had even been taken up by EMI's American label Capitol, but the results were hardly infused with teen spirit.

The biggest record shop in the country at the time, by some considerable distance, was the EMI-owned HMV in London's Oxford Street. This was an emporium of recorded music. The staff wore uniforms. With its various departments devoted to musical equipment and music of different genres it was the only place in the country where somebody could come in off the street and make contact with the music business. One of the special services the shop offered was the opportunity to make a simple recording which could be used as a demo to drum up interest in a performer. One day in the spring of 1958, following payment of the requisite £10 by a friend of the band who happened to have a job at the local sewage works and was presumably feeling flush, five youngsters from the Hertfordshire suburbs came in and recorded their own stabs at the American rock and roll songs 'Lawdy Miss Clawdy' and 'Breathless'. Unaware that in America there was already an established band of the same name, the group had called themselves the Drifters. The singer had recently changed his name from Harry Webb to Cliff Richard.

The demo did its job, and on 24 July of the same year they came to Abbey Road to make their first record for commercial release. Columbia's Norrie Paramor had decided the time was right for the label to have a young act of its own. This was a strategic decision by the company, much as they might have felt their roster would be bolstered by the addition of a dance orchestra or a honky tonk piano player. Because this was a youth product aimed at the youth market they had decided that his first single had to be a cover of a youth song, an American composition of great insipidness called 'Schoolboy Crush'. In the course of the song we learned this crippling condition afflicted the singer 'at the candy shop, at the record house' and even 'at the drive-in show', all places you would have sought in vain in the Britain of 1958. To ensure the record should not be found wanting when it came to the shoo-be-doos, finger clicks and whistles which seemed a characteristic of the genre they made sure the Mike Sammes Singers, England's foremost close-harmony jingle merchants, were standing by to help. 'Schoolboy Crush' may have been about teenagers but it was anything but a teen record. In fact it was a most middle-aged notion of a teen record.

Having gone to all this trouble, the company was forced to concede that 'Schoolboy Crush' was nothing like as appealing as the tune which had been written by the band's guitarist Ian Samwell and recorded for the B-side. This song, the notion for which had alighted on Samwell as he sat on a Green Line bus stuck in traffic near Cheshunt, has some claim to be the first proper British rock and roll record. It was certainly the first one that was the product of actual flaming youth rather than another act of Olympian condescension perpetrated by slumming jazz musicians, as in earlier British rock and roll hits such as Tommy Steele's 'Rock With The Caveman'. That said, session guitarist Ernie Shear was nonetheless standing by to play the twiddly bits when they recorded it. Norrie Paramor wasn't yet ready to hand over his studio to a bunch of kids, particularly when he had to be sure he emerged with two releasable sides from a three-hour session. The plan to switch sides worked. 'Move It' went into the chart in September. It turned out to be the first of decades of hits Cliff Richard would provide for EMI.

The gatekeepers of 1958 still thought in terms of professional standards. Recording songs written by either the performer or the people in his band – the players that even a young engineer such as Malcolm Addey thought of as 'amateurs' to distinguish them from the sight readers and trained musicians he was accustomed to dealing with – was unknown at the time. Songwriting was one of those things British musicians seemed to have little business with. The UK charts were overwhelmingly dominated by hits from America – the same records by Elvis Presley, Fats Domino, Guy Mitchell, Harry Belafonte or Johnny Ray that were popular on the other side of the Atlantic – or by hit songs from the USA covered by British artists, like 'Green Door' by Frankie Vaughan or 'A White Sport Coat (And A Pink Carnation)' by the King Brothers. Even the hits George Martin produced with the Vipers at Abbey Road during the skiffle boom of 1957 were based on American folk songs. Rock and roll was American by definition in much the same way that flamenco music was Spanish.

Cliff had been brought to Abbey Road by Norrie Paramor. Norrie preferred to project him as presentable son-in-law material rather than the bit of rough hinted at every time he curled his lip or adjusted his quiff. Paramor was sufficiently in touch to realize that the company ought to have some sort of stake in rock and roll, even at a time when dance band musicians were lining up to pile earth on its casket, but he didn't have much of an ear for what worked. Happily, the public seemed to decide for him. Cliff's first film role in *Serious Charge* the following year did its best to project him as a threat to good order but the success of the song from that film, the finger-snapping Lionel Bart tune 'Living Doll', lit Cliff's way to a long career in the middle of the road – which was good for Cliff, for EMI and for Norrie, who rarely missed an opportunity to slip one of his own compositions on to a B-side. This was not something encouraged by senior EMI management, but since they didn't permit the people who found and recorded the talent to participate in any royalties from those records there wasn't much they could do about it.

The first long-playing record from Cliff Richard was in a sense a concept album. The powers that be in the post-war recording studio rarely got near enough actually to hear what was causing a stir among audiences so they were more concerned to record the evidence of the stir than the sound of the music. To that end, in February 1959 Abbey Road's management erected a stage in Studio

Two, brought in an audience, plied them with orange juice and sandwiches and then put Cliff Richard and his newly named Shadows on stage in front of them. In the event the young Cliff, who didn't have enough experience of singing live to know how to husband his vocal resources, was reduced to a croak. Since EMI had already invested the not inconsiderable sum of £200 they were not prepared to postpone the event until he could sing, and thus it went ahead. Ten years later EMI was still rubbing the same lamp when it invited fans of the Edgar Broughton Band to bring their greatcoats and grandad vests into the same studio, where a similar attempt would be made to bottle the kind of performance with which they were delighting polytechnics up and down the M1.

The music business was becoming the record business. Sound was becoming as important as song. A tension was beginning to arise between the label bosses, who were by and large sons of Denmark Street's sheet music trade, and their young seconds-in-command, represented by George Martin, John Burgess and others who had come on board and were increasingly excited by the commercial and creative possibilities of records. Records could be about something more than tuneful songs, pleasantly performed. They could offer drama. They could offer excitement. They could take you away from all this. In this new world it was possible to make movies with sound. On record, it turned out that the strangest things captured the imagination. Kids growing up in Britain in the fifties might be able to take or leave Dick James's plummy rendition of the theme from the TV series *The Adventures of Robin Hood* but they couldn't get enough of the sound of the arrow piercing the oak which preceded it. This had been achieved by George Martin with the aid of a ruler on the edge of a desk and a very close microphone. In the new age of recording this kind of trouble would evidently be worth taking.

What was holding them back was not just the cultural disconnect between the music that was stirring up the teenagers and the instincts of the people at EMI charged with finding and recording talent. It was also the studio itself. When George Martin visited the USA in 1958 with engineer Peter Bown, Martin may have been impressed with the professionalism of the Frank Sinatra session they visited but Bown was taken by the fact that American studios somehow sounded different. Bown was a most interesting character. Flamboyantly gay at a time when this could mean prison, Bown, who had joined the studio in 1951, carved an unusual path through the organization, graduating from recording *The Dream Of Gerontius* with Sir John Barbirolli to *The Piper At The Gates Of Dawn* with Pink Floyd, and proving equally good at both. He was sufficiently interested in the technical side of things to discover that what made American studios sound different was something called audio compression. This had been developed in the United States for the radio business but then spread into recording studios. It was a way of controlling the peaks and troughs of recorded music, particularly at the disc-cutting stage, where there was a danger of a sudden peak making a record jump, or in radio to make one station sound punchier than the station next door. Basically it raised the level of the quietest parts of the music and brought the loudest parts down to meet them. Compressors were soon being used in the studio itself to manipulate sound during the recording process. They made everything sound punchier, harder, more urgent. Their introduction did for sound what processes like Technicolor did for film. They made records that leapt out of the radio. They made things sound otherworldly. Much as Technicolor rendered such pictures as nobody had actually seen in normal life, the compressor created sounds in the studio that were more exciting than would be possible in the outside world. The compressor was the reason American records seemed louder and more brazen. They made the sounds cut through. They seemed to move the air around.

The absence of this technology was one of the reasons why an Abbey Road rock and roll record such as Johnny Kidd and the Pirates' 'Shakin' All Over', released at the end of the decade, was not half the record the performers and the song deserved. Heft was what it needed and at this point in time Abbey Road didn't do heft. The best pop records coming out of there were by the Shadows, records which had their own insinuating charm, or the twisted *café au lait* sound of John Barry's 'Hit And Miss', the theme tune for *Juke Box Jury*. Barry even produced an entire 1960 LP called *Stringbeat* in which his guitarist Vic Flick had to record twelve tunes in a day in Studio Two while lined up with a music stand before the pitiless gaze of violinists who felt they should be doing something more becoming their talents than plucking their strings to make the pizzicato sound that had become Barry's trademark. Around this time Barry went to the West Coast, where he met with Phil Spector, who was just beginning to enter his imperial phase, and Lee Hazlewood, the man whose records with Duane Eddy were as full fat as Barry's were frothy coffee. The only British pop records of the time with that other-worldly density were those being made in Holloway Road by Joe Meek, records such as 'Telstar' by the Tornados, which seemed to be made up of sounds nobody had ever heard before. That was about to change.

It would take time for this kit to reach Abbey Road. They didn't rush into anything. EMI wasn't the kind of company to just buy this kind of thing off the shelf. There would first have to be a certain amount of preliminary tyre-kicking and some sceptical sucking of pipes on the part of the gentlemen from the record engineering development department out at Hayes before an American machine could be successfully adapted to achieve the standards of sound quality they demanded. It's said that by the time the men in the lab had finished with the American Altec compressor its only remaining original feature was a single VU meter on the front. Only then could it be installed in their studios, and even then you can imagine the whimpering sound arising from the boffins as they were finally forced to let go. But once they had done so they never let the RS 124, as they affectionately termed their processor, off the premises. Which is why, come the sixties, records made at Abbey Road didn't sound like records made anywhere else.

7

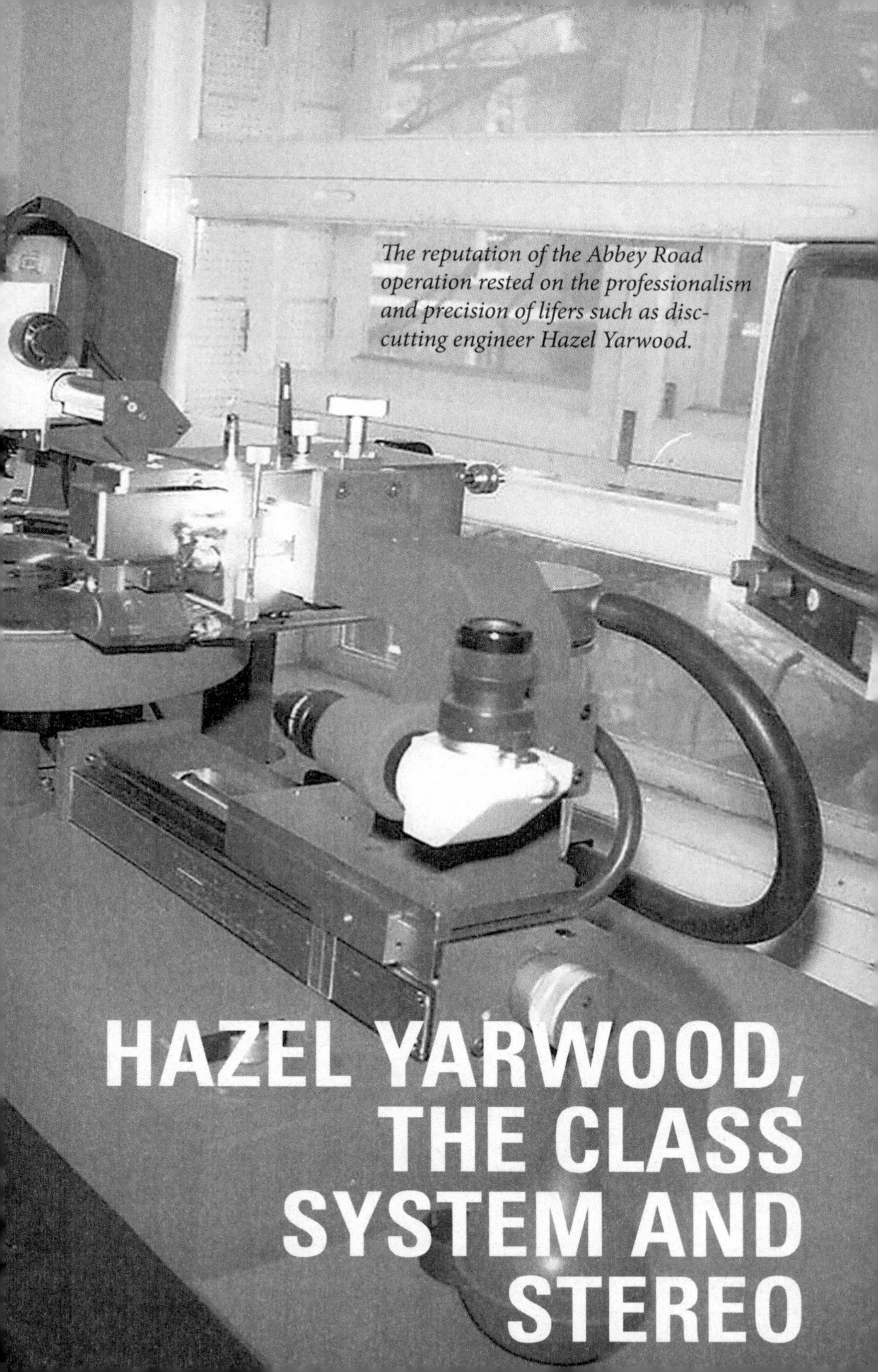

The reputation of the Abbey Road operation rested on the professionalism and precision of lifers such as disc-cutting engineer Hazel Yarwood.

HAZEL YARWOOD, THE CLASS SYSTEM AND STEREO

In the years following the Second World War there were no places you could go to learn about working in the business of recording. Anybody who knew anything about the business of recording was already fully occupied in the business of recording. In those first years of peace, when London was pockmarked with bomb damage and everything was still in short supply, three young people found their way to employment at the studios in St John's Wood, which was one of the only places you could learn. All ascended the same whitewashed steps and passed before Sgt Wells, the First World War veteran who guarded the portal. Each one took their turn perching nervously under the painting of the listening dog in reception while awaiting their interview. Happily they all secured the jobs they applied for, even though none of them knew much about the jobs they had applied for because each function of the recording process was a mystery known only to the people inside. None of them could have predicted how momentous a day this would prove to be. All would remain with the company for the rest of their working lives, watching technologies come and go, empires wax and wane, and hairstyles and behavioural norms change more dramatically inside the building than they did in the world outside.

They came from different backgrounds. What they had in common was a certain steadiness of temperament, a commitment to exactitude in all things which was apt to irritate the slapdash, an ability to absorb and understand technical information, an appreciation of music, and the uninterrogated belief that spending one's working life taking something as evanescent as music and translating it into a thing as tangible and precious as a record was a privilege. These were not flamboyant people. The Second World War had seen to that. They had no difficulty fitting in with the studios' codes of dress and deportment. They were people of the suburbs and they had suburban attitudes. They were cricketers and gardeners and table tennis players and leading lights of their local amateur operatic societies. They were not given to excess except in the pursuit of the standards they felt should be associated with their place of work. They were not dazzled by starlight. On his retirement, one long-serving classical engineer liked to recall the day he loaned half a crown to a Beatle for the cigarette machines but couldn't recall which one it had been. Through the many changes they would see through their working lives they would continue to provide artists of all kinds with the benefit of their expertise. They would do their best to give those artists what they wanted. As is often the case with people who spend their lives learning things others cannot be bothered to learn, they often gave those artists what they wanted before they realized they wanted it.

Hazel Yarwood was one. She began work at Abbey Road in 1947. When she applied for the job she had no relevant experience but she was well brought up, clearly dependable, familiar with her father's collection of classical recordings and could read music. She had been working as a travelling actor in the years after the war and the studio seemed like a good place to settle down. Since she remained there, at first editing tape and then cutting master discs, for the next thirty-eight years, she was correct in that assessment. In those days No. 3 Abbey Road was an eminently respectable place to work. The steps leading up to the front door were kept spotless to create the right impression. At work, Hazel wore a white coat to denote her status as one of the technical staff. She didn't mind the uniform because it had a pocket in which she could keep the yellow pencil she used to mark the place where the edit needed to be made, and another for the scissors which would make the fateful incision.

The management of EMI in the early fifties was less than forward-looking. In 1948, when the two big American companies RCA and CBS combined their resources to launch that exciting new product, the long-playing record, the boss at the time said there was no point confusing the public by having records going round at speeds other than 78 rpm. EMI would not be doing new recordings for this new format and therefore the first work Hazel did involved going back to piles of 78s, painstakingly transferring them to tape, splicing them together and then cutting fresh discs for reissue on LP.

When Joseph Lockwood took over as chairman in 1954 EMI finally overcame its prejudice about the LP and the first artists keen to take advantage were the classical musicians. Now, at last, they could perform their pieces as they would do on the concert stage. But was it as simple as that? They wanted their work to be heard to best advantage, but what did that mean? Hazel was in the studio with the pianist Solomon in 1956 when he was having trouble with the double fugue in Beethoven's Hammerklavier sonata. She attempted to reassure him by saying that since this was being done on tape it would be perfectly possible to edit the slip. He refused her offer of help on the grounds that 'I cannot take you with me on my concerts'. Therefore it was decided they would stop for supper before resuming. This time he got it right. A stroke later that year which robbed him of the use of one arm meant Solomon never finished the complete cycle of sonatas. The recording he made after dinner, however, remains in the catalogue seventy years later.

In 1960 Hazel asked to be moved to the part of Abbey Road where the discs were cut. There she remained for the next twenty-five years, supplying a key link in the lengthening chain of record production, taking what had been done in the studio using the latest and most expensive equipment and bringing to bear all her experience to judge how to translate that sound on to a record which would provide a satisfactory listening experience on gramophones ranging from the most high-end to the kind you might take on a picnic. This was a job which married her exactitude of manner with her love of music. In each case she began by listening to the tape while reading the score at the same time. She did this in order to note any unusually loud or quiet passages where some assistance might be required in the cutting process; she was simultaneously deciding how much music could be happily accommodated on how many discs. Any more than twenty minutes a side and quality would be lost. If she cut the record at too high a level there would be distortion. If she didn't attend to the sibilants the sound might break up on certain players. It was a tense process.

When Hazel was listening she was not to be disturbed. The telephone was switched off. Questions of vulgar commerce did not intrude on her priestly work. When things were finally in place she put the platter – in this case an aluminium disc coated with a layer of lacquer with some of the consistency of wet paint – on the turntable beneath the arm, started the tape and engaged the machine. Once the arm contacted the surface of the disc its heated cutting stylus took the musical information coming through from the tape and inscribed it on the lacquer. The cutting lathe is like a record player whose pickup works in reverse. Rather than taking the information from the disc, the lathe cut the information into the disc. These lacquers were then sent off to the factory at Hayes, where they would make a few test pressings to be approved by the company. Hazel would always make sure she heard these before the artist did. If they weren't right she could require them to be done again. She saw her work with cutter and lathe and highly tuned human ear not as the first step in a mechanical process of manufacture but as the last one in an artistic process of creation. It was not surprising that she never felt the need to move on, retiring in the same job in 1985. When Hazel died in 2013 there were obituaries in the heavy papers.

Unlike Hazel, Francis Dillnutt, who joined the studios in 1945, had been born to the trade. His father had been a recording engineer working for HMV from the turn of the century, spending a lot of time accompanying his precious straight-to-wax recording equipment around the world. To India by sea. All across the Continent. He was even sent to record a speech given by a prominent Italian who went on longer than the four minutes fifty seconds the machine could accommodate. This is how Francis's father earned the right to boast that he told Mussolini to do it all over again.

Francis was a classic example of the men who built Abbey Road, a grammar school boy who began his apprenticeship at the EMI factory in Hayes at the beginning of the war, shuttling between the foundry and the department where the electronics people were developing the means to track aircraft. At the time Hayes was a city in itself, with its own fire brigade and its own Home Guard. They generated their own power on-site. They had two Artesian wells. They had a railway siding with two engines to transport the coal to the factory. At the age of twenty-one, helped by the fact that his father had worked for the company, he got a job at Abbey Road. It was a tight ship in those days. You wore a suit for work. If you were called upon to work on a weekend only then were you permitted the brazen informality of a sports jacket and flannels.

In those pre-electric days a young recording engineer like Francis would have to deal with lathes, spindles, cutting tools, flammable materials and dangerous chemicals rather than buttons and faders. When he began, recordings were still being made direct to disc. There was no actual recording machinery in the studio where a full orchestra of musicians would be playing. Nor would there be any tackle in the control room, where the executives from the record company would be listening. All sound would be directed to the Machine Room. This was where the actual recording was made.

With this technology there was as little room for error as there was at the time with a car gearbox without synchromesh. The Machine Room would signal its readiness with one buzz to call for silence. A second buzz would announce that the cutter had engaged. A red light would signal the beginning of the performance. The engineers were not silent witnesses to a musical performance. They had to know precisely how long the performance was going to be before it began. Four minutes fifty seconds was about as long as a disc could manage. More likely it would be around four minutes. If something went wrong during the performance it was more than any mere musician's life was worth to put a hand up and call for a do-over. Once it was decided a performance was satisfactory the musicians moved on to the next selection without having the satisfaction of hearing a playback. The lacquer would be packaged up to be sent to the factory where a negative image of it would be used to make the stamper from which the finished 78s could be made.

In any disagreement between the recording artists and the recording engineers, the latter would tend to win because they could always predict the dire consequences that would arise should this machinery be placed under greater pressure than it was designed to handle. When Francis began in the years after the war his boss, the senior recording engineer, was not above hitting the machine to make it jump at the point where the conductor had insisted on fortissimo and claiming that the peaks would make the record impossible to manufacture properly. At the time the recording engineers belonged to a priesthood who held as much sway over what was or was not possible as the coders of today's digital industries. EMI was a manufacturing business; these boys had trained at the factory and their job was to ensure above all that the minimum standards of manufacture were being observed.

When the company first began issuing records made in stereo it adopted a belt-and-braces approach and Francis was charged with supervising the two different microphone set-ups and two separate control rooms required to record the mono and stereo versions simultaneously. He also did a lot of travel. On the occasions when there could be no question of bringing in an overseas orchestra, Francis would be dispatched to cities such as Vienna and Berlin with the boxes of equipment needed to set up a recording unit in a symphony hall. These trips could last as long as eight weeks and were known within the company as 'Recording Expeditions', as though they were being undertaken by a district officer in a far-flung corner of the Empire from which they might not return. The employees being deployed overseas in this manner were on a similarly tight leash, being permitted just one phone call home on arrival and another prior to their return.

It was that kind of organization. At EMI, the daily struggle to maintain standards and to assert one's position within the organization was conducted via formal memos. These were produced by the armies of typists who far outnumbered the company's executives dictating them. On 25 August 1961, for instance, classical supremo Walter Legge fired off one such pained communication to J. D. Bicknell at Hayes. It began: 'As you know, no singers like recording in No. 1 studio and both my Wife and Callas hate it.' His wife just happened to be Elisabeth Schwarzkopf, the soprano so unafflicted by modesty that when guesting on BBC radio's *Desert Island Discs* she chose seven of her own records. Legge wrote that he had been casting around for alternatives and had rejected the Wigmore Hall on grounds of noise from the sewing machine factory next door. Three years later Sir Malcolm Sargent, referred to behind his back as 'Flash Harry' for his open and frank admiration of his own gifts,

To: Mr. J.D. Bicknell, Hayes. 25th August 1961

c.c. Mr. E. Fowler, Abbey Road.

From: Walter Legge WL/ED

As you know, no singers like recording in No.1 Studio and both my Wife and Callas hate it. For solo voice with piano it is much worse since its last treatment, and I feel that we shall never get first-class Lieder records out of Schwarzkopf until we have found another hall.

The Wigmore Hall is impossible, both on the grounds of noise from the sewing machines from the wholesale clothing establishment next door and because empty it does not produce good sound.

Mr. Beckett and Mr. Larter both feel that Battersea Town Hall would require extensive acoustic treatment, but I believe that with screens and some damping it might work. Are you prepared to go to the expense of a test session with Schwarzkopf and Moore at the earliest possible date, or have you any London alternative to No.1 and No.3 Studios ?

Walter Legge

Classical supremo Walter Legge and his wife Elizabeth Schwarzkopf were unhappy with Studio One in 1961.

took his beef higher, dashing off a letter to Sir Joseph Lockwood, by then the boss of the whole EMI shooting match, which began with those words every chairman dreads, 'I am sorry to have to write this letter'. It went on to detail his disappointment with the changes which had been made to the studio since he last recorded there. Poor Sir Joe, who probably hoped to get through the rest of his career without being party to a conversation with a sound engineer about reverberation intervals, found himself forced to adjudicate between the venerable baton wielder and Mr G. F. Dutton, who headed up his own research department and placed inverted commas around the word 'pop', as though it had been coined earlier that day. There is no indication that the disagreement was ever sorted quite to everybody's satisfaction but Sir Malcolm's next session for EMI was moved to the Kingsway Hall. At one point in the correspondence Sir Joseph wrote to Sir Malcolm thanking him for his letter on acoustics, a letter which he described as 'interesting'. In the genteel world of classical music this is tantamount to inviting someone to step outside.

The last of our three, Ken Townsend, arrived at Abbey Road in 1954 after four years learning a trade at Hayes. Here he was immediately struck by the gulf between the classical and pop sides of the business. This, he found to his amusement, often mirrored the class differences among the staff. The classical side was dominated by those to the manner born who made an unquestioned assumption that pop was for common people and therefore it was best left in the horny hands of sons of toil. Ken was a grammar school boy and so, like the man in the middle in the famous *Frost Report* sketch about class, was quite used to explaining one class to another. Over the next ten years the pre-war culture of the studios would be revolutionized by just such grammar school boys.

The overall boss of the studios at the time was 'Chick' Fowler. Ken wondered why he was so-called. It took him a short while to work out that the culture of the place was such that anyone with a poultry-derived surname had to be issued with a matching nickname. Fowler was the man who had recorded Artur Schnabel's Beethoven marathon in the thirties. He was not one for managing by wandering around unless it was to turn off lights. He would turn up if they were recording an opera in Rome but he might not be too visible around Abbey Road on a daily basis. Fowler's background was entirely on the classical side. As far as the company was concerned the priorities were classical. If they bought new equipment it was most likely to be for classical recordings. There still wasn't that much thought given to the pop side.

From his position in what was then known as the Amp Room, which was where the people who dealt with the equipment were quartered, young Ken was ideally placed to see what was going on. He worked from 8.30 a.m. to 5 p.m. He would start by setting up all the equipment for a session, according to the layout provided by the studio engineer (this individual was actually known as the balance engineer and often didn't know very much about the technical side of recording). Like Hazel Yarwood and Francis Dillnutt, Ken remained at Abbey Road until retirement, so if anybody is in a position to know what changed in the way the company was run during those decades it's Ken. 'In the early 1950s there were almost no studios in this country,' he recalled. 'There was Decca in West Hampstead, Phillips at Marble Arch, and then there was EMI. Each company recorded its own artists in its own studio. There were a couple of independents but the amount of recording being done was relatively small. For EMI the studio was a service, not a profit centre. At Abbey Road we did everything possible for the artist to get the best record. We didn't have to worry in any shape or form about how much it cost.'

In the course of his career Ken worked both sides of the Berlin Wall dividing pop from classical and became familiar with how the twists and turns of outrageous fortune left their mark on people other than the stars. 'If an artist was doing well and then suddenly didn't, he would never accept the fact that the public didn't want his records any more. It wasn't ever him that was wrong. It was either the producer or the engineer.' Ken held back his true thoughts during such conversations and made sure he maintained good relations with everybody. This wasn't simply the good manners of a grammar school boy. This was also because you never knew whose star would be the next to rise.

One Sunday evening in the summer of 1962 Ken came home to his wife and family. He had been playing cricket against a side called the Gayfarers. At home there was a message from George Martin asking if he could possibly make himself available the following Wednesday evening because Parlophone had a group coming in for a test recording. These sessions were an occasional feature of studio life and were widely regarded as a waste of time because nothing ever came out of them. The idea that any bunch of untried youngsters would turn up with anything you hadn't heard many times before was a very long shot indeed. These test recordings were more for the benefit of the company than the turn. Much like the BBC at the time, EMI felt it had to be reassured that the musicians it engaged came up to certain basic standards of competence. To that end George was asking for Ken to be standing by because he had never worked with the group or the engineer, Norman Smith, before.

Ken, who kept in with everyone, put it in his diary.

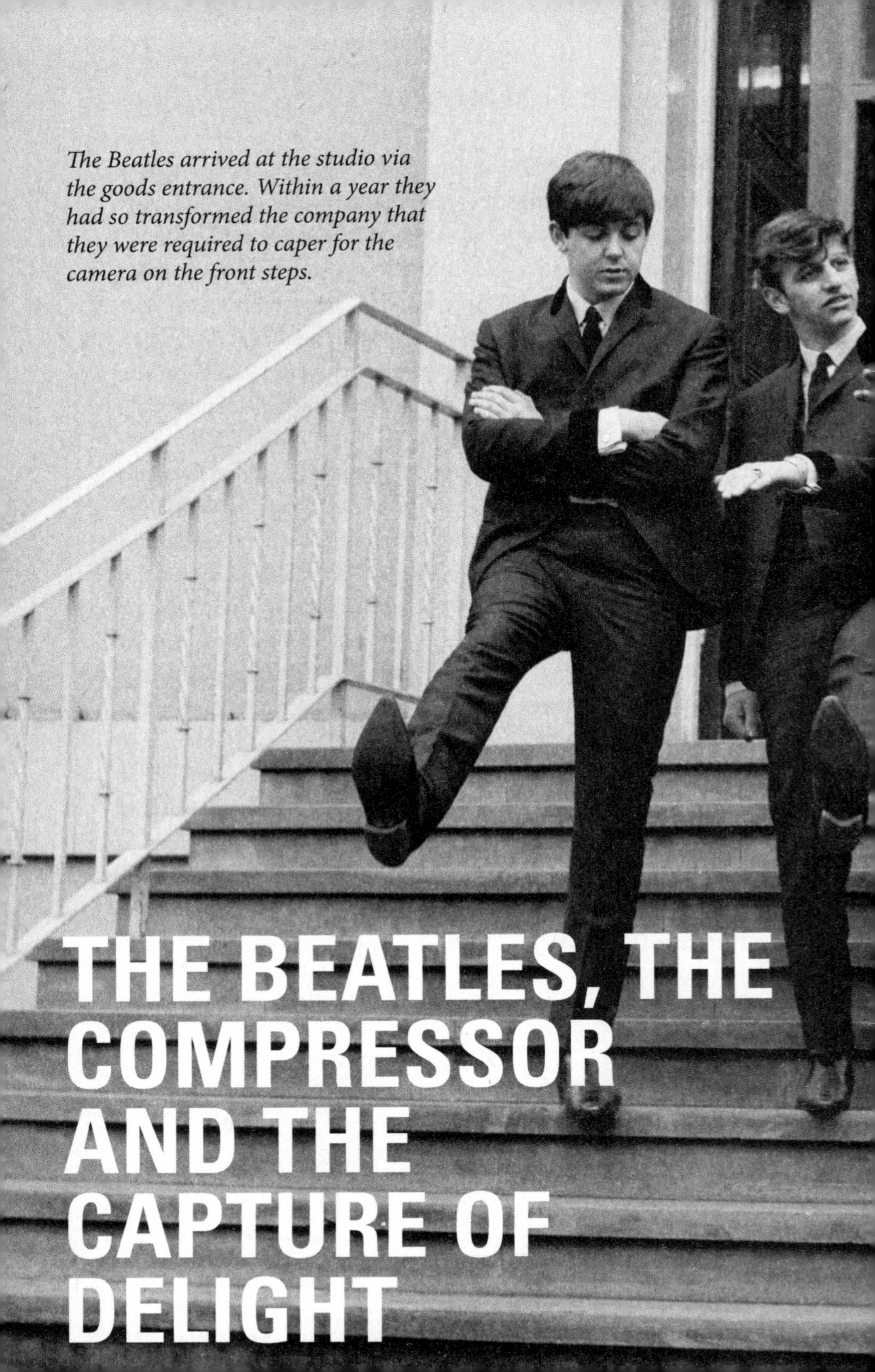

The Beatles arrived at the studio via the goods entrance. Within a year they had so transformed the company that they were required to caper for the camera on the front steps.

THE BEATLES, THE COMPRESSOR AND THE CAPTURE OF DELIGHT

8

When Norman Smith applied for a job at Abbey Road in response to an ad in *The Times* in March 1959 he felt the need to subtract eight years from his actual age in order to qualify. By that time he was already thirty-six and had even trained as a glider pilot during the war. In the course of the interview he wasn't asked about that. He was asked instead what he thought of Cliff Richard, who was obviously a wedge issue within EMI. Not a lot, said Norman – an unsurprising answer for someone who prided himself on being a jazz musician. Then he expanded. Well, actually, he said, that sort of music nauseates me.

His interviewer smirked confidingly that while he personally felt the same, any applicant for a job at EMI Recording Studios must understand that were they to be successful they might actually have to work with people like Cliff Richard. Just imagine that. The degree of condescension implicit in this statement underlines how wide was the gulf that separated the studios' dalliance with pop and its proper work, which was classical.

Norman got the job and began as an assistant engineer, although the organization was so keen to make sure that the newcomers didn't get above their station that this role was widely referred to within the studio as 'button pusher'. His first session was on Victor Silvester's *Dancing To Victor Silvester*. After three months he had made it into the good graces of Norrie Paramor and became an actual engineer. He had learned that while technical proficiency might be what got you hired, people skills were what got you ahead. 'I kept my eyes and ears open and my mouth shut because that was the best thing,' he later recalled.

On 6 June 1962 the rota which ruled the life of everyone but the most senior people informed him that he was assigned to work on a test recording. These sessions, which were effectively auditions, were a chore for the people who worked in the studio because so few of them resulted in anything. The majority of EMI's pop hits came from cover versions of records that had already been hits in America, records such as that week's highest flier, Cliff Richard's cover of Bobby Freeman's 'Do You Want To Dance', and therefore the quality they were seeking from this walk-in trade was the kind of polish that might be called for in covering an imported hit. In a sense they weren't looking for people to be themselves. They were looking for people who had a talent for presenting themselves as somebody else.

The session for the evening of 6 June was booked in Studio Two. This space had been designed with small groups and dance bands in mind and therefore it was more reverberant than the 'drier' classical studios. It looked and felt like the kind of school hall with which anyone educated in Britain after the war would have been familiar. It also had an unusually high ceiling, and the control room in which Norman sat was at the top of a flight of stairs leading from the studio parquet, meaning that the powers that be literally looked down on the musicians far below. Studio Two had been used more recently by contemporary groups like Cliff Richard and the Shadows but in many senses the same division of labour established in the thirties was still observed, with the musicians carrying on to the next selection on the instruction of the producer. They would rarely be encouraged to come up the stairs and listen to what they had done. That was none of their business.

Norman Smith was surprised to see that George Martin turned up to supervise this particular session. He would have expected Ron Richards, who was his number two at Parlophone. The presence of the senior man on this occasion seemed to indicate that this might be a little out of the ordinary.

George Martin could have been forgiven for having more than the usual swagger that day. His label Parlophone was having a pretty good 1962. Their hot artist was Bernard Cribbins. His records had been made in this same studio. When Noël Coward, who had also recorded in the same place, was the guest on *Desert Island Discs* in January 1963 he picked two George Martin productions among the eight gramophone records he wished to accompany him if he were cast away. One was Peter Sellers and Irene Handl lampooning the reviewing class in 'The Critics', the other was 'The Hole In The Ground' by the comic actor Cribbins, which had spent many weeks in the British charts. The record was more than a catchy tune. It was also one of those microcosmic studies in class conflict with which British entertainment is studded. It enacts a situation where a hapless workman is being informed by one of his betters that the hole he has recently dug is in the wrong place and also entirely the wrong shape. When asked to pick the one out of the eight records he liked most it was Cribbins that Coward picked. He said that it was the only one he never got tired of listening to and therefore he planned to spend his time on the island translating that song into French.

Coward was not aware that George Martin was the producer. Like the rest of his generation of artists he would not have known what a producer was and he would have been surprised to learn that the work of a producer could continue after the session was over. 'The Hole In The Ground' was a very good song, provided by jobbing writers Myles Rudge and Ted Dicks, and Cribbins, one of the most distinguished NCOs of British comedy, gave it a masterful reading. But what made the difference was the work George Martin did on the record once all the singers, musicians and writers had left the studio. Returning to it at regular intervals over a period of weeks, he added the sound effects of an electric drill and a spade attacking the ground until the record blossomed into something as satisfying as a comic sketch. And unlike a comic sketch, the advantage of a record was you could play it again. Martin went to town on the follow-up, 'Right Said Fred', which told the story of two furniture movers managing to destroy a house in their determination to install an old piano in a certain room. In both cases Martin managed to place the effects in the soundscape so that they became part of the music. In both cases he came up with something which remained a joy to listen to even after you might have tired of the actual jokes. In both cases he went to more trouble than anybody had previously considered it worth going to for a mere pop record. It was the first time he had worked on something with true finesse, and finesse seemed to be the quality that kept bringing Noël Coward back to listen again. Clearly it would not be the last.

The young men who entered Studio Two via the goods entrance would see to that. Norman Smith was the first to clap eyes on them. 'I looked down into the studio, a door opened at the back, and in walked these four lads,' he recalled later. 'And of course I did a double take on them because they looked so different to any young guitar groups I'd seen.'

The story of how John Lennon, Paul McCartney, George Harrison and their drummer Pete Best came to be at EMI Studios that night, and the more consequential fact that they were being auditioned by George Martin rather than Norrie Paramor, was recounted hundreds of times over the years by eyewitnesses who agree on very little. As McCartney was fond of saying many years later, there are a million stories about the Beatles and they're all true. What seems likely is that the band had found their way there because their manager Brian Epstein was an important retailer in the north-west whom EMI didn't wish to upset, he had pitched them to an EMI-owned song publisher who were keen to show off how much juice they had with the record company, and Parlophone was not such a sure thing that George Martin could afford not to let the people upstairs have their own way from time to time. Hence he had agreed to give them an audition. The calendar of an executive at any good-sized company is littered with similar appointments, placed there as a consequence of a half-hearted sense of obligation with no expectation of it ever resulting in anything. This one in George Martin's diary was no exception.

The thing that struck Norman Smith, apart from their oddly uniform appearance, was their Liverpool accents. This instantly made him think of comedians. At the time, comedians were the only entertainers who didn't seek to conceal their regional accents, and Liverpool had loads of them. He went downstairs to introduce himself as they brought in their gear and set it up. The equipment looked as though it had seen a lot of service. The Beatles had just returned from Hamburg. There they had played their standard marathon sets at the Star-Club literally every night for six weeks. This hadn't left them a lot of time for the care and maintenance of their equipment, as Norman was about to discover. 'I came back into the control room, opened up the mics, and I couldn't believe the extraneous noises, particularly from Paul's amplifier. I called for a technical engineer and Ken Townsend came down. He brought his soldering iron with him.'

Ken later recalled that at the time he was so unfamiliar with the set-up of even the most rudimentary kind of amplified beat group that he had difficulty telling which instrument was the bass. George Martin said that if he couldn't find a way to do something about the buzz the session would be a disaster. So Ken and Norman lugged a huge Tannoy speaker out of another studio, Ken put a jack socket on it – a measure which was so contrary to all Abbey Road studio regulations that he could have been fired for doing it – and miraculously it worked. When Ken went home that night his wife asked what he'd been working on. The name was what had struck him. 'Normally you don't want to bore her to tears but I said, "We just recorded the Beatles!"'

By the time the band began recording they only had time to play three numbers. Nobody felt it was going well. 'At the end they were summoned to the control room to be given feedback,' recalled Norman. 'George Martin started to address them because it was not a very impressive session. They stood over there while he told them that the company would only record them if they were really impressed with their performance. Then he handed them on to me and I said, "You've got to get new amplifiers." I advised Pete on the best kind of cymbals to buy. They stood there, stunned, listening to everything they were told. Then George said, "Look, we've been lecturing you for some time. Is there anything you want to say to us?" It was George Harrison who said, "Yeah, I don't like your tie." And a string of comedy came out of them from then on. When they had gone, George turned to me and said, "Well, what do you think?" And I just said, "George, in my view they're very different. There's something there personality-wise."'

That June, Bernard Cribbins was about to release 'Right Said Fred', his follow-up to 'The Hole In The Ground'. This would also do very well, but Cribbins would as a consequence of this Beatles session find that he was no longer foremost among Parlophone's priorities. The career of the Beatles took off that winter, and in such a way that it took Parlophone, EMI and Abbey Road with it. When they came back that September to make their first single, 'Love Me Do', they had taken George Martin's advice, fired Pete Best and brought in Ringo Starr, but the producer still took the precaution of having a session drummer standing by in case the new boy couldn't keep time. This was standard operating procedure with bands. A three-hour session had to produce an A- and a B-side and nothing caused more delay than a drummer whose playing couldn't stand up to the pitiless scrutiny of the playback. They got better. By the time they had recorded 'Please Please Me' in November George Martin had such confidence in them he was promising them they had recorded a number one. By 11 February 1963, when the Beatles returned to Abbey Road, this had been proved correct.

In the light of this preposterous success they were now being allowed to proceed to the previously unimaginable reward of making a whole long-playing record. Because this would naturally include their hits they only needed another ten tracks to have enough for an LP. Two three-hour sessions were earmarked for this work, which seemed more than generous by the standards of the time. There was no possibility of overrunning into the following day as that was when they were booked to play two shows. At different venues. On different sides of the Pennines.

As the engineer of two hit records, one of which had been a number one, Norman now felt he was sufficiently established to have an idea not just of how the Beatles' sound might be captured but also of how it might be enhanced. It was obvious to anyone who was paying attention that the Beatles generated excitement on a scale which was unprecedented in British pop music and Norman wanted to reflect some of that. 'I wanted to produce a sound which was like being in a venue, in that you could hear a mixture of the direct sound of the group and the ambient sound of the venue. So I set them all up much closer together, so that they could all hear each other, and I did away with all the screens which were usually used to achieve separation. I said, "Set yourselves up, set your levels according to what you're happy with. You can play as loud or as soft as you like." It took me some little time to experiment but eventually I got a sound that I was happy with. I suppose you'd call it a live performance sound.'

As it turned out, on that day they didn't finish the work in the morning and afternoon sessions. In fact they were still there at ten o'clock at night, the point in the evening when Abbey Road neighbours were inclined to complain, particularly if a band was using the echo chamber on the outside of the building. Most of what they had recorded that day would go on the first LP but George Martin decided that 'Hold Me Tight' was not quite strong enough yet and therefore he needed another tune to complete the record. They took a break in the canteen in the basement to decide what it might be. It was Alan Smith, a journalist friend from Liverpool who was with them that day writing a story for *NME*, who suggested they do 'Twist And Shout' – or, as he said at the time, 'the thing you do that sounds like "La Bamba"'. This seemed as good an idea as any. They returned to Studio Two and took up their positions. They were exhausted by the demands of the day and thinking about how early they would have to get up in the morning. John was further wondering whether his flu-racked voice could possibly hold up for the performance ahead.

'Twist And Shout' had been recorded by American R&B groups the Top Notes and the Isley Brothers. Both recordings are in their different ways very American and twist-worthy in a decorous way. You could imagine advertising men dancing to it in New York's Peppermint Lounge. In the hands of the Beatles in Studio Two that night in June 1962 the song was not so much transformed as transcended. If Norman Smith required any vindication of his quest for a new, live sound, 'Twist And Shout' provided it. While the combined vocal and instrumental attack of the other three shut off any possibility of retreat, John Lennon sang the song like it was the last he would ever sing. Since they abandoned a further take, this was what 'Twist And Shout' proved to be for that night and for every other night of their touring years. It became the closing track of the LP they were making that day. It became the closing song of every show they would do in that year of Beatlemania. It became the song that more than any other the Beatles always had to do. In the sense that the record's less about the song than it is about the delirium of the delivery it is the record you could use to explain the Beatles to a Martian. And although it didn't strike anyone at the time, it turned out that between them the Beatles, George Martin and Norman Smith had stumbled upon a sound which was about to give old American rock and roll a new birth of freedom in north-west London.

Thirty years later writers like Ian MacDonald were still trying to understand what they had managed to do at the end of this session. The intensity of 'Twist And Shout' didn't simply come from the performance. It also came from the manner of the recording. At the height of the beat mania of the winter of 1963 lots of young bands would be going into the studio for the first time to turn their live act into their first album. Most of the time that would result in little more than at worst a sobering reminder of their shortcomings and at best a useful audition tape. 'Twist And Shout' by the Beatles was something more than that. It communicated how their music felt, which was a different thing entirely. It conveyed the excitement the Beatles could generate. It also seemed to communicate how excited they felt about that excitement. It conveyed *them*.

In the wake of the desire to install the Beatles securely in the pantheon of so-called serious artists has come a tendency to place too much emphasis on their songwriting and not enough emphasis on the way they performed songs, even when those songs were written by other people. 'Twist And Shout' is the key example of this. By the time they had finished with it, it was their song. It was the perfect vehicle for them to put over their special sauce, which was what happened when they sank their individuality into the group. Once you had heard them do these American songs you no longer had much time for the so-called originals. This was no longer a group trying to sound like anyone else. This was a group who wanted to sound like themselves. That was what shone right through 'Twist And Shout'. As Ian MacDonald was to say of the record in his book *Revolution in the Head*, 'nothing of this intensity had ever been recorded in a British pop studio'.

It was also, along with the song that started the album, 'I Saw Her Standing There', the first of their records that could be called great in the sense that it would have stood against those coming out of Motown or Nashville at the time. Just five months later, on 1 July 1963, they were back in the same studio with a new song they had written and rehearsed in the previous four days. Norman Smith later remembered taking a look at the song's words, which had been written out and left on a music stand. He was dismayed at their seeming banality, much as Paul McCartney's amateur musician father had been when it was performed for him in their living room. Neither of them were wrong. As a song, 'She Loves You' was banal. Staggeringly so. But when you heard the people who had written it play it, that was no longer the case. When you heard them sing it, a whole new dimension opened up. You heard what they had been imagining when they were writing it. When you heard the way their performance sold this scrap of nothing there was no alternative but to surrender. And when you heard the recording back you realized that this group was not only more of a confederacy of equals than any group had been before, it was also capable of getting more of its mystery ingredient on to tape than any group had previously done. That was 'She Loves You', the record that brought a world to its knees.

No short era of recording has been as pored over as the Beatles' time at Abbey Road in the 1960s. Everybody who had even the most glancing acquaintance with them and their deeds during this time has their anecdotes, small chapters in the greater creation myth with which they understandably do not wish to tamper. Memoirs have been written, often many decades after the events, which do not always square with other memoirs. In each case there is a tendency to place the author at the centre of the most momentous events, a tendency which is entirely understandable. In other cases entire episodes have been recalled which others who were there do not remember at all. Everyone has their anecdote, the culmination of which is the blob of solder they applied, the edit they made, the suggestion they put forward which played some part in nudging in this direction or that a piece of music with which we are all familiar, deep in our bones.

Geoff Emerick, the engineer who was to be to the second half of the Beatles' recording career what Norman Smith was to the first, was in the studio that day helping out. In his memoirs, written in a different century, he describes how on this particular day the Beatles were doing a photo session outside the back of the building which resulted in a stampede of fans which in turn led to the building's security being breached and hysterical girls tearing through the offices in search of a Beatle before being eventually evicted. He describes how the excitement of these events may have fed into that day's recording, how 'She Loves You' was the way it was because it was made with the hot breath of Beatlemania upon its cheek.

He also describes how Norman Smith used a compressor, which had finally been released from the clutches of the boffins at Hayes and was now available for use in a British studio, on the bass and drums separately instead of together, as had been the usual practice. The next thing he did, which he had never done before, was suspend an overhead microphone above Ringo's brand-new Ludwig drum kit, a celebrity perk with which the drummer was well pleased. This immediately had the salutary effect of putting the drums, which are the first thing you hear on the record, at the forefront of the sound, which seemed to lend the entire enterprise a wholly new energy. Suddenly the very air of Studio Two seemed charged with particles that had not been present before.

Sometimes confidence flows from an improvement in performance. Sometimes an improvement in performance is the outcome of an increase in confidence. Sometimes both occur so close to each other, as they did on 1 July 1963, that it's impossible to tell which way the molecules are bouncing. At times like these, like the very specific golden hours between 2.30 and 5.30 when they cut 'She Loves You', you have to call it magic.

9

The Hollies look up to Studio Two's control room to hear producer Ron Richards' advice, more often than not 'Don't stop'.

'THE GREATEST RECORDING ORGANISATION IN THE WORLD'

At the end of 1962 the word 'pop' was still presented in inverted commas on the occasions it appeared in internal memos in EMI. By the end of 1963, when EMI chairman Joseph Lockwood was dazedly informing the City that a staggering 80 per cent of the number ones on that year's pop singles chart had been recorded in their studios in St John's Wood, it was clear that the boot was suddenly on the other foot. The country's favourite music was now home-grown, EMI was the great British company providing the bulk of it, and the home of Edward Elgar and Thomas Beecham was now the home of the hits.

Never before and certainly never again was one place to have such a lock on the nation's ears. If a Golden Age is, as they say, a time when things work in such a way as to make you think they're going to work the same way for ever, 1963 was the Golden Age of EMI's primacy in pop music. Studio Two's hegemony over that year's top spot had begun with Cliff, continued with the Shadows and Frank Ifield, and then taken wing with the Beatles and their Scouse compatriots Gerry and the Pacemakers and Billy J. Kramer and the Dakotas, all of whom had been produced by George Martin at Abbey Road and gone on to have number ones.

It was the year that the EMI factory in Hayes was having to operate twenty-four hours a day seven days a week to keep up with the public demand for singles and EPs. These were now produced with black labels because now that the quantities being demanded were so unprecedented, who could possibly afford to produce colour ones? They sold in such numbers that their flimsy paper covers were newly in demand as advertisers sought to interest their teenage buyers in Morphy Richards hair driers or Miner's make-up. Going into a record shop every Saturday morning, looking at the new entries on the chart pinned up behind the counter and pointing to the ones you wanted to take was by 1963 the standard habit of most young people. The first to recognize this sea change, with music buying suddenly becoming as mainstream as TV viewing, were chain stores Boots and WHSmith, who quickly gave over key parts of their retail estate to the merchandising of records, meaning that you could buy the hot new platters in every high street in the country. Each one of these EMI records bore the legend 'The Greatest Recording Organisation in the World'.

For a lot of the bands making the records, who had come out of the north of England where at the time it was simply not possible to make any kind of record, Abbey Road was the nearest thing they had to a base in the capital. They would point their vans down the A1, head to the Finchley Road and take a right towards Abbey Road for a place where they could get away from screaming girls, catch their breath and enjoy the feeling that they had somehow arrived. Liverpool groups the Fourmost, Billy J. Kramer and the Dakotas, Gerry and the Pacemakers and the Swinging Blue Jeans all recorded at Abbey Road at this time, as did a group from Manchester, the city at the other end of the East Lancs Road, called the Hollies.

The Hollies did successful work at Abbey Road throughout the decade. Because they were never royalty the way the Beatles were royalty they didn't manage to change the system to suit their ends. They wrote some of their own material later on, but initially their hit songs came from America. The Hollies never quite reached the point of convincingly authoring their own records in the way that the Beatles were doing as early as 1964 with the soundtrack of *A Hard Day's Night*. Not that they didn't have the equipment. Picked up during one of EMI's post-Beatles talent sweeps of the cities in the north in which the company had previously rarely set foot, they were probably the most accomplished of all the beat boom groups when it came to live performance. The Hollies' front line could sing, their back line could play, and they were almost remorselessly professional. But their experience at Abbey Road throughout the decade was very different from the experience of the Beatles.

An early line-up of the group came down to Abbey Road to audition for George Martin's number two, Ron Richards, thus beginning a working relationship that endured for almost twenty years. By the time they returned to Abbey Road to record on 11 October 1963 they had been boosted through the addition of guitarist Tony Hicks and drummer Bobby Elliott. Both were seasoned performers but small-time in the sense that neither had ever seen the inside of a recording studio before their van rolled up to Abbey Road. Everything about the experience was overwhelming. 'Just to go into the control room and hear ourselves was staggering,' recalled Hicks, sixty years later. 'We sounded so big and powerful. There must have been two speakers but it wasn't even stereo.'

'We were in awe because it was like going into a cathedral,' says Elliott. 'You might be rubbing shoulders with Malcolm Sargent and John Barbirolli. I was queuing up in the canteen one day to pay for my tea and rock bun and on one side of me was John Barry, on the other was André Previn, and just over there was Hank Marvin. It was very like the BBC. Very British. You might go past the commissionaire and you wouldn't salute but it definitely felt a bit military.'

The first recordings the Hollies did were captured on a two-track quarter-inch tape. This meant using a stereo machine to capture the entire band on one track and the vocalist on the other. These two tracks could then be copied to another tape machine while adding further elements, and then be mixed down to mono, which is the form in which they would be heard on the radio and on people's record players at home. In most cases the original two tracks were junked once the mono mix had been completed. In later decades, during the rush to reissue everything on CD, the few two-track recordings that survived would be presented as a singularly unsatisfactory form of stereo that left the singer in one ear and the band in the other.

At the time the studios were as rudimentary as a kitchen with just the one stove. Nonetheless the members of the Hollies were amazed at what the balance engineers could do using very basic tools. 'We only did a couple of takes of our second single, which was the Maurice Williams song "Stay", and somebody made a mistake so we stopped,' recalls Elliott. 'Ron Richards said, "Never stop. We can always fix it." When we played two tracks back, we preferred one guitar solo to another. So the engineer Peter Bown just got the tape and spliced it with a razor blade. He did it in seconds. We were amazed.'

At the time there was a widely accepted way to record pop music, which was to concentrate on capturing the top end of the sound, because this was after all what the listener sang along with, at the expense of the bottom end, which was what encouraged the younger listener to move. Bobby Elliott, who had more of a bag of tricks than the average beat band drummer, understandably felt this didn't do him any favours. 'They only had one microphone on the drum kit, which meant my bass drum wasn't as punchy as I wanted it to be. Ron Richards was a great one for his breaks so about six o'clock we go round to the Abbey Tavern for a pie and a pint. I made sure I bought the engineer his whisky mac. Then I told him I'd been to the BBC and they'd put a huge great microphone such as Winston Churchill might have used next to my bass drum. And I bought him another whisky mac. When we got back he'd got out another microphone and rigged it up next to my bass drum, which is why "Stay" turned out to be so punchy. I was told years later that I was the first drummer to have more than one microphone on my kit at Abbey Road.'

The Hollies liked coming to Abbey Road but tended not to make their visits any longer than they needed to be. This was an approach which also suited Ron Richards, a Tin Pan Alley-bred character who didn't like musicians who put on airs and was always keen to pick the right song, get it recorded quickly and then get to the pub. Thus each Hollies recording trip had a purpose. They would go in knowing exactly what they were going to record – mainly songs by established American writers like Chip Taylor and Carole King, most of which had been identified by Richards – and would not spend much time getting up to speed. Tony Hicks quickly realized 'there's a power you lose if you have to do something again. "Bus Stop" [a Graham Gouldman song which was a hit for them in 1966] was the third take. Even if we had to do a few repairs on a track it was often based on the first take. After that we could play around with the vocals a bit. We were big believers in eye contact. We'd set up facing Bobby's drums. When we were doing harmonies me, Graham Nash and Allan Clarke would have to be gathered round the same microphone. It wouldn't have sounded the same if we'd been on different ones.'

It could be the Hollies' let's-do-the-work-and-get-to-the pub attitude that explains the crackle of records like 'I'm Alive', 'Look Through Any Window' and 'Here I Go Again', which are certainly among the most effervescent singles to come out of St John's Wood in the sixties. The rest was down to the fact that their producer Ron Richards was, unlike the schoolmasterly, classically trained George Martin, a song man who, according to Elliott, 'could smell a hit'.

'In our early sessions when the red light came on we would

perform like chimpanzees. Our first album, which like everybody's first album at the time was our stage show, was done in a day. Listening to it now it's a bit fast, but there's an atmosphere to it because it all went down in one take. Ron would be looking at his watch. Later on when we had a bit of money we got very lackadaisical in the studio. The truth is you need a bit of pressure.

'Later on in the sixties we wanted to do things differently. We would say, "Ron, can we record through the night?" He'd say, "You can, but I'm going home at ten o'clock." One night when we were left unsupervised Graham arrived with one of the Walker Brothers and it turned into a party. Graham found this film projector and we were watching *Wind in the Willows*. We were spending money on a session and we were just watching *Wind in the Willows*. That would be 1967.'

However, most of the time the Hollies worked under strict supervision, in many respects like contract players in the studio system of old Hollywood. In other respects working at Abbey Road was much like operating in a superior head office with executive comforts such as the pot of tea brought to the studio during sessions. It resembled proper work in one further important respect, as Bobby Elliott recalled. 'In those days you got a session fee of seven guineas. As you finished, a guy in a suit would arrive with a briefcase, set up a table at the studio door and he'd get little pay packets out and we'd each have to sign for our seven guineas. The drummer would get a pound extra for what they called "porterage". Allan Clarke didn't get anything because he was a singer.'

Recording in the middle of the sixties was a matter of making choices from a relatively narrow range of options. Hicks remembers that since he did not have an array of effects pedals ranged around his feet, the basic track generally recorded itself and novelties would be added later. 'On "Carrie Anne" we got some steel drums in Studio Two. There was one track where we had a bass harmonica. Then we would get things from the cupboard under the stairs in Studio Two.'

'That was the sound effects cupboard,' Elliott recalls. 'There were all these things they'd accumulated over the years to use on comedy records or recordings of stage shows. You opened it and it was a treasure trove. There was a ship's bell – "And the fireman rushes in . . ." There was a gravel tray which you shook to make the sound of footsteps. We used that on an album track called "Crusader". The cupboard got somewhat plundered over the years sadly. We would record in Studio Three and there would be orchestral instruments like glockenspiels and tubular bells all around the walls. What's that? A celeste? Let's try that. We experimented because we could.

'In 1966 Burt Bacharach wanted us to do the theme for a film called *After the Fox* with Peter Sellers. Burt was conducting the orchestra. Our bass player didn't turn up that day so we got Jack Bruce, who was just about to start Cream. Then George Martin came in with Peter Sellers. We thought, this is going to be funny. But he just looked a bit glum. The only thing he did was pretend to karate chop the piano. That was the only laugh he got.

'We were once in there the same night that Phil Spector was in recording and the drummer was Jim Gordon. They asked to borrow a tom tom. We were packing up and going to the pub – Ron liked to finish in time for last orders – and we said fine. The next morning we came in and the head of that drum, my Ludwig blue-sparkle eight-by-ten tom tom, was destroyed. It was as if they were hitting it with a hammer, overdubbing something, trying to get some effect. Anyway, Ron was furious. He went into the studio where they were and came back later, smiling and rubbing his hands.

'Ron was the one that people like George Martin looked up to because he had a business head on his shoulders. They were all artists but he was shrewd. It was Ron who said, "We're all making this money for EMI and we're on a salary. We should start our own studio and sell our wares." What eventually became AIR studios started as Ron's idea.

'When we were doing "He Ain't Heavy" in 1969 we needed a piano and so Ron said, "There's this guy Reg Dwight who's just been signed to Dick James." He had a little pub band but he also did sessions. He was a young chap and shy. There was no small talk when he came. Ron thought that if you booked a musician you were paying him and therefore you got on with it. The grand piano was near the bottom of the steps in Studio Two. We didn't move that because you can easily knock them out of tune. So I dragged my drums over to where he was. There were no click tracks in those days. You had to keep time. We were flying by the seat of our pants. We ran it through and then recorded it second take. I made a slight mistake and said to Ron, "Can we do it again?" And he said, "When we get the strings on you won't hear it." My drum kit was usually below the window in Studio Two. When it got to ten o'clock I would look up and see Ron's arm going into his raincoat. In those days the pub closed at ten thirty, you see.'

The Hollies never successfully made the transition to the albums that would dominate the seventies but the string of hits they had in the decade of the seven-inch black vinyl 45 are unlikely ever to be emulated. At the end of the sixties Graham Nash left because for him this was no longer quite enough. The recorded legacy of Crosby, Stills & Nash may be more celebrated but it doesn't stand up against the crackle of the Hollies singles, all of which have a let's-do-the-show-right-here quality which remains eternally in the moment.

Across sixty years in the record business, and through having a son who engineered records in the twenty-first century, Tony Hicks was to see a lot of changes in the way things were done. He would come to appreciate the beauty of the limitations of those early days in Abbey Road. These limitations meant that they gathered in the same room around the same microphone at the same time, knowing they had the same three hours to achieve some kind of result; from that a very special form of human energy would flow and, if they were very lucky, find its way on to a record. At that point all the energy is going into the collective rather than into how good each individual contribution sounded. They weren't seeking perfection because perfection was never an option. That grand illusion came later. The Hollies began in the days of recording on two tracks and were still recording when the number of tracks began to proliferate to the point where there was no longer a reason to do things in the way they had once been done.

'It got to other extremes,' reflected Hicks. 'Once you moved on to twelve-track, excuses could always be made. You'd all go in and record and then you'd say, "I think we can improve on it all except for the cowbell," then you'd start again, building the track from the cowbell. You'd think you could play the bass a bit better or the guitar a bit better, and you might do, but you might lose the naturalness of what you were trying to do. That was the end of it for me. I find that when things stop you instantly have too many opinions. Which was what Ron used to say. Don't stop.'

They continued working with Ron Richards until the end of the seventies. In 1979 they were back at Abbey Road doing their best to make an album called *Five Three One Double Seven O Four*. The old two-track machine was now sixteen- and twenty-four-track digital machines linked together. Such are the almost infallible signs of energy being directed within the collective rather than outside to the paying customers. There were the usual signs of fatigue. The singer had left the group. Then they recorded with another singer. Then the old singer came back. They were all over the place. The number of tracks they had to choose from meant they suffered from the phenomenon increasingly known in studios as option paralysis. The consequent inability to make a decision and then move on may have been what finally led Richards to crack and bring in the landlord of his local pub to ask his opinion on what the Hollies had recorded the previous night.

'The guy was wearing carpet slippers,' recalled Bobby Elliott wonderingly forty years later.

That was the last record Ron Richards made with the Hollies.

SGT PEPPER, J. S. BACH AND BENDING THE CURRENT

10

In 1966 the Beatles gave up touring, grew moustaches, moved into Studio Two and began making the kind of records nobody had ever made before.

When the Beatles left the stage of San Francisco's Candlestick Park on 29 August 1966 it was the end of their touring years. The beginning of their studio years, effectively an entirely different career, did not begin for another three months. First they each took holidays. This was the longest time they had spent apart since they had been a group.

When they had first entered Studio Two as EMI artists in 1962 it had been to record 'Love Me Do', which was the very model of an elementary pop song of the time. When they returned to Studio Two at EMI a mere four years later it was to begin making a record based on a new song of John's called 'Strawberry Fields Forever'. The distance between these two was a dramatic indication of how, in less time than the gap between World Cup competitions, these four studio beginners had changed what was possible even to consider as a pop record. It also reflected the part that the studios at Abbey Road had played in that Great Leap Forward, not simply as the facility which happened to be owned by their record company, not solely as the place where their producer happened to be based, but more importantly as a massive musical and technological resource which had quickly grown to rather enjoy meeting their often vague demands for something that had never been done before with surprisingly practical solutions, the kind of solutions they would never have thought of themselves.

In the early days they didn't draw attention to the artful tweaks that were quietly introduced by George Martin. Fans knew that the theme song from *A Hard Day's Night* had been written overnight by John Lennon to fulfil the need for a single. They didn't know that its urgency owed so much to the producer's insistence on boosting the rhythm with bongos; nor were they aware that the distinctive instrumental break was achieved by recording at half-speed the two Georges in unison on guitar and keyboards and then overdubbing it at normal speed. However, as they grew more confident they began to make a feature of any interesting novelties which had gone into making their records: the feedback at the beginning of 'I Feel Fine', the strings on 'Eleanor Rigby', even the packing case played by Ringo on 'Words Of Love', the sitar on 'Norwegian Wood (This Bird Has Flown)' and Lennon's in-drawn breath on 'Girl'. The Beatles were the first group to draw attention to the way they did what they did.

To be fair they weren't the only people who were making big moves during this period of steady escalation. During 1965, the annus mirabilis of the seven-inch pop single, it seemed that every week had seen a release which had the effect of somehow rendering the previous week's crop passé. Whether these new sensations were from the Rolling Stones, James Brown, the Byrds, the Kinks, Phil Spector or Tamla Motown, the Animals or Bob Dylan, they all seemed to have put something on a record that had never been put there before, each one raising the stakes for those following in its footsteps. Most of those records had been made on the run by artists whose main priority was getting out and playing live or appearing on television. That was about to change.

The week the Beatles reconvened, the number one single on both sides of the Atlantic was the Beach Boys' 'Good Vibrations', a record which was a dazzling advance on even the giant leaps of 1965. 'Good Vibrations' wasn't even a song at all so much as a montage

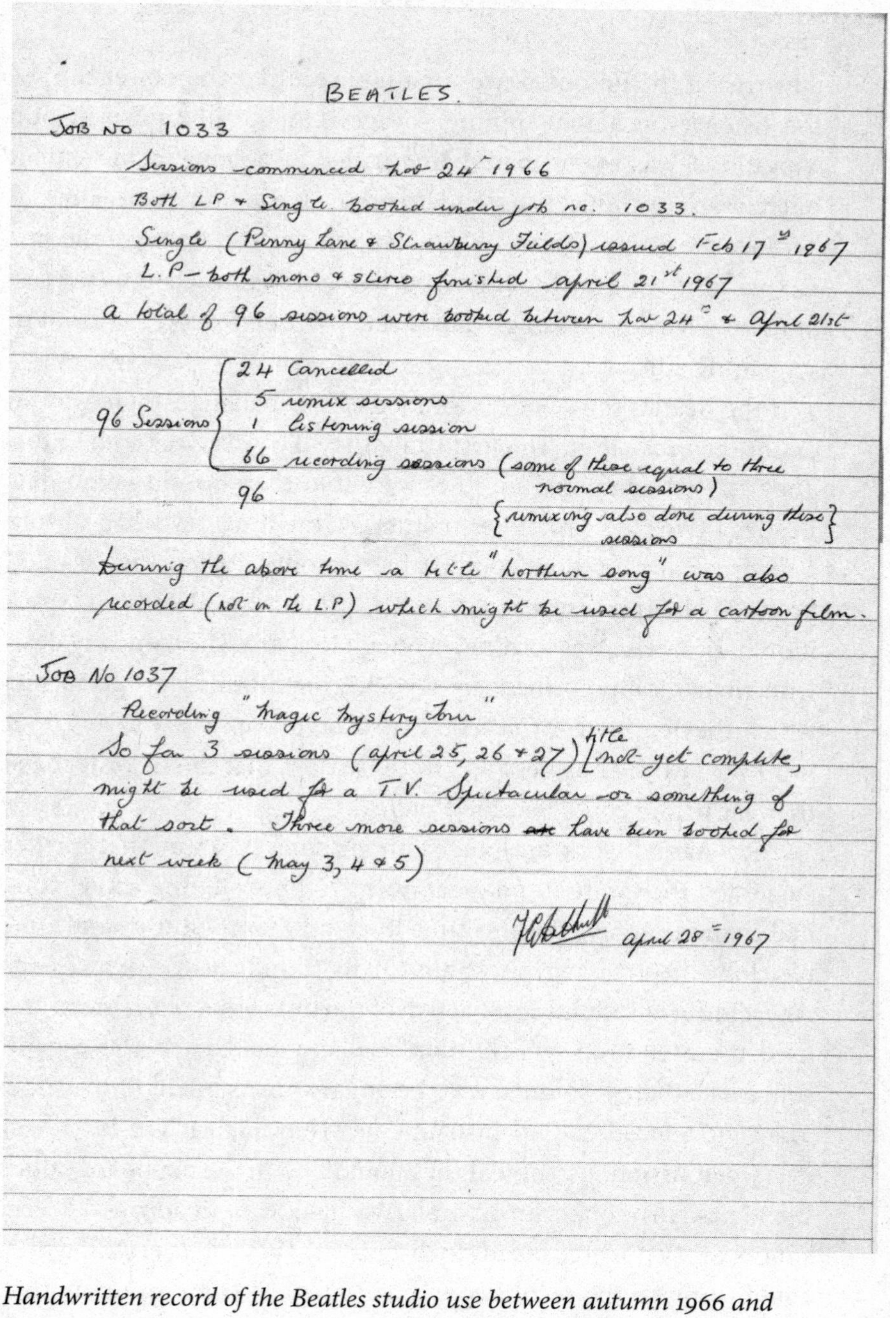

BEATLES.

JOB NO 1033

Sessions commenced Nov 24th 1966

Both LP & Single booked under job no. 1033.

Single (Penny Lane & Strawberry Fields) issued Feb 17th 1967

L.P – both mono & stereo finished April 21st 1967

a total of 96 sessions were booked between Nov 24th & April 21st

96 Sessions {
24 Cancelled
5 remix sessions
1 listening session
66 recording sessions (some of these equal to three normal sessions)
96

{remixing also done during these sessions}

During the above time a little "Northern song" was also recorded (not on the L.P) which might be used for a cartoon film.

JOB No 1037

Recording "Magic Mystery Tour"

So far 3 sessions (April 25, 26 & 27) [title not yet complete, might be used for a T.V. Spectacular or something of that sort. Three more sessions ~~are~~ have been booked for next week (May 3, 4 & 5)

April 28th 1967

Handwritten record of the Beatles studio use between autumn 1966 and spring 1967.

advertising the unique power of a pop record – the power to take the listener on a four-minute voyage into the unknown. 'Good Vibrations' was everywhere being hailed as a signal achievement but it wasn't a product of a standard group. It had only been achieved because the group's Brian Wilson had remained at home in the studio working with the best Los Angeles session musicians as the rest of them played increasingly unsatisfactory one-nighters in front of screaming fans.

If the Beatles saw 'Good Vibrations' as a challenge, there was no doubt they rose to it. The first thing they did was clear some time. They started by saying no: EMI were told there would be no new Beatles LP for the Christmas market. At the time nobody ever told a record company they couldn't have product when they wanted product. Nobody else was the Beatles. They were already in a position nobody else was fortunate enough to share. The company dealt with their disappointment by repackaging a bunch of recent hits which they entitled *A Collection Of Beatles Oldies*. It was a sign of just how fast the business was in those days that the records made the year before could be called 'oldies'.

They started work on John Lennon's song in a way that further suggested they were in no great hurry to finish it. The actual song had a simple appeal but this time they didn't want it to sound simple. John kept saying he wanted it to sound 'heavy', which was emerging as the defining adjective of the time. Their early stabs at it used the Mellotron, which, thanks to the fact that it was a good source of ethereal sounds, was the voguish instrument of the time. They introduced Indian instruments. They had a free-for-all on every percussion instrument they could find in the cupboard under the stairs. Lennon, who had always hated his unadorned voice, sought every possible means to disguise it. They did everything they could to make the record sound as though it came from another world.

At this time their records were still being made on four-track. If they wanted more than four instruments and vocals they would have to 'bounce down'. This meant mixing the four tracks they had already recorded to a single track on another machine. Then they could erase the tracks they had recorded first and start again, adding new instruments and vocals. These would then be added to the mix that had been bounced down to the second machine. It was a process that had more in common with painting than with any of the recording usually done in EMI's studios. Rembrandt would have recognized it. Once something had been bounced down you might be able to obscure it with another layer of sound but you couldn't remove it. At every stage you had to commit yourself. There was no underlying grid. There was no click track. There was no safety net. There was no undo facility. If you made a mistake you had to cover it up with something better and hope nobody noticed.

They ploughed on with 'Strawberry Fields Forever' through November and December. This took steady nerves. The Monkees, who had been invented as a Beatles for the younger brothers and sisters of Beatles fans, were occupying the number one slots in both the LP and singles charts. These were places which would have been theirs had they not decided to work on John's song. In an effort to achieve the heaviosity he sought, Lennon asked George Martin to provide more layers. Horn and string sections were called in, scored and recorded. Mixes were tried, acetates produced and taken home to houses in the stockbroker belt. Eventually, having pressed on in search of some quality he couldn't define, Lennon announced that he preferred the opening section the way he had done it on the first day and suggested to George Martin that he stitch together takes seven and twenty. When Martin pointed out that these two versions had been done in entirely different tempi and keys, Lennon said he was sure George would be able to find a way to fix it. Having said this, he went home.

'Strawberry Fields Forever', which was released as a double A-side with 'Penny Lane' in the middle of February 1967 (so seriously did Brian Epstein take the threat of competition from the Monkees), is often cited as one of the greatest pop records ever made. For the technicians working in the studio over the Christmas of 1966 this would have seemed preposterous because they understood that it had strayed so far from the standard way of doing things that other professionals would even have considered it an irredeemably botched job. Inspiration may have been its starting point but it wouldn't have reached its triumphant conclusion without a greater weight of perspiration, most of it from the brows of George Martin, Geoff Emerick and Ken Townsend as they laboured on in the studio, attempting to find a way in which these two takes, incompatible in both rhythm and pitch, might be married.

They eventually found a solution in a frequency changer, an enormous machine which was capable of actually bending the alternating current in the tape machine's power supply, thus allowing the early part of the song to speed up imperceptibly until it met the second part almost exactly at the one-minute point, just after the words 'let me take you down' occurred in the vocal. This shotgun marriage broke every established rule of recording. Happily to Lennon's ears, which were the only ones that mattered, it sort of worked. (He may well have been seizing on the prospect of a way out of his self-inflicted impasse. At this stage in a complicated production any kind of solution offering closure tends to be eagerly embraced.) The fact that it magically achieved the sought objective of making the record sound as though it came from a different world was just another one of those serendipitous miracles which happened to the Beatles all the time but never seemed to happen to the Hollies.

This combination of hallucinogenic drugs on the one hand and Heath Robinson practicality on the other was added to the list of things that could only have occurred at this Ministry of Recording in St John's Wood. This was a place where the new school met the old, where the *Tibetan Book of the Dead* met the *Handbook of Practical Electronics*, where the dreamers posed the problems and the doers came up with the solutions, where the bacon of musicians whose reach would oft-times exceed their grasp would from time to time be saved by a man with a soldering iron and a steady temperament. In his autobiography, George Martin further wondered if the thing that made the Beatles' records work so triumphantly at the time was that while the band might have been exposing themselves to all kinds of inputs, he and Geoff Emerick remained straight and sober. This was a division of labour the band themselves respected. They would not have had it any other way.

When on 21 March 1967 they were overdubbing vocals on 'Getting Better' it was obvious to George Martin that John Lennon was feeling ill. The producer, who was innocent of the reason for Lennon's queasiness, suggested that he take him outside for a breath of fresh air. Because the permanent presence of fans meant it was out of the question for he and Lennon to take a turn down Abbey Road he suggested they go on to the roof above Studio Two. He didn't realize that this climb might be more than usually hazardous because the reason for Lennon's untimely peakiness was that he had taken acid when he had intended to take amphetamine. This meant that when he got on to the roof – it was a lovely night, Martin recalled, with a sky full of stars – he was in imminent danger of tripping over the six-inch parapet and falling to his death. It was then that Martin realized the best thing to do was call it a night. Lennon later recalled that this was the only time he took acid in the studio.

The songs that were to make up *Sgt Pepper's Lonely Hearts Club Band* were unlike any of the Beatles songs that had gone before. They didn't actually exist prior to the studio sessions and they would only exist subsequently within the context of the record. In more than one case – 'She's Leaving Home', 'A Day In The Life' – whole songs were magicked up straight out of the newspaper the group happened to be reading while in the studio. Never in the entire history of recording have whims been elevated into masterpieces to such lasting effect. Songs invented in seconds were fashioned into records over months. Lennon took down the words from a Victorian circus poster to make 'Being For The Benefit Of Mr Kite' and then pretty much handed it over to George Martin and Geoff Emerick with instructions to make it sound circus-like. This they achieved with a combination of bass harmonica, Wurlitzer, Hammond organ and recordings of Victorian steam organs which were dubbed on to tape, cut into random strips, thrown up in the air and reassembled. In some respects making this record was like a student art project suddenly being presented with the budget of a feature film.

Because the new LP would not be accompanied by a tour, the release of a single or a TV special it could only be publicized by releasing photographs of the band at work in the studio. For the first time the key piece of information which was being pushed about this new record was that it was the result of hundreds of hours in the studio. This and the title that referred to a fictional band were both attractively novel ideas at the time. Anything which had taken so long, anything which had required so much work, people were inclined to think, must be worthwhile. The interviews they did around its release were, for once, about the music because there was so much about the music that people wanted to talk about. It is often said there are three degrees of difference. There's difference that is recognized by the creator but not the audience. There's difference which the audience recognizes but does not appreciate. The third degree, where the creator and audience both recognize and appreciate the difference, is rarely achieved. It was achieved with *Sgt Pepper's Lonely Hearts Club Band*.

When the finished LP came out in May 1967 people bought it in unprecedented numbers and played it almost as they would play a single. In fact they played it as though it was a longer 'Good Vibrations'. It had been put together almost as though it were a movie and, as in a movie, it was the junctions, the mixes, the cross-fades, the witty juxtapositions, the kaleidoscopic shifts in focal length, in other words the things that could only be done in the studio and could only be done by people versed in what the studio could or could not do, that made it land with so many people. It was an act of audio illusion. It began with the sound of an audience and a pit band. The first song was an advertisement for the titular group, which then segued into a featured solo number by a fictional member of that group. The first song was reprised near the end, its percussion intro emerging out of the animal noises at the end of the previous song. The album was an exercise in the capturing and retention of attention. No group other than the Beatles could have conceived it. No producer other than George Martin, with his background in formal music, his instinct for variety and the taste for summoning imaginary worlds which he had first explored on his comedy records, could have lent it the psychedelic lustre that made it so satisfying. The whole LP sold the whole idea of the whole LP. It was, like 'Good Vibrations', an advertisement for itself.

Like all too few movies it had an ending worthy of its beginning. John had come up with the basic verse of 'A Day In The Life' and he looked to Paul to provide a contrasting middle eight. It contrasted so much that it was scarcely the same song at all. However, they quickly decided to make a virtue of the difference by presenting it as almost a dream sequence. This worked well, but it still left them needing some way of getting from the bridge back into the song. Had it been three years earlier, when they had been in the same studio recording *A Hard Day's Night*, they would have come up with some neat and cheap trick. Now that they had all the time, money and cheek in the world, the solution could be on an altogether grander scale. John decided he wanted a symphony orchestra and he wanted them to make a grand noise, a noise which grew from nothing to a chord that sounded like the end of the world. He told George Martin to get an orchestra and told him they would take it from there. Martin, a classical oboe player by trade, knew that ordering up a symphony orchestra and then expecting them to make a non-specific musical sound without precise instructions was about as reasonable as asking the Beatles to play a slow foxtrot. Hence the sound that Lennon thought would be as simple to produce as one of the freak-outs which ended a live set by the Who was eventually arrived at by Martin patiently writing out a score for each player which showed them exactly what was required of them.

Because this recording was to take place in the larger Studio One, the Beatles decided they would add to the specialness of the occasion by asking the members of the orchestra to turn up in full evening dress as though they were appearing in a concert at the Albert Hall. Not all the members of the orchestra took to this, fearing, with some justification, that the Beatles, who turned up wearing their own spangled civvies for the occasion, were being faintly disrespectful of the classical players. This impression was accentuated by the fact that they invited Mick Jagger, Marianne Faithfull and a few more of their fabulous friends along to watch just what these Lords of Misrule could command when they put their mind to it. They brought with them more party equipment. George Martin turned round at one point to see the lead violinist wearing a false red nose, another distinguished player with his bow hand in a giant gorilla's paw, and every single member of the orchestra wearing a funny hat. This was clearly where making music met a Happening.

The recording on the other side of 'Strawberry Fields Forever' had hinged on a similar meeting between two worlds. If Lennon's memory of his Liverpool childhood was characteristically dark, McCartney's recollection of the roundabout where he used to change buses on his way to John's was characteristically cheerful.

'Penny Lane' was built on layers of piano parts all supplied by McCartney and then compressed into one track by Geoff Emerick in order to leave room for contributions by the rest of the band and session horns and strings. Its recording was a trying time for the rest of the band, who had to spend most of their hours mooching about the control room as Paul worked to record it to his satisfaction. The record was effectively finished and its release date set when McCartney just happened to tune in to one of the three television stations Britain could boast at the time and caught a performance of Bach's Brandenburg Concertos during which one David Mason played the piccolo trumpet. The next day in the studio he asked George Martin if they could secure the services of this mysterious instrument and the musician who was its master. No other band would have asked. No other studio would have responded in the way Martin did. He, of course, knew Mason, so Mason was given a call.

He arrived in the studio like a well-prepared assassin. He had nine instruments arrayed before him from which to choose. Like every other highly trained classical musician finding himself in the studios with the Beatles he had to bite his lip as McCartney sang the kind of solo he had in mind and George Martin wrote it down on manuscript paper. Had he been inclined to let his professional pride be injured he only needed to think of the special fee of £28 which had been negotiated for him.

Musicians like Mason take pride in being supreme technicians. Often they don't even think of themselves as artists. They don't need to be warmed up. They don't need to be in the mood. They don't need to be in sympathy with the project. Just give them the right marks on the stave and there is a good chance they will perfect their contribution the first time through. This was certainly the case with Mason's solo on 'Penny Lane', which is arguably the most high-wire demonstration of musical mastery to be found on any record in the Beatles catalogue.

Of course musicians who play in beat groups, where they speak of 'feel' and set great store by warming up and entering into the spirit of the thing, simply don't believe in that way of playing. It was an anathema to them that this man could turn up, hit his marks and be done in less than a minute. When McCartney, who was in the control room, hit the talkback and asked, with all the insouciance of a twenty-four-year-old who couldn't read music and didn't even have Grade One piano, if the virtuoso could give it 'another pass', it was explained to him that a performance such as the one Mason had just committed to tape was physically as well as artistically taxing. Therefore there would be no second pass.

Mason packed his weapons and left.

PARTICULARS

OF THE

VALUABLE UNRESTRICTED

Freehold Building Site

KNOWN AS

No. 3, ABBEY ROAD

ST. JOHN'S WOOD. N.W.8.

Opposite the junction of Grove End Road and Abbey Road, close to Lord's Cricket Ground and about six minutes' walk from St. John's Wood Road and Marlborough Road Stations (Metropolitan Railway) and a litte over a mile from the West End.

The Motor Omnibus Services 53 and 153 pass the site and there are numerous other services within a short distance.

At present occupied by a Detached Residence containing:–

Nine Bed Rooms, Bath Room,
Five Reception Rooms, Kitchen,
Two Servants' Rooms, &c.

arranged as follows:—

ON THE SECOND FLOOR—

Two Attic Bed Rooms.

ON THE FIRST FLOOR—

Seven Bed Rooms, approximately 18-ft. by 15-ft.; 18-ft. by 15-ft. 6-in.; 24-ft. by 16-ft. 3-in.; 15-ft. 6-in. by 15-ft.; 9-ft. 6-in. by 6-ft. 6-in.; 15-ft. 6-in. by 15-ft.; 16-ft. 9-in. by 15-ft. 3-in. W.C.

Bath Room on Half-landing.

ON THE ENTRANCE FLOOR—

Dining Room, about 23-ft. by 15-ft. with Service Lift to Lower Floor.

Handsome Drawing Room, about 39-ft. by 18-ft. with parquet flooring.

Library, about 15-ft. by 14-ft. 6-in.

Morning Room, about 23-ft. by 16-ft.

Study, about 15-ft. by 10-ft.

W.C.

IN THE HALF-BASEMENT—

Kitchen, Scullery, Servants' Hall, Pantry, Two Servants' Rooms, Larder, Wine Cellars, etc., W.C.

LARGE GARDEN AT REAR.

THE PROPERTY has a FRONTAGE of about 91 ft to Abbey Road, and a DEPTH of about 250-ft.

There is therefore an Area of approximately

22,750 Square Feet

and offers an exceptional Site for the erection of

AN IMPORTANT BLOCK OF RESIDENTIAL FLATS FOR WHICH THERE IS A STEADY and INCREASING DEMAND in the neighbourhood.

or alternatively

FOR STUDIO RESIDENCES, BIJOU HOUSES OR FOR A PRIVATE RESIDENCE or INSTITUTION, INCORPORATING THE EXISTING BUILDING.

The Building line will be defined by the London County Council upon submission of a Building Scheme.

Vacant Possession will be given upon Completion.

*When property people working for the Gramophone Company first set eyes on the large house at No. 3 Abbey Road, St John's Wood, in 1929 (***top***), it was by no means clear that it was worth a company investing in a building dedicated to recording. By the time it opened two years later the massive Studio One had been erected in the back garden and the new parent company was now Electrical and Musical Industries (***above***).*

Left: *The sixteen-year-old Yehudi Menuhin came from the United States to record Elgar's Violin Concerto under the baton of its composer.*

Below: *Billy Cotton and his band were one of the many dance bands catering for less elevated tastes.*

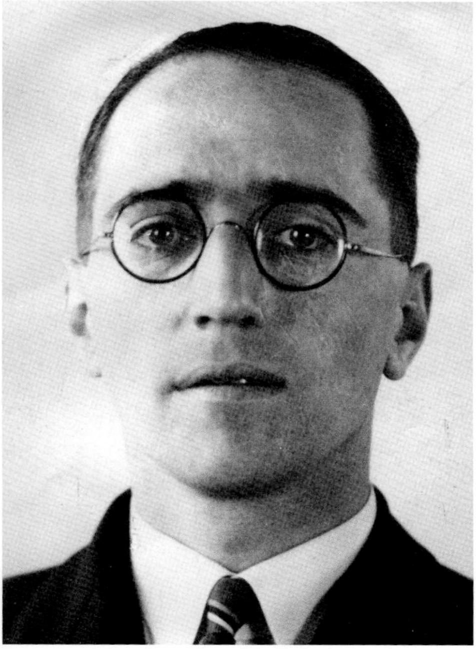

Left: *Alan Blumlein, one of the young geniuses who worked for the studio in the 1930s, invented stereo twenty years before the business had any use for it. He died during the war.*

Below: *Stravinsky conducted an early recording of* Les Noces *in Studio One, which was known as the HMV Studio.*

Jack Hylton with his dance band recorded at the studio under the Columbia branding in 1931.

Studio boss Edward 'Chick' Fowler with what passed for a mixing desk in the 1940s.

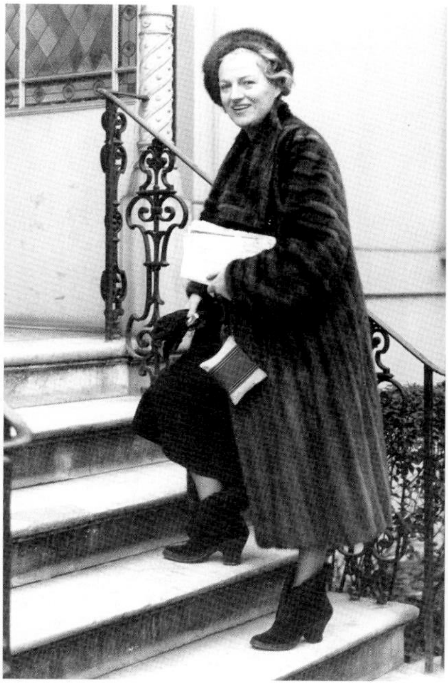

Gracie Fields was one of the musicians cum weapons of war who ascended the famous steps during Britain's finest hour.

Fats Waller recorded part of his 'London Suite' on the Compton organ, at the time a fixture in Studio One, in 1938.

The deployment of band leader Glenn Miller and singer Dinah Shore to record at Abbey Road in 1944 had to be cleared at the highest level. Miller disappeared a week later.

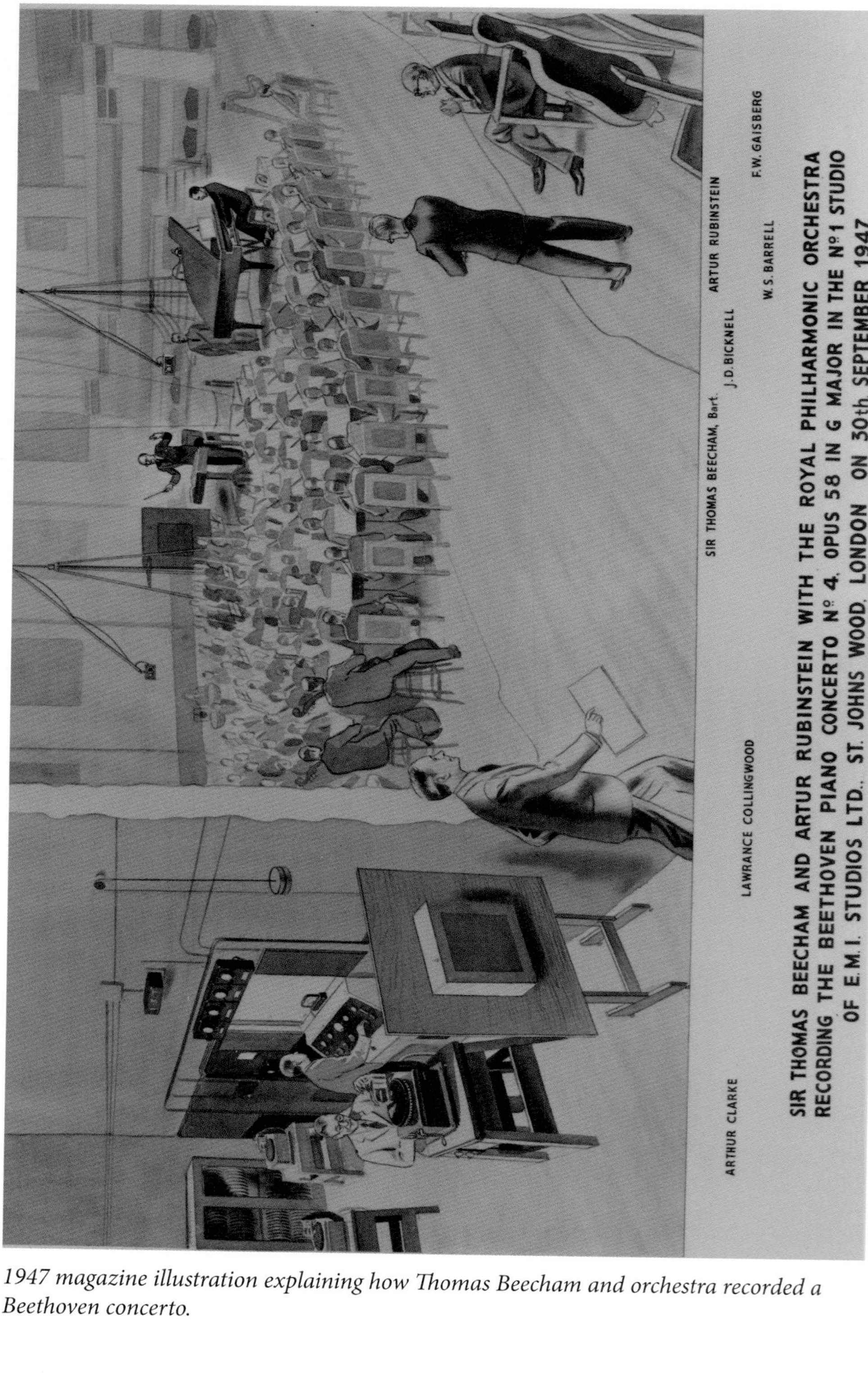

1947 magazine illustration explaining how Thomas Beecham and orchestra recorded a Beethoven concerto.

Left: *Peter Sellers' 1959 hit* Songs For Swingin' Sellers, *which included his extraordinary improvisation with Irene Handl (***below***), paved the way for George Martin's later work with the Beatles.*

In the same year Cliff Richard and the Shadows recorded their first album 'as live' on a stage in Studio Two. The audience had their inhibitions loosened with orange squash and sandwiches.

Left: *The Beatles often worked out the arrangements of their songs in Studio Two with the help of George Martin but they gradually moved into the control room* (**above**) *where, they learned, the true record-making power lay.*

Left: *The Beatles did most of their work with two engineers. Norman Smith (pictured here with McCartney and George Martin) engineered their moptop smashes while Geoff Emerick, who cut his teeth with pianist John Ogdon and Sir John Barbirolli* (**above**)*, realized their psychedelic visions.*

11

Pink Floyd make themselves at home in Studio Three in 1973 as the equipment becomes more sophisticated and control rooms begin to resemble telephone exchanges.

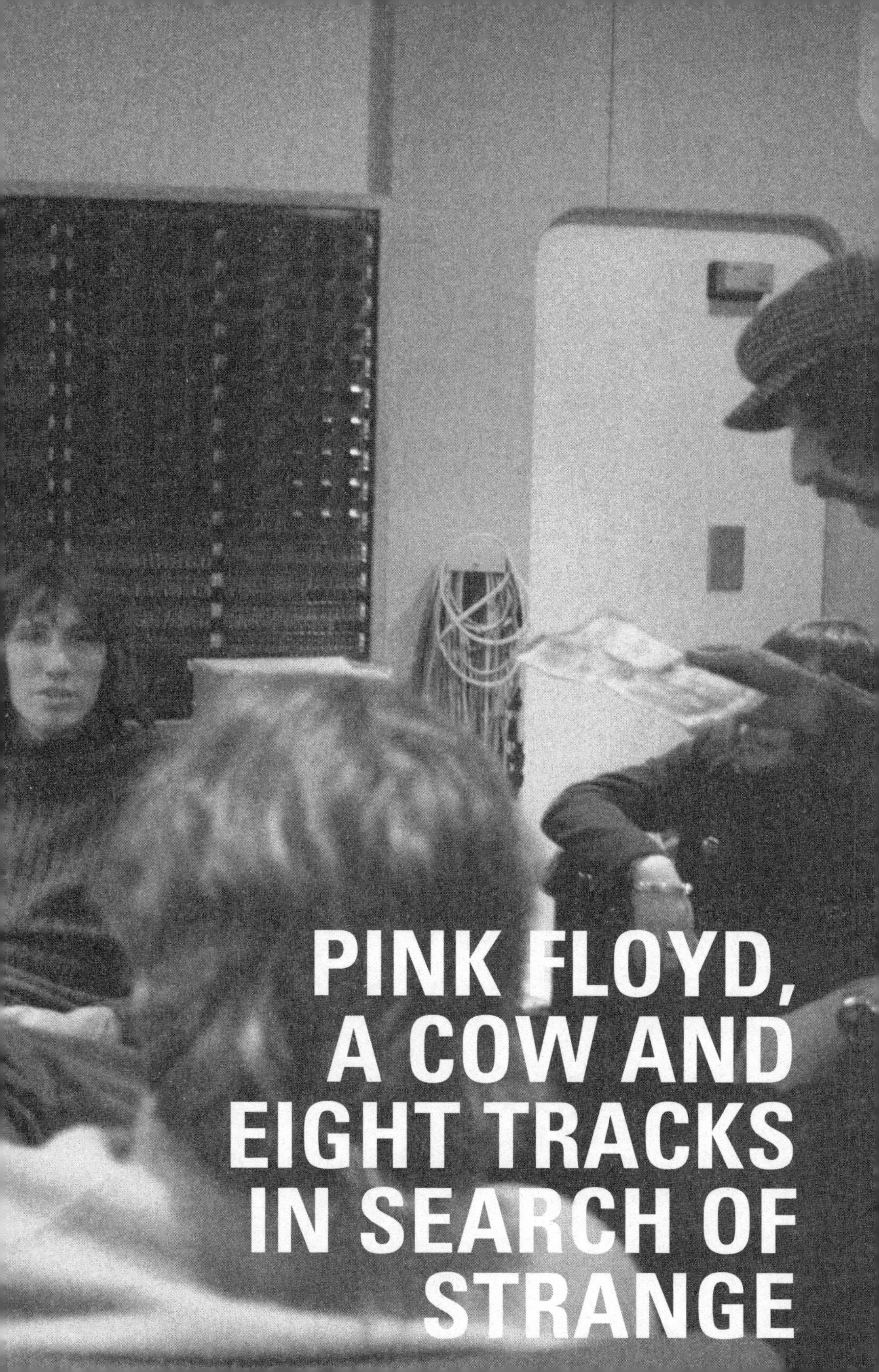

PINK FLOYD, A COW AND EIGHT TRACKS IN SEARCH OF STRANGE

Nobody knew for a fact what had been going on behind the door of Studio Two during the winter of 1966 and spring of 1967. The group, always described in the bookings diary as the Dakotas, laboured night after night with no apparent deadline in mind. Towards the end they started to share samples of their work with selected musicians in the hope that word would get out, and presumably because they were so unused to working this long without any feedback.

David Crosby of the Byrds was invited into Studio Two during a visit to London in 1967. He was placed on a stool between two large speakers while the Beatles retreated up the stairs to the control room and rolled the tape of 'A Day In The Life'. Since Crosby was as baked on that occasion as he was on most days in 1967, he could be relied upon to communicate his unrestrained enthusiasm to anybody he stumbled into. Graham Nash of the Hollies received a tape from Brian Epstein just before the album's release. He was simultaneously dazzled and disappointed: dazzled by what the Beatles and George Martin had managed to do and bitterly disappointed that his own group hadn't demonstrated the same sort of ambition.

Sgt Pepper turned the heads of everybody with a recording contract, much as 'I Want To Hold Your Hand' had done a mere three years earlier. Suddenly they all wanted to be in this new game the Beatles appeared to have invented. *Sgt Pepper* made them think of themselves differently. Every other band from that hectic decade, whose fantasy had previously been one of cavorting just beyond the imploring fingertips of panting young women, were now driven by an equally powerful fantasy of being able to spend the time it clearly took in the studio to have a *Sgt Pepper* happen to them. Some thought this would happen by magic. Much as even the most short-form scribblers are tempted to believe that they too can write a mighty novel if only they were seated at a picture window overlooking the sea, many could not conceive of not being able to bring forth a similar masterpiece if only they too were allowed to spend an extended period 'in the studio'.

Most shifts of emphasis in popular music are telegraphed by parallel shifts in the barbering arrangements of the people who play that music. Thus it was on this occasion. The first thing the Beatles did once they stopped touring – and they did it so abruptly it seemed to be in response to a memo only they had been sent – was to grow moustaches. This bristling of the upper lip announced the beginning of their studio years and saved them the trouble of calling a press conference to announce that henceforth they would prefer to be regarded as artists rather than pop stars. Since nobody ever screamed at a musician with a beard or moustache, it was also a subliminal way of getting over the message that henceforth they were more interested in being admired than in being idolized.

Where the Beatles led everybody else followed, or at least tried to. In this new phase of the 1960s photos of bands at work in the studio started to appear in the news pages of music papers. This time the sharing-a-joke poses of yore were supplanted by shots of these newly moustachioed men gathered around unfamiliar instruments, brows wrinkled to give the impression that they were no longer in the fast and furious work of pop picking. Now they were carrying themselves more like painters or sculptors. In these pictures they were looking newly serious. They were thinking. They were obviously engaged in exploratory work. Pioneering work. Studio work. The Lord's work. This was now what they did. The mental picture of a pop group, which had previously summoned the image of a bunch of strolling vagabonds, was now more likely to be of a bunch of serious young men apparently entertaining big thoughts behind closed doors.

More importantly, it threw into disarray the old studio system, wherein the job was to use the resources of the place to come up with a reasonable proportion of hits, thereby ensuring that the business could continue. Bands that had previously written songs outside the studio and then taken them in to commit them to tape now began to treat the studio as the place where songs would magically arise. Suddenly there were hundreds of examples of this new breed, and many of them seemed to be heading for Abbey Road. Their transit vans would pull into the car park and disgorge their cargos of chronically unfit, undernourished young men wearing Kensington Market fancy dress, sporting vaudeville moustaches, and keen to make the most of their shot at making an album that was a big statement. They appeared to be wired differently from the members of the Hollies or the Fourmost who had come just three short years before. They had different dreams. They wanted something more than a single in the charts. They craved the immortality that could only come from an album.

One of the key people who interfaced with this new generation was Norman Smith, the man John Lennon christened 'Normal' to indicate that he was very much at the straighter end of the spectrum of EMI engineers. George Martin's moving on in 1966 to start AIR studios had left a vacancy for a head of Parlophone. This was offered to Norman. He was happy to move on from the Beatles because he didn't feel the atmosphere was as familial as it had been. He was persuaded to stay until they had completed *Rubber Soul*, following which they expressed their gratitude with the gift of an inscribed

USE OF MELLOTRON DURING LAST SIX MONTHS

Instrument on six months hire

AUGUST

Koobas: 5th, 6th.

Beatles: 7th - 9th, 12th - 16th, 21st - 23rd.

Nocturnes: 11th.

SEPTEMBER

Beatles: 3rd, 5th, 6th, 9th - 13th, 16th - 20th, 23rd - 27th.

OCTOBER

Beatles: 3rd, 7th - 12th.

The Gods: 14th - 16th, 21st.

Pink Floyd: 22nd, 23rd, 28th - 30th.

NOVEMBER

Pink Floyd: 4th.

Liza: 15th

The Gods: 25th - 29th

DECEMBER

Pink Floyd: 2nd - 4th, 9th - 11th, 16th - 18th.

The Gods: 12th.

JANUARY 1969

Cliff Richard: 3rd, 8th, 11th.

John Rowles: 9th.

Dobie Gilles: 13th.

Pink Floyd: 16th, 21st.

Edward Hand: 17th.

Cost: £350

Note: next six months hire to cost £250.

Additional instrument hired for sessions as required.

AUGUST

Koobas: 7th.

Pretty Things: 21st, 22nd.

The Gods: 19th, 22nd, 23rd, 24th, 29th, 31st

SEPTEMBER

Pink Floyd: 16th - 20th, 9th - 11th, 23rd - 25th, 30th.

OCTOBER

Pink Floyd: 1st, 2nd.

The Lace: 7th, 8th.

JANUARY 1969

Nocturnes: 13th, 21st, 22nd.

Cliff Richard: 17th.

Pink Floyd: 23rd.

Cost: 19 gns. per session.

In 1969 everybody from Pink Floyd to Cliff Richard wanted to put a Mellotron on their record.

carriage clock, much as Brian Epstein's NEMS music company might have presented to the head of bought ledger on the occasion of his retirement.

Norman didn't seem altogether cut out for the alternative society, which made it all the more puzzling that the next act he should be asked to work with was Pink Floyd. For their part, Pink Floyd were not ones to turn down an opportunity to work with the man who had worked his magic with the Beatles; and Norman was not one to pass up the group who appeared to be exciting a lot of the right people.

'The first session was in Number Three,' he told Abbey Road archivists. 'We were going to start an album called *Piper At The Gates Of Dawn*. Syd Barrett was the writer. So we got along fine. A door opened, who should walk in but Paul McCartney? He didn't have to introduce himself of course. Eventually he put his hand on my shoulder and said to the boys, "Well, you won't go far wrong with this guy. He will do you right." Which I thought was extremely nice of Paul, and it certainly helped an awful lot to develop this sense of friendship and trust between myself and Floyd.'

Smith tried manfully to mould Pink Floyd for the commercial fray. He spent a lot of time talking to Syd Barrett about how he might improve his performances. He soon realized that nothing he was saying seemed to be manifesting itself in the takes and so he took to talking first to Roger Waters and ultimately to Dave Gilmour instead. When the band were booked to appear on *Top of the Pops* to mime 'See Emily Play' in 1967 he went so far as to set them up in Studio One to practise miming in preparation for what was bound to be an odd experience. It did no good. 'Syd went on *Top of the Pops* and he didn't perform at all. And then the second time when they went on he just stood there with his guitar hanging down, doing nothing. And that was coming towards the end of Syd Barrett's career with Pink Floyd.'

The people who worked in the studio at the time were starting to make the acquaintance of what seemed to be a wholly new variety of musician. Some of them seemed actively to resist popularity, or at least to pretend that it played no part in their calculations. This had never been the case with the Beatles and their ilk, who rarely shrank from catchiness. For the first time it wasn't possible to work out what the bands who came into the studio wanted and it was dangerous to assume their aims were aligned with the business. Whereas the members of Pink Floyd actually thought that Norman Smith did a good job of directing some of their wayward impulses into an album that at least some people bought, Norman, as befitted a man who had come up thanks to the greatest hot streak in recording history, was frustrated that he couldn't get chart singles out of them.

The members of Pink Floyd were, as far as EMI Studios were concerned, a new kind of people. These were confident young men from upper-middle-class backgrounds in Cambridge. They were not intimidated by the prospect of entering an institution which had a uniformed commissionaire at the door. They rather liked it. They were entirely comfortable with an environment which in some respects resembled the schools they had all been to. They quickly worked out how to talk to people to make sure they got what they wanted. One of the main things they wanted was to spend time in the studio. In fact they were so keen to spend time in the studio they negotiated a reduction of their royalty rate in exchange for free studio time. As far as they were concerned this, not the road, would be the place where they did their real work.

Their drummer Nick Mason later wrote approvingly of the 'odd mixture of conservatism and radicalism' about the place. 'Recording took place on four-track machines, which were then mixed down on to quarter-inch either mono or stereo tape,' he recalled. 'All editing was carried out by trainees using little brass scissors, in order to prevent any magnetism affecting the sound. The whole

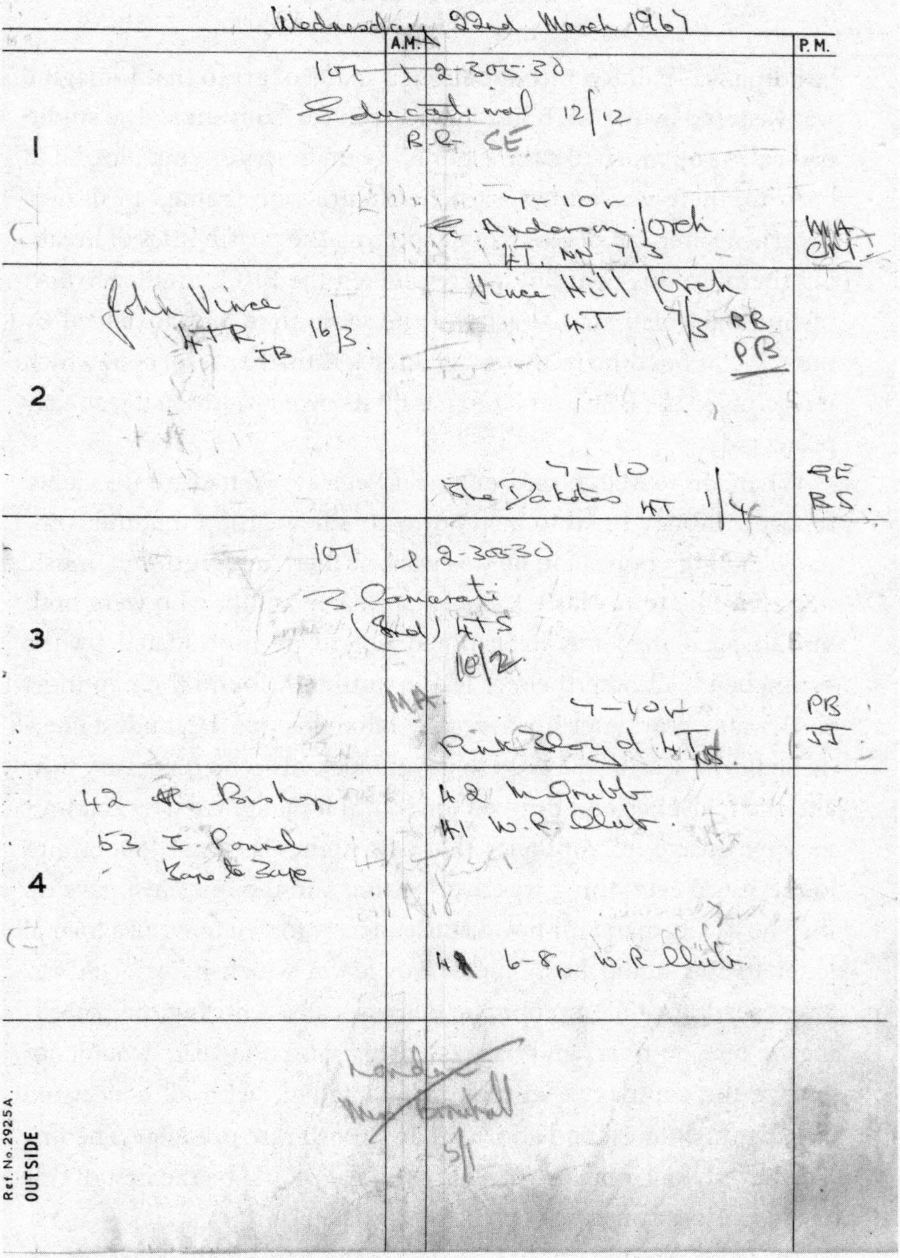

22 March 1967: the Beatles often appeared in the bookings diary as 'The Dakotas'.

building was painted throughout in a shade of green that I imagine was inspired by the KGB headquarters in the Lubyanka.' The studio had rules but, much like the schools the members of Pink Floyd had been to, there was always a teacher figure who seemed to draw a surprising amount of glee from exploring the possibilities of breaking them. In this EMI Studios resembled the BBC, another British institution which started around the same time and advanced by breaking or bending its own regulations. A further respect in which it resembled the BBC was it often built its own kit, which it jealously protected.

When, on 16 March 1967, engineer Peter Bown had got the call to report to Abbey Road to help out with a new group that the company had high hopes for, he was warned their 'underground' music might not be to his taste. He and producer Smith, who were both middle-aged men but determined not to be intimidated by the young band, allowed them to let rip until they found their comfort level. Many years later Bown recalled that this was the loudest noise he had ever heard. 'Syd used to go and kick his echo box every now and then, just because he liked the sound it made. We wrecked four very expensive microphones that first night. They got louder and louder until everything was overloading and the mics just gave up the ghost.' Norman Smith was subsequently forced to write a formal letter to the studio boss 'Chick' Fowler in which he said he was 'most sorry for the microphone damage caused during the recording of one number' and expressed his wish that this would not change the company's attitude to new talent, 'with all concerned sharing the interest and effort needed'. With rare prescience he finished by saying, 'I believe "The Pink Floyd" could be the first of this eagerly awaited success.'

There was something to be said for the perceived squareness of the place, as there was for the fact that staff were as used to making classical records as rock records. Since this was a full service studio

MS/3/NS/CSP

28th March, 1967.

MR. E. FOWLER,
ABBEY ROAD.

c.c. Mr. K. East.

RE: THE PINK FLOYD

As I am responsible for the introduction of the above group and their future records, I feel it my duty to stress the desire for strengthening the relationship between A & R and the studios, with this group in mind.

I am most sorry for the microphone damage caused during the recording of one number, but the group are in no way to blame for this and full responsibility must be shared by myself and Peter Bown, for an unwise choice of microphone for this particular purpose, although I hasten to add that we were not aware of the level at which the bass guitar was playing at this time. I should however, be most grateful for your tolerance in this matter, as I have nothing but praise for Peter Bown and his assistant for all the very hard work they have put in so far.

I must also mention the ban put on the use of the full grand piano in No.3, even though a very delicate piano passage was being played at the time and neither the baby grand or multi-tone came up to the required standard. However, I have no complaint against this decision, only at the manner in which it was administered, causing me some embarrassment with the group and great disturbance over the apparent inference of lacking faith in control over the treatment of studio equipment.

This memo is intended with great respect and with the earnest wish for EMIR to be concerned with the successful promotion of new talent with all concerned sharing the interest and effort needed.

I believe 'The Pink Floyd' could be the first of this eagerly awaited success.

Norman Smith

NORMAN SMITH
A&R Producer.

RECEIVED
29 MAR 1967
E.M.I. STUDIOS

Norman Smith apologizes for microphone damage sustained in an early Pink Floyd session.

all manner of instruments were close at hand, from pianos of all shapes, sizes and timbres to a million and one curious objects just begging to be struck. These could be employed for the quality that groups like Pink Floyd sought more than any other, which was colour. If they couldn't provide that pigment themselves then somebody in the studio would know a man who could. For instance, by the time they came to do the second album, *A Saucerful Of Secrets*, in 1968 it was clear that Syd Barrett, who had previously been the group's driving force, could no longer operate within the confines of a group. His one contribution to that second album, 'Jugband Blues', was placed at the end. This had been recorded a year earlier. When asked if he had any ideas what if anything might be overdubbed on the track, Syd had suggested a Salvation Army Band. Norman Smith took him at his word and hired just such a band. The musicians had been waiting an hour when Syd finally turned up to the date. When asked what they should play, Syd said they should play what they felt like playing.

This was beginning to be standard operating procedure. At this time, once given a choice between a considered response and an extravagant gesture the performer, who was now being regarded as an artist and as such could never be wrong, would unfailingly choose the extravagant gesture. As the older generation of record company talent managers followed George Martin and his colleagues by setting up on their own, many of these new groups were now working with engineers who weren't an awful lot more experienced than they were themselves. These juniors, in the flowery shirts they were suddenly being encouraged to wear for work, were quite enjoying the riskless freedom of allowing the acts to have their own way. It made as much commercial sense as anything. In the spring of 1968 a record called *The Hangman's Beautiful Daughter* by the Incredible String Band was in the top ten between the soundtrack of *The Sound of Music* and the latest by Andy Williams. Since clearly nobody knew how the new best-sellers had got to be the new best-sellers, it seemed you had to be prepared to try everything. By the end of the decade Norman Smith was one of the people who reasoned that since he was a musician and had been at the centre of making some of the biggest records of all time, he ought to have a go himself, and he was preparing his own songs which would come out under the name of his alter-ego Hurricane Smith.

At the same time as Norman was envisioning his future as a performer, Pink Floyd were wanting to produce their own records. Since they often entered the studio with only the most nebulous idea of what they were hoping to achieve it helped not to have to explain it to anyone. Pink Floyd's fifth album, which came out in the autumn of 1970, was a classic case. Its cornerstone was intended to be a composition known variously as 'Theme For An Imaginary Western', 'The Amazing Pudding' and 'Untitled Epic', a composition which they had originally worked up at a gig. They began recording it from the bottom up with drummer Nick Mason and bassist Roger Waters laying down a twenty-minute-long foundation. Because this was their first use of EMI's new eight-track console and the company had decreed there would be no tape editing, everything they subsequently did to the track had to adjust to the less than disciplined time signature they had put down. As Mason later admitted, they weren't particularly accomplished musicians at the time. In fact the people in whose name all this work was being done were, compared to the classical musicians who were brought in to play on the record, hardly musicians at all. They couldn't read music. They could play their own music but not much more. The only thing that made them professional musicians at all was they happened to be members of Pink Floyd, who were a professional band.

Because they had no producer they had nobody to turn to when they became stuck in the summer of 1970. Committed to an American tour, they asked composer/arranger Ron Geesin, a friend of

Roger Waters, to see if he could write something over the top of what they had already done, something that would make it all somehow add up. All summer Geesin laboured, stripped to his underwear because of the heat, until he had something ready to present to them when they returned from tour. A date was booked to record ten brass players and a twenty-piece choir performing this arrangement. Pink Floyd attended but there wasn't much they could add because, as Geesin reflected, they were the only people in the studio who couldn't read music – a state of affairs which was bound to place them at a certain disadvantage. Legitimate musicians, called in apparently to do the unclear bidding of some bunch of longhairs who couldn't even tune their own instruments, were apt to cut up rough from time to time. This was one of those times. Geesin, who was supposed to be conducting, made the mistake of asking the brass players what they thought rather than simply telling them what he wanted. When things became so heated with one musician that it appeared Ron was about to punch him, somebody in the control room suggested he withdraw to a safe distance. The rest of the session was conducted by John Alldis, the very experienced and most distinguished director of the choir.

The record, which was belatedly named *Atom Heart Mother* after a newspaper story the band happened to be reading, appeared in the shops late in 1970 wrapped in a cover starring a Friesian cow which sleeve designers Hipgnosis had talent-spotted in a field near Potters Bar in Hertfordshire. There was no indication on the outside of the package of the name of the group or the album. There was no hit single. Here was a piece of music which was disowned by most of the people who worked on it, all of whom had passed it down the line as though it was some kind of fizzing cartoon bomb. The title it was eventually given was entirely unrelated to the business of its composition. It arrived in the marketplace in a form deliberately designed to confuse. None of this seemed to be a problem in this new world order since the album went straight into the charts at number one in the week of release.

There was no official link between Pink Floyd and EMI. The company quickly accepted that this was the way things were going to go in the future. There was no way they could lay their hand on the tiller. Because there was no leader there was nobody they could call in and sweet-talk. Because there was no producer there was nobody to take the praise or blame, whichever was applicable. Roger Waters was outright derisive on the subject of *Atom Heart Mother*. David Gilmour put it down as an experiment that didn't work. There were subsequent attempts to perform the piece live, most of which rather foundered on the difficulty of transporting a choir of proper singers to muddy fields where the logistics could be sub-par. Hence the piece rather fell away from Pink Floyd's repertoire. It was never one of the strongest sellers in their catalogue. Even so it performed an invaluable role in their unfolding CV by reminding people just how strange they could be and just how little that appeared to put anybody off.

In 2008, such was the halo effect of Pink Floyd and the seemingly Elysian era out of which *Atom Heart Mother* had sprung, and the power of what we have all gradually come to recognize as the canon, there was a recital of it in a posh hall in Chelsea. David Gilmour turned up and played guitar. In time, it seemed, there would be a reverent recital of everything done in Studio Two back then. By then the place would be every bit as famous as the people who worked in it.

ROY HARPER, HARVEST AND ENDLESS OVERTIME

12

Roy Harper recorded 'When An Old Cricketer Leaves The Crease' with the Grimethorpe Colliery Band under the direction of David Bedford in Studio One in 1975.

By the end of the 1960s most of the grown-ups, the salarymen who had previously mediated between the bean counters at corporate HQ in Manchester Square and the music makers in St John's Wood, had departed the scene. Ballad specialist Norman Newell had left EMI in 1965, returning occasionally to produce records as a freelance. Cliff Richard's producer Norrie Paramor began his own operation in 1968, taking the young Tim Rice with him as a personal assistant. Both Newell and Paramor had belatedly come to the conclusion that it was the only way to be paid what they felt they were due.

George Martin had left the employment of EMI in 1966, having realized he could no longer afford to remain on the payroll. During the never-to-be-repeated madness of 1964, when even the richest and most powerful figures in the worldwide entertainment business urgently needed above all to know when they could next expect a record from the Beatles, the only person who knew the answer was this junior executive paid a salary of £3,000 a year. As a member of EMI's officer class, albeit in the junior ranks, Martin actually did less well than the infantry of the sales department. They at least banked a commission on the millions of Beatles records they had been knocking out. When, at the end of the studio's annus mirabilis 1963, the company announced that all its employees would be getting an extra four days' pay as a bonus, the man who more than anyone else had been responsible for this amazing year was sufficiently short of funds to wonder why this hadn't yet shown up in his pay. It was upon enquiring that he found out his £3,000 salary made him simply too senior to qualify. This clearly couldn't go on.

By the waning years of the decade this old system, wherein the avuncular men with the expense accounts came over from head office and told the musicians what kind of records they would like them to make, could no longer hold. Any individual whose touch on the tiller could claim in the smallest way to be golden was now no longer on EMI's payroll. At the beginning of the sixties the record companies had been able to assert, with some justification, that they knew more about what made a hit than anyone else. By the beginning of the seventies they could no longer make that claim. Suddenly even a company like EMI had to turn for answers to its newer, younger employees, people who had been attracted to the company in great numbers by the boom of the previous decade. Maybe they would know where the hits of the future would come from.

The new generation were made of a different timber. In the place of the men in shirts and ties with wives and children – men who had served in the war or played in dance bands, who could read sheet music and locate middle C on a piano – came a new generation of young men who had been born in the early years of the Baby Boom. The backgrounds of these young men were more likely to have been in practical electronics or the beat band circuit. As the technology of recording grew more sophisticated there was an increasing need for people who were as interested in what the various buttons could do as they were in dealing with the musicians. These young men were sufficiently starry-eyed to have fantasized about landing a job in a recording studio but also green enough not to have a clue what that would mean in practice. They could wire a plug, fill in a studio time sheet, turn up on time and express themselves in clear English, but this being the late sixties they were unlikely to have gone to university. This was not a problem since the EMI operation had a seemingly limitless appetite for clean, honest youngsters who could relieve the senior people of a large amount of day-to-day drudgery in exchange for the remotest chance of a career at the end of it. In the main they resided in London, which meant that there was a greater than average chance of them knowing that such places as recording studios existed and of being able to find their way to St John's Wood station.

Thus as the likes of George Martin and Norrie Paramor were moving on, a small army of polite, quiet young men with hair just slightly over their collars were finding their way to No. 3. Some stayed there for decades. All were destined to spend the rest of their lives recalling the time they worked there. For instance there was Alan Brown from Carshalton, who was working in a language lab in 1967 when he answered an ad in the *Evening Standard* to begin work at the studio as a trainee engineer. Two years later Alan was pointing his Singer Vogue in a northerly direction on an errand up Abbey Road. Since this was the precise moment the Beatles were stepping on to the zebra, Alan found himself driving that car into immortality.

There was west London grammar school boy John Leckie, who was on his way home from the Klooks Kleek club in West Hampstead with his mates on the summer evening in 1967 when the Beatles filmed 'All You Need Is Love' and actually saw George leave in his Rolls. John began work at the studio in 1969. Within a year he was tape operator on an *All Things Must Pass* session in Studio Three. He remembers looking around and seeing George Harrison, Klaus Voormann, Rick Wright, Donovan, Eric Clapton and Ringo Starr. He remembers bottles of Jack Daniel's stretching to the horizon.

Brian Gibson applied for a job as maintenance engineer in 1967.

Brian was working in Studio Three one day the following year when the engineer Ken Scott asked him to sit in his chair while he took a break. Brian took over without blinking, determined to prove he was not impressed by the celebrity of any musician, not even John Lennon. On this occasion John had decided he wished to record his vocal flat on his back on the studio floor. Brian dutifully positioned a microphone in the right place and found a pillow for Lennon's head.

Jeff Jarratt, another west London grammar school boy who at the age of nine had been the champion piano accordionist in London, and who early in his tenure at the studio was sent home for not wearing a tie, found himself working on Syd Barrett's *The Madcap Laughs* in 1969 and noting how David Gilmour and Roger Waters seemed to be just trying to get their old friend, who but two years earlier had sparkled, through what appeared to be a difficult patch which would surely pass.

Such encounters made a deep impression on these green young men. Whereas the earlier generation of EMI's producers or recording managers or whatever they were called had been music people, the new generation were more likely to be hardware people. The earlier generation knew how to foxtrot. The new ones had grown up with amplification. The earlier generation were drawn instinctively towards moderation. The new one was attracted by excess because it seemed the way of the future. In the absence of anyone more qualified, it fell to them to tell EMI what kind of records it should be making next and how it should do it.

In 1967 a young man called Malcolm Jones was taken on to EMI's graduate trainee programme. People like Malcolm, part of the generation who were spending the majority of their university grants on longhair records, could see at a glance that as a record company EMI had something of an image problem. Suddenly it seemed important for record companies actually to have an image,

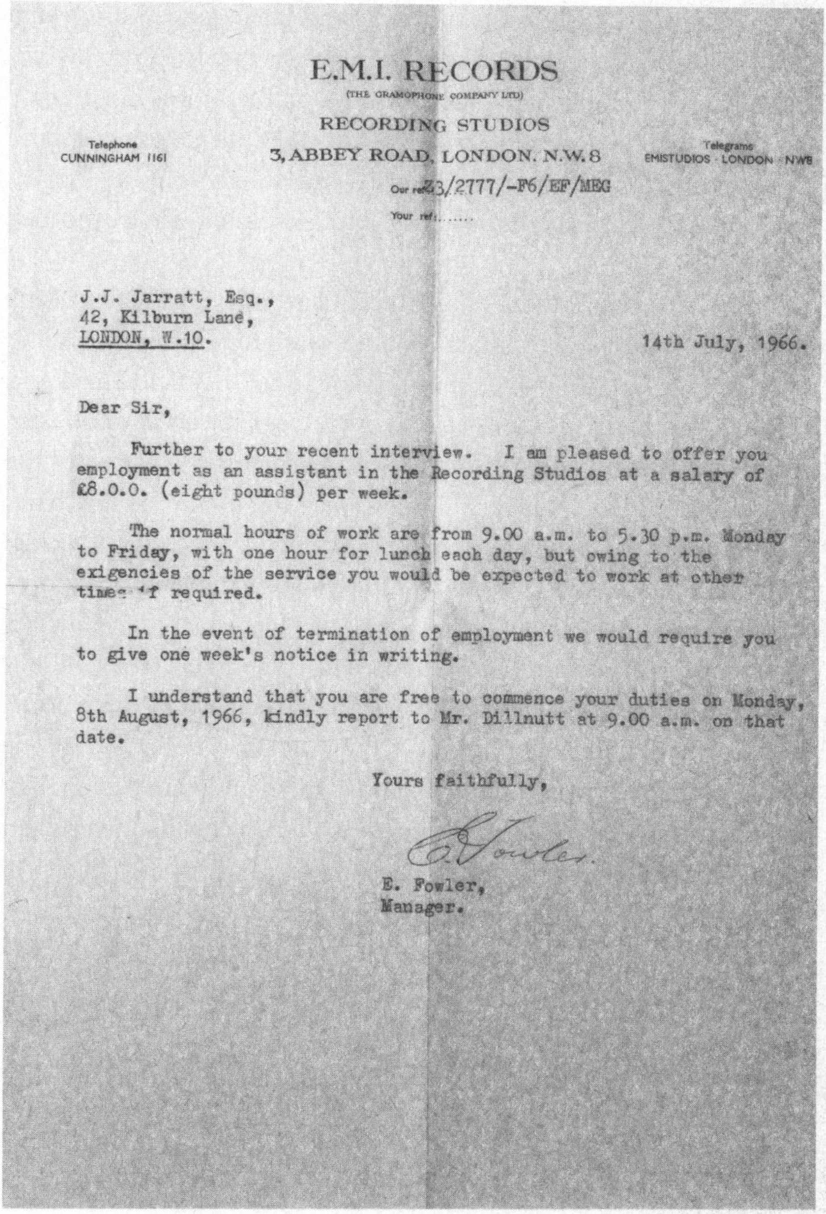

E.M.I. RECORDS

(THE GRAMOPHONE COMPANY LTD)

RECORDING STUDIOS

Telephone CUNNINGHAM 1161

3, ABBEY ROAD, LONDON. N.W.8

Telegrams EMISTUDIOS · LONDON · NW8

Our ref. Z3/2777/-F6/EF/MEG

Your ref. ......

J.J. Jarratt, Esq.,
42, Kilburn Lane,
LONDON, W.10.

14th July, 1966.

Dear Sir,

Further to your recent interview. I am pleased to offer you employment as an assistant in the Recording Studios at a salary of £8.0.0. (eight pounds) per week.

The normal hours of work are from 9.00 a.m. to 5.30 p.m. Monday to Friday, with one hour for lunch each day, but owing to the exigencies of the service you would be expected to work at other times if required.

In the event of termination of employment we would require you to give one week's notice in writing.

I understand that you are free to commence your duties on Monday, 8th August, 1966, kindly report to Mr. Dillnutt at 9.00 a.m. on that date.

Yours faithfully,

E. Fowler

E. Fowler,
Manager.

Jeff Jarratt's 1966 appointment letter used the word 'exigencies'.

preferably one like the independent Island label. Jones was given a job acquiring catalogue from other companies to release on the Parlophone or Columbia labels and was finding that it was not an easy sell. Therefore he proposed to his masters that the company should develop a new, hippy-friendly imprint and quietly fold the longer-haired artists from the Parlophone and Columbia labels into this new label.

Malcolm wasn't content to sit around and wait for the next Pink Floyd to drop into the company's lap. He was prepared to go out and scare one up. This is what led him first of all to Rockfield Studios in Monmouth, where the independent operators Charles and Kingsley Ward were recording with some local musicians in what was little more than a converted feed loft. Jones was keen to have a blues band on EMI, because blues bands like Fleetwood Mac and Chicken Shack were tearing up trees at the time (to such an extent that parodists had written a song called 'I Got The Fleetwood Mac Chicken Shack John Mayall Can't Fail Blues'), and if the musicians he identified did not have the blues he was prepared to buy them some records from which they might acquire some. The musicians he found in Wales dutifully came to Abbey Road and equally dutifully made an album called *Blues Helping*. By then events had overtaken them. They had performed their party piece, a high-velocity version of Khachaturian's 'Sabre Dance', on John Peel's programme on 8 October 1968 (he was so impressed he played it twice) and it quickly became a national obsession. By then they were called Love Sculpture. The record went to number five.

Flushed with this success Jones got his own label to run, into which were seemingly swept all the acts from the college circuit not considered quite strong enough to survive on their own and therefore in need of the shielding arm of a label, plus Pink Floyd. This label was named Harvest after polling all the acts on the label, one of whom already had the name Barclay James Harvest. The bulk of

Harvest's releases in those early days, the majority of which were recorded at Abbey Road by bands absolutely thrilled to have any time in a proper prestige studio, were often notable for their covers, a great deal of which were produced by the deliberately transgressive design collective Hipgnosis. Many of these covers – such as the one where the Edgar Broughton Band were represented by slabs of meat dangling from hooks, and another where the attractively named Toe Fat were shown naked on a beach with huge thumbs where their heads should have been – seemed to dare you to listen to the records inside. In their first year of operation they put out a record by Tea & Symphony called *An Asylum For The Musically Insane*. There was another by the Third Ear Band which had just four tracks, called 'Air', 'Earth', 'Fire' and 'Water'. They went in for records with titles such as *Things May Come And Things May Go But The Art School Dance Goes On Forever*, the kind of names long-haired students could quote approvingly to each other while pretending to be stoned.

So many acts were signed to Harvest between 1969 and 1971 and so many of them desired nothing more than to get into a proper studio and make their mark that all these young engineers found themselves pitched into the front line sooner than they were expecting. Like medical students being let loose on live patients, this late sixties intake were asked to provide services that probably wouldn't have been required of them in any other studios at the time. Their job was to check the rota and dutifully turn up to do duty for whoever they were asked to assist, whether that meant Manuel and the Music of the Mountains or Pete Brown's Battered Ornaments.

Peter Mew was one such engineer who was looking to establish himself, both in the studio and on the domestic front, in the late sixties. 'When I started it wasn't unusual for an album to be made in two or three days,' he stated when being interviewed for the Abbey Road archives. 'When EMI introduced the Harvest label it was all very experimental and they wanted young engineers to work on it. That meant people like Edgar Broughton, Roy Harper and the Third Ear Band, people who have actually now become cult figures but at the time were a bit of a joke.

'Suddenly we were looking at a situation where you might have two weeks to make an album, which gave you a lot of time to experiment and learn your trade as an engineer. But the wonderful thing was, it was all overtime. All these groups preferred to work overnight. You didn't have to deduct the morning when you weren't there, but we were being paid time and a half, double time for being there at night. I've always said that the Edgar Broughton Band bought my first house. I would never have been able to get a deposit for a house if it hadn't been for all this overtime I was working.'

At the time there were outposts of EMI's operation in various territories overseas and staff were occasionally posted to distant lands to help with the installation of some new item of technology. When Abbey Road's Tony Clark did one such stint in Nigeria he was particularly impressed by Fela Ransome-Kuti, a national as well as a musical hero, and plans were made to record Kuti and his band in St John's Wood during a visit to London in the summer of 1971. The twelve-piece Africa '70 had an admirably brisk attitude to work, recording two albums in Studio Three on two consecutive days in late July. Some members of the band had difficulty acclimatizing to the temperature of British summer. Engineer Jeff Jarratt discovered that three of the conga players had to spend time in the Gents running their palms under hot water before they were able to play effectively. On the second day they were joined by Ginger Baker, at the time a demi-god because of his stint with Cream, and an audience of no fewer than a hundred and fifty souls, many of them smoking enthusiastically, were somehow crammed into Studio Three.

The early 1970s were a curious time for a record company like

EMI, which was still awash with cash and treated their studio operation as part of the cost of doing business rather than a cost centre which had to be controlled. Inflation did not begin raging through all such businesses until 1972. In the boardroom of a public company like this they had to accept that it was impossible to predict where public favour would next alight. The people who signed the cheques at EMI really had no earthly idea why a group as difficult to grasp as Pink Floyd had somehow connected with the nation's furnished flats but they were pleased they had done. Hence they had to be prepared to believe that an artist like the acoustic singer-songwriter Roy Harper, friend and fellow management client of Pink Floyd, might also be worth a fair crack of the whip. This was the start of a beautiful if not golden friendship. For a period of ten years during the seventies Harper enjoyed privileged access to Abbey Road to record his iconoclastic musical rambles. 'The technicians used to thank me for helping them pay their mortgages,' he later recalled.

At the time there was no network of independent labels making records with artists who had a small but clearly finite following. If you were on one of the big labels you got the big treatment and were allowed to make an album as though you were one of the big acts. If it didn't work then the money that had been spent could be kicked down the road to be added to a debt that would probably never be paid off.

For artists like Harper, the studio was not the place where they took their inspiration so much as the place they went in order to be inspired. Led Zeppelin called one of their songs 'Hats Off To (Roy) Harper' in order to pay tribute to the fact that this low-rise troubadour seemed to operate above and beyond the calls of petty commerce. The seventies seemed to be the first decade when it was possible to wear this apparent lack of popularity as a badge of honour. In all likelihood artists like Harper, and others on EMI's prickly

Harvest label would have been perfectly happy to yield their commercial virginity if only they could find paying customers wishing to relieve them of it.

Even Harper's most appealing songs, such as the ones on 1971's *Stormcock*, tended to eschew brevity, leaving the people in EMI's promotion department complaining, not without justification, that there was literally no way to bring them to the public's attention beyond waiting patiently for word of mouth to perform its miracle. There was a further practical difficulty in the studio in that Harper's songs were often too long to be accommodated on a single reel of tape. 'A tape only lasts for fifteen minutes maximum and so a lot of those things I couldn't record in one take. And nobody was going to let me do that. So we had to use two tapes and then edit. On one I remember we had to edit on an oboe solo, in "Me And My Woman", which was incredibly difficult. We ended up having to get the oboe player back in.'

In this decade a certain amount of vagueness had to be priced in when it came to artists like Harper. For a start, such people regarded themselves as artists rather than performers. Harper remembers that on no fewer than three occasions he had to go to Hank Marvin to borrow guitar strings. Not all his encounters with the legends he met in the halls of the studios were so happy. Harper claims that he once found that his studio booking had been usurped by Paul McCartney, who needed to do something in a hurry. 'I lost it and went down to the canteen and ripped the food vending machine off the wall.'

Looking back in the twenty-first century, Harper has no hesitation in calling Abbey Road 'the best studio I'm ever likely to record in with the best atmosphere and the best energy. It was full of very techie people. They used to call themselves "bods". I remember once me and John Leckie called the Amp Room because there was something wrong with the desk. A guy came down, put his Kit-Kat on the mixer and went to work behind it. After a while we heard a voice say, "Please don't eat my Kit-Kat." That's the sort of people they were.'

The musicians who recorded at Abbey Road, who had killed time at school in art classes and left as soon as possible in order to chase girls, were dependent on the technicians of Abbey Road, who had followed the sciences route and had found their way to their employment thanks to the fact that they were never happier than when taking some crude electronic device apart. An affection developed between the two, one which rarely blossomed into socializing. The studio people were men of a certain kind. The contemporary term 'nerd', with its suggestion of the colourless and odourless world of digital, does not do justice to a tribe who could invent things few normal human beings could but who were not always quite so sure-footed when it came to deciding where their invention might be best employed. This applied to play as well as work.

There had been no better illustration of the Abbey Road *esprit de jeu* than the great lavatory joke of Christmas 1969. Looking for a seasonal prank to play on their rivals at Decca in West Hampstead they fell upon the idea of putting a full lavatory including cistern and giveaway roll of EMI toilet paper in a large packing case in which a piece of studio equipment had been delivered and then dispatching it to the Decca studio in Broadhurst Gardens. When this delivery was effected, using the van belonging to the group Orange Bicycle, who were recording at Abbey Road at the time, the Decca staff were such rule followers themselves that they naturally assumed that since they had not ordered any equipment from this particular manufacturer they would not open it and would instead do the responsible thing, which was to ring management at Abbey Road and say that this had been mis-delivered. They only got round to opening it when the EMI people insisted, which rather robbed the joke of some of its force. Such touching efforts to be seen as wild and crazy guys only underlined that this was precisely what they weren't.

During the recording of his 1975 album *HQ*, Harper found himself in a position that artists of his marginal commercial standing no longer find themselves in. He had booked session guitarist Chris Spedding to come in and add a guitar solo to opening track 'The Game'. When Spedding arrived the only studio available was the vast Studio One, as opened by Sir Edward Elgar in 1931 and patronized by grandees ever since. Spedding happened to be wearing a cream suit with a red carnation, as though on his way to a fancy dress event. His hair was slicked back Memphis-style. He placed his amp in the middle of the vastness of the studio floor. Its power lead snaked back all the way to a socket in the wall. The engineer rolled the track. Spedding listened. He nodded to indicate that he had the idea. The engineer took it back to the top, rolled the tape, and Spedding improvised over the top. When it was completed, Harper nodded his approval. The guitarist put his instrument in its case and was out of the door. It was less than twenty minutes since he had arrived.

HQ's other magic moment, and by common consent the zenith of Harper's entire career as a recording artist, also took place in Studio One. Harper had a passion for cricket, one he shared with Ken Townsend and the members of Pink Floyd. This had led him to write a song about the strange vibrations which thoughts of the game set off in the English breast. It was decided, with more thought for history than accountancy, that what would set this song off a treat was a brass band. Thus no less august a body than the entire Grimethorpe Colliery Band was brought down from South Yorkshire and set up in Studio One, where they performed under the baton of David Bedford. The resulting record, 'When An Old Cricketer Leaves The Crease', is one of the dozen greatest records ever made at Abbey Road.

The Grimethorpe Colliery Band was formed in 1917, back in the days when men who made a perilous living on their bellies in the dark elevated their souls at weekends by mastering the overture from *William Tell* or the 'Londonderry Air'. Their fame spread and led to residencies on British radio and appearances at the annual brass band festival at the Albert Hall. The sound of a brass band, particularly when falling upon the ear of anyone brought up in the north of England, is freighted with a sadness and sweetness which few other sounds can equal. It was ideally employed in the context of Roy Harper's song. No sound was more suited to summoning the shades of batsmen long dismissed, stalking away into their lengthening shadows, regretfully swinging their bats.

It's conceivable that this sound could have been supplied by some musicians from Rickmansworth or even in due course by a machine, but in this case it seemed to gain greater power because we had read the sleeve notes and knew it had been delivered in Studio One, and we knew it had been delivered by a bunch of burly men in their best cardigans, men who sprang from the same soil as the song. In the short term, 'When An Old Cricketer Leaves The Crease' was not the hit it probably should have been. It is, however, played to this day at the funerals and wakes of cricketers. It seems doubtful that this would be the case if the sound of the brass band had been digitally flown in. It lives in our hearts not simply because it is an exquisite piece of music. It endures in the imagination because when hearing it we can close our eyes and imagine the performance taking place in a certain room at a certain hour on a certain day under a certain clock. It is proof, for those who require proof, of the genius of the studio system.

13

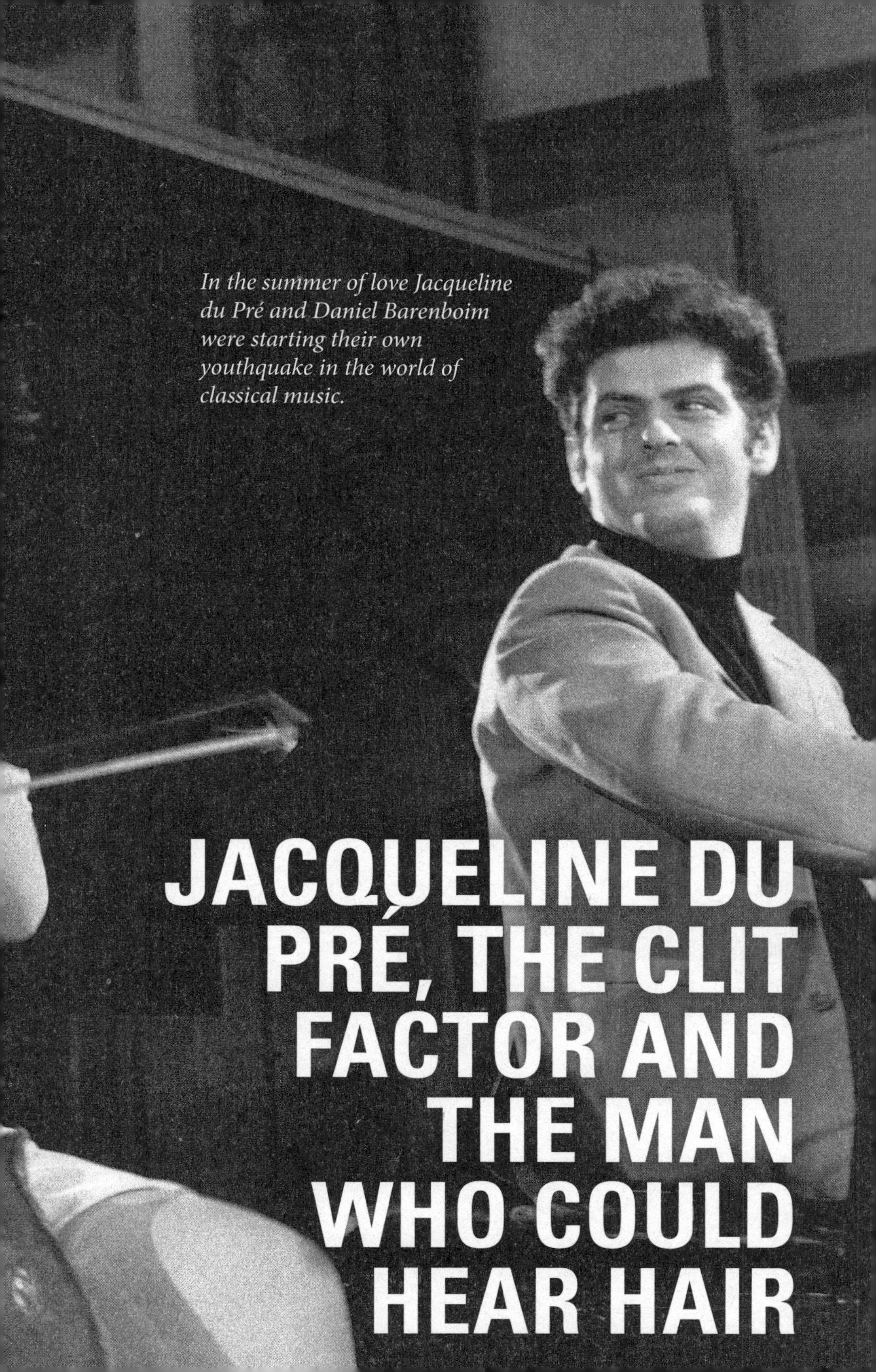

In the summer of love Jacqueline du Pré and Daniel Barenboim were starting their own youthquake in the world of classical music.

JACQUELINE DU PRÉ, THE CLIT FACTOR AND THE MAN WHO COULD HEAR HAIR

Jacqueline du Pré burned through her first cello teacher in just a year. She was four at the time. She left school in 1960 at the age of fifteen to devote more time to music, practising at least four hours a day. Jackie stood out, even among the prodigies. When she played her first professional concerts as a teenager the critics would note that the only thing letting her performances down was her accompanist. The accompanist was her mother, a professional pianist. When she played for the Spanish master Pablo Casals he refused to believe that anyone who put so much of themselves into their playing could possibly be English. The violinist Pinchas Zukerman remarked that she 'played from the stomach'.

As she grew, her mentors noted that she had a power to put herself over in performance which sometimes seemed in danger of overshadowing the works themselves. She came into the public eye in the sixties, when the manner in which she carried herself on the platform seemed to have something in common with the way the rock stars of the time presented themselves. Other musicians envied the way she could turn up, be reminded what she was slated to play, and then instantly be in the moment. When she appeared, people came to see her perform as much as they came to hear her play. She would sway back and forth, tossing her hair as though she would really prefer to pick up her instrument and carry it among the audience. She loved an audience, flinging her music towards them. They loved her in return. She knew about audiences. According to the British conductor Jeremy Dale Roberts, she and her early accompanist Stephen Bishop would talk about what they called the 'clit factor' in music, thanks to which she knew exactly how to time a phrase to send a particular frisson through the listeners.

She first recorded a recital of cello music at Abbey Road in July 1962, but what really made her name was her 1965 interpretation of Elgar's Cello Concerto. First performed in the wake of the First World War, the piece was interpreted as the resigned work of an old man who had witnessed far too much sadness. When Jackie first played it on a concert platform she turned the world of classical music on its ear. People were so keen on hearing this elegy performed by a young person that she was hired to play it at the Proms for four consecutive seasons. On 19 August 1965, at the age of twenty, she recorded it for EMI at the Kingsway Hall near Holborn. This venue, which was pulled down in 1996, was used by all the record companies that needed to be able to accommodate an orchestra, even though the sound of passing tube trains could drive recording engineers to distraction. The staff of EMI's classical division deserted their offices that day and sat in the back of the stalls just to be able to say they were there. They had a lunch break after the first two movements, during which interval Jackie popped out into Holborn to find a chemist where she could buy something to fend off her headache. At the end of the recording the London Symphony Orchestra burst into applause, which was not a courtesy they extended to most soloists. There were Elgar purists who thought du Pré's recording failed to deliver the proper restraint. They criticized her tempo rubato, the classical term for varying the tempo and tone in search of a more expressive performance. Nobody at the time pointed out that this was exactly what rock musicians like Jimi Hendrix and Steve Winwood were doing. The

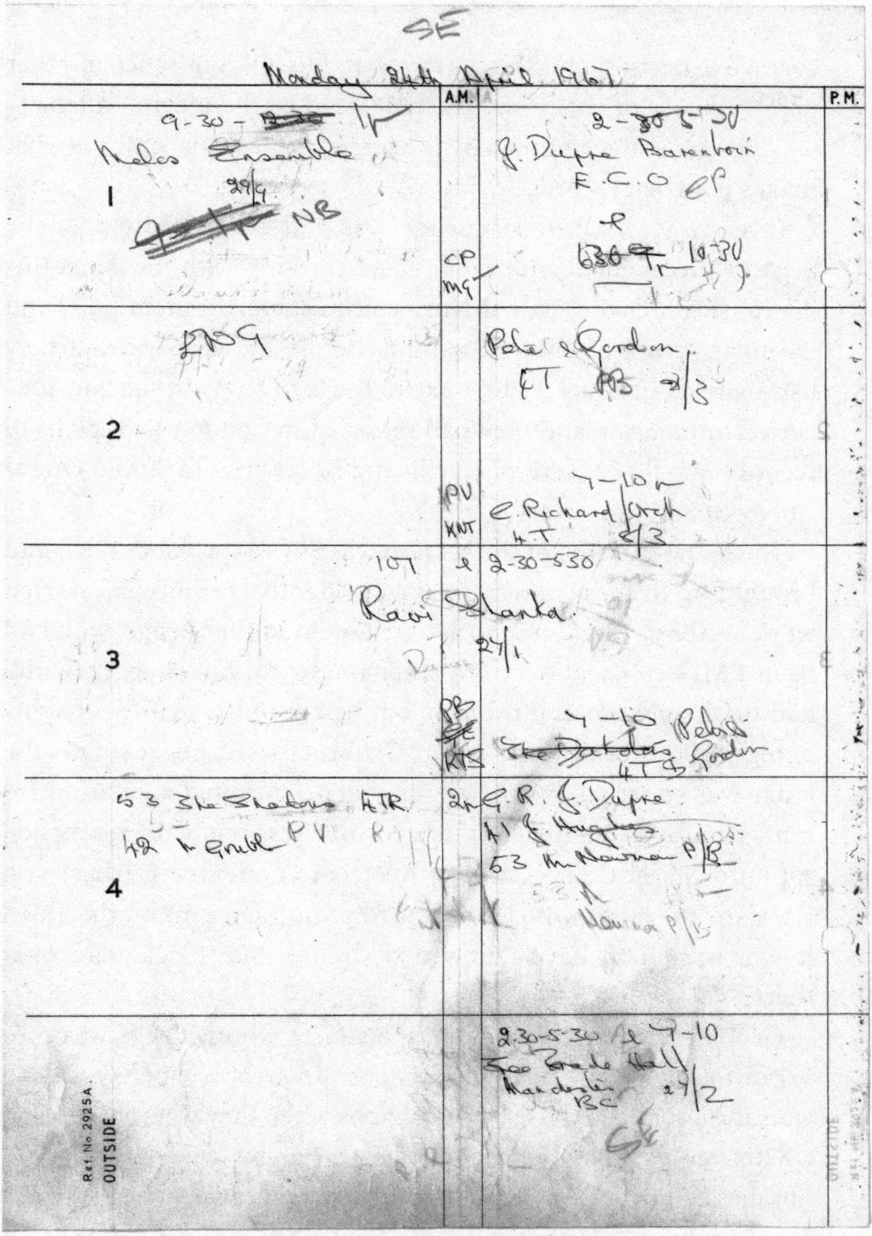

1967: while Jacqueline du Pré was recording a Haydn concerto, Peter and Gordon and Ravi Shankar were next door.

average listener, then as well as now, in blissful ignorance of other performances of the piece, reacts instead to the blazing intensity which is generated as much by the singer as the song, which is what makes it a great record.

In early 1967, when Jacqueline was still only twenty-one, she began a professional and romantic partnership with the Argentinian musician Daniel Barenboim, which catapulted them both into the mainstream of public attention. Before the year was out they had married in Israel in the wake of the Six Day War, she had converted to Judaism, and they had returned to London with plans to record the cello concerti of Haydn and Boccherini in Studio One at Abbey Road.

The man in charge of the session was Suvi Raj Grubb. Born and brought up in India and trained as a scientist, Grubb had started work at Abbey Road in 1960 as assistant to Walter Legge, who had been EMI's classical overlord since the 1930s. Like Legge, Grubb had no formal musical training but had read himself to a frightening peak of erudition. When Grubb crossed Legge's path the latter was so struck by his talents that he invented a position for him. He was immediately plunged into sessions with renowned soprano Maria Callas and the Austrian conductor Herbert von Karajan. The latter, who had come to prominence under the Third Reich, is said to have demanded, 'Who's that black man over there?'

Grubb soon became the only person to whom Legge was prepared to outsource musical decisions. This wasn't merely during working hours. On those rare occasions when they were at home on a Saturday morning and neither Legge nor his wife (the soprano Elisabeth Schwarzkopf) could recognize what was playing on the Third Programme they would give Suvi a bell. From a mere snatch over the phone Grubb could identify Bizet's Symphony in C. As academic Andrew Blake pointed out, both Legge and Grubb, who played a significant part in shaping what the producer of a classical record could be expected to achieve, were fundamentally musical appreciators rather than musicians. They were producing records for the man – and it usually was a man – who wished to have the experience of sitting in the notional middle of the equally notional row 15. They had no use for the meretricious gimmicks their colleagues on the other side of the wall were introducing into pop records, but they were similarly shaping listening experiences which were not actually available in the material world. The records that came out on EMI's classical imprints were every bit as much the product of their decisions as the records that had George Martin's name on them.

They were certainly not in the market for change, even if their masters might appear to be keen. In the late 1950s EMI had bought the lease of a cinema in the northern reaches of the city with a view to starting another studio in which they would do all their pop recording, thus allowing them to dedicate Abbey Road to classical. The plan was quietly dropped a few years later but there were clearly people at a senior level in the company who felt there had to be other ways of doing things, even if they were not clear on how. In *Music Makers on Record*, his illuminating 1986 memoir, Grubb even recounts the occasion when the chairman of EMI turned up in the studio with a couple of recording engineers and insisted on doing a parallel version of that day's recording, the implication being that this would be done in a different way, 'with sound effects', as Grubb, in his rather loaded manner, puts it. It's not explained precisely how this alternative recording should differ, and Grubb clearly has little interest in finding out, or how it might have arisen within the company and possibly been used as a focus for discussing whether the recording of classical music might be revolutionized much as the recording of pop music had been. He is merely content to say that nothing further was heard of it, which suggests that as far as the classical side of the work at Abbey Road went, a certain conservatism went with the territory.

Recordings at the time were being made on two-track with a view to stereo. The engineer's job on these sessions was to use all his experience to position microphones in relation to different instruments, using his judgement about how the sound might be affected by factors such as the humidity and temperature in the hall. In other respects the staff were less fastidious about the atmosphere. The cigarettes Legge smoked during takes could actually make it difficult to see across the control room.

Grubb kept his eyes fixed on the score during takes, noting every few bars which would require re-recording and which take could be merged with another in the subsequent edit. He didn't consider this to be cheating the listening public. Whereas a live performance was an emotional experience in which a peak passage might make the listener forgive a plodding section that came afterwards, the record buyer sitting at home with their hi-fi needed to be treated to the best all the time, even if that had to be assembled from takes captured hours or even days before. Consequently, making recordings of the great works by the great orchestras with the great conductors was a job calling for a level of musical knowledge and fastidious bookkeeping such as was probably not required with Johnny Kidd and the Pirates.

It also called for levels of diplomacy not needed elsewhere in the building. Grubb hadn't been long in the job when he was involved in a stand-off with the fearsome conductor Otto Klemperer over the necessity of redoing certain parts of the piece they were recording. A studio recording was one of the few occasions in the professional life of a major conductor when their judgement might be called into question, and this was made more difficult if it happened in full view of the orchestra. When the producer needed to stop the recording he would literally have to ring the phone on the conductor's podium. The conductor would pick it up and hear the reason why he had been stopped. This way the orchestra didn't have to overhear any mild reproof being communicated.

Grubb was famous for going the extra mile in order to have an answer to the most unlikely objection. When recording opera, he claimed to be aware of the menstrual cycle of one singer who could not be expected to hit a high C on certain days. He even went so far as to make a note of the serial number of any individual piano in case so much as a single note needed to be re-recorded and inserted at a later date. His job was to make sure the editors would have all the acceptable takes they required to put together an acceptable master tape. Then he had to listen to and pass the master tapes which were subsequently produced for each of EMI's major markets. Once the test pressings were made he was required to audition those as well.

Walter Legge left the company in 1964. He was tired and he didn't like the way things were going. If there had been any doubt that EMI Studios would no longer be dominated by the classical side of its work the annus mirabilis of 1963 had dispersed it. Henceforth new recordings would have to be sanctioned by a committee which would balance the likely expense of the undertaking with the revenue it was likely to generate. Unlike with pop music, where there seemed to be no ceiling to what a gigantic hit could bring in, the sales of a new recording of a well-known work by a reputable orchestra with a celebrated conductor could be predicted down to the last few hundred, even if it was recorded in what was apparently the last word in stereo. When Jacqueline du Pré and John Barbirolli recorded the Elgar in 1965 it was cheaper to hire the LSO than to pay for hotel rooms for Barbirolli's usual band, the Manchester-based Hallé Orchestra. Now that the stature of the classical side seemed to be reduced, there would be more such decisions. Walter was not about to tangle with any committee and so he moved on, leaving Grubb to take over his lifetime's work.

Thus, on 24 April 1967, he found himself in charge when du Pré came into Studio One to record the cello concerti, Haydn's C major and Boccherini's B flat. His first challenge was to site the soloist somewhere she was comfortable and also audible. Because the cello is played sitting down, it is on the same sonic plane as the orchestra and therefore can easily be overpowered by the rest of the strings. Having tried facing away from the orchestra and from the side, they eventually settled on placing her on a rostrum which put her at the centre of a horseshoe, raised above the orchestra but facing the conductor. When they resumed after lunch Grubb thought that the tone of the cello had changed. He was the only one who thought this way but he was most insistent. All the obvious things were checked. The cello was the same. The microphones were the same. Their position had not been changed. They stopped and checked every piece of equipment. Eventually du Pré confessed that she had changed her bow for the afternoon session. Even this minor alteration, which was effectively the substitution of one horse's tail for another, which had not been apparent to any of the musicians and technicians, had been all it had required to trigger the eerie sonar of Suvi Raj Grubb.

Whereas so many of the leaps being made in pop recording in the neighbouring studios at the time had been achieved thanks to the gleeful embracing of the distorting effects of amplification, in Grubb's sound world the technicians were dealing with music-making technology that had been perfected in the eighteenth century. On her classic Elgar recording Jacqueline du Pré had played an instrument which had come out of Stradivari's workshop in 1712. She eventually abandoned this one-in-a-million instrument because it did not respond to the way she liked to push against its limitations. (It is now played by Yo-Yo Ma, who observes that you have to coax the music out of it rather than demand it, but it is so precious that it is owned by a multi-national company as an investment.)

When it was first presented to Jackie by a wealthy friend it had been with the idea that it could be sold to finance her retirement, as is the traditional fate of the fiddler's tool. Her retirement was to turn out to be tragically early.

Playing the cello calls for prodigious reserves of muscle memory. There are no frets or keys telling the musician where to place the left hand to achieve a particular sound; the hand simply knows where to go, and that knowledge stays with it until some other force, most often old age, intervenes. With Jacqueline du Pré, a feeling of numbness that began to manifest itself in the late sixties eventually resulted in 1971 in her not wanting to play at all. Concerts were called off on the grounds of 'mental exhaustion'. She had a trial separation from Barenboim. She was treated for depression. Since the age of four she had lived to play and now there didn't seem to be much reason to live.

One morning in early December 1971 she woke up feeling for some reason much better. She got out her cello at home and started playing for the first time in six months – a very long time for somebody who in better times was in the habit of playing for many hours a day. Recognizing that something had come over her which might not remain for long, Barenboim called Grubb to ask if there was any chance they could come into the EMI studios and try recording a few sonatas that they liked playing together. No orchestra, no fuss, nobody need know. They would be in and out. No pressure. Grubb checked the bookings. The only available studio was the giant Studio One. He booked it for 10 and 11 December, and in they went.

Grubb was impressed by how undiminished du Pré's playing seemed to be. She had always been a quick study and this time she rattled off pieces by Chopin and César Franck by lunchtime on the second day. They had enough for an album in just those pieces, but Jackie was keen to have a go at recording the Beethoven cello sonatas in the afternoon. When the time came they played the first movement and then, apparently taken over by tiredness or a presentiment of the multiple sclerosis that would kill her at the age of forty-two, she stopped. She put her cello back in its case, snapped it shut and said, 'That's all for today.'

She was twenty-six. She was never in a recording studio again.

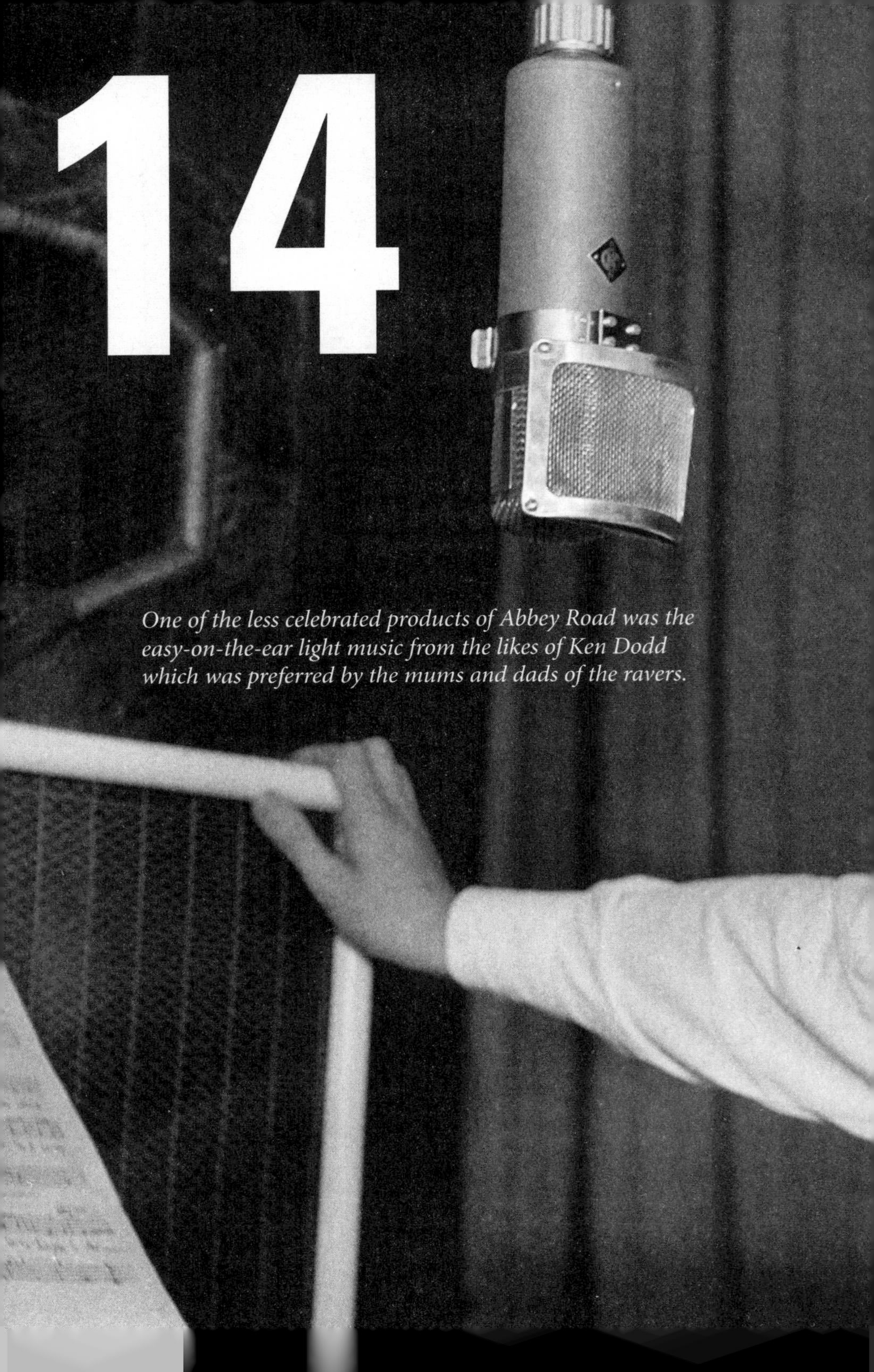

14

One of the less celebrated products of Abbey Road was the easy-on-the-ear light music from the likes of Ken Dodd which was preferred by the mums and dads of the ravers.

PINKY, PERKY, MANUEL AND LIGHT MUSIC BY THE YARD

1965 had been the peak year for the seven-inch 45. It was the year of Bob Dylan's 'Like A Rolling Stone', the Rolling Stones' '(I Can't Get No) Satisfaction', 'You've Lost That Lovin' Feelin'' by the Righteous Brothers, 'In The Midnight Hour' by Wilson Pickett, 'California Girls' by the Beach Boys, and numberless gems from the studios of Motown and Stax. To this roll of honour EMI Studios in St John's Wood were able to add 'If You Gotta Go, Go Now' by Manfred Mann, 'I'm Alive' by the Hollies, 'Ferry Cross The Mersey' by Gerry and the Pacemakers and, from the Beatles, the small matter of 'Help!', 'Ticket To Ride', 'Yesterday' and a dozen deathless album tracks.

However, the biggest UK hit single of that year of hit singles, and also the biggest record made at EMI's studios, was 'Tears'. This was a ballad of the most old-fashioned kind, originally brought to prominence by crooner Rudy Vallée in the 1920s and here being interpreted by Ken Dodd, a comic entertainer best known for his buck teeth and tickling stick. The production of this single had been supervised at Abbey Road by Norman Newell. Norman had played his part in the pop revolution that had recently changed the studio by bringing in Peter and Gordon with their Paul McCartney-penned hit 'A World Without Love' but he was not about to have his head turned by any fads. Norman was old school. He continued to bring in the companies of West End shows to make their original cast recordings on Sundays, the day when London's theatres were dark. He also remained a believer in the enduring appeal of the big ballads, which were still popular below the olive line and which, in those pre-Abba years, regularly scooped first prize at the Eurovision Song Contest. While people of John Lennon's generation sought to make records which were above all heavy, Norman Newell knew there was a huge market for light music in all its myriad forms of lightness. Norman had been the man responsible for handling Judy Garland when she recorded at the studio in the late fifties. He was the person who prodded the reluctant piano star Russ Conway into the limelight. He took care of Shirley Bassey. He wrote Matt Monro's first and biggest hit 'Portrait Of My Love', provided English lyrics for 'More', the theme song for exploitation film *Mondo Cane*, and even produced the first records by the Leeds *chansonnier* Jake Thackray. Every session he supervised was conducted as it would have been ten years earlier.

There was always a particular kind of tension about any session that called for the recording of a singer with an orchestra. It took a deal of self-belief to mount the dais and try to perform an unfamiliar song in front of forty middle-aged white males for whom this was simply another day at the office. It might have been no skin off their noses if they had to play the same arrangement repeatedly because the singer apparently couldn't do his or her part, but it took a great deal of self-confidence for a singer to persuade him- or herself that they wouldn't go away from that session muttering that you weren't in the same class as Vera Lynn or Donald Peers.

When Cilla Black entered Studio One on 22 February 1966 to record the title song for a major new motion picture, she was only twenty-two years old, untrained and inexperienced. She had to sing this song 'Alfie', which called for all her range and then some, in front of Burt Bacharach, the man who composed it, a forty-eight-piece orchestra, three backing singers, her producer George Martin

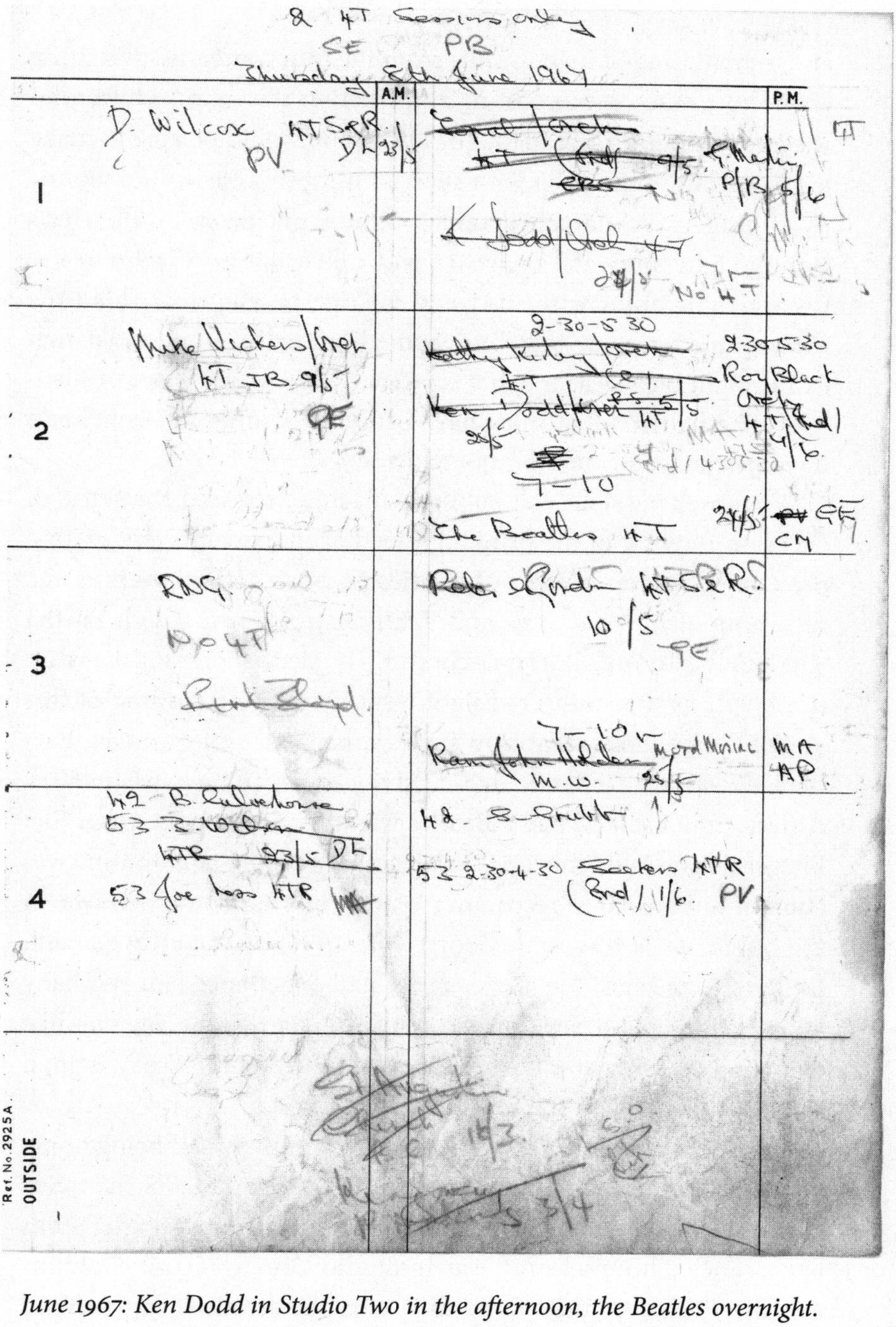
2 4T Sessions only
SE PB
Thursday 8th June 1967

	A.M.		P.M.
1	D. Wilcox 4T S&R PV DL 23/5	~~Signal Orch~~ ~~4T (End) 9/5~~ ~~CBS~~ G. Martin P/B 5/6; ~~K. Dodd/Orch 4T~~ 24/5 No 4T	4T
2	Mike Vickers/Orch 4T JB 9/5 PE	2-30-5-30 ~~Kathy Kirby/Orch 4T~~ ~~Ken Dodd/Orch 4T~~ 5/5 24/5; 7-10 The Beatles 4T 24/5	2-30-5-30 Roy Black Orch 4T (End) 4/6; ~~PV~~ GE CM
3	RNG No 4T ~~Pink Floyd~~	~~Peter & Gordon~~ 4T S&R 10/5 PE; 7-10 ~~Ram John Holder~~ Mord Moire M.W. 25/5	MA AP
4	42 B. Culverhouse ~~53 S. Wilson 4TR 23/5 DL~~ 53 Joe Loss 4TR	42 S. Grubb; 53 2-30-4-30 Seekers 4TR (End) 1/6 PV	

Ref. No. 2925A. OUTSIDE

June 1967: Ken Dodd in Studio Two in the afternoon, the Beatles overnight.

and a smattering of men in suits from the film company, all fretting about how much it was costing and whether this gawky child, who was only a couple of years out of Liverpool, would be able to make anything out of the song with such an unlikely title. It took hours. According to Bacharach it took twenty-eight takes in all. That's twenty-eight times the orchestra was called upon to begin again, twenty-eight times with Burt and George praying that this time Cilla would produce that little something extra – and what that extra might be was as much a mystery to them as it was to Cilla – while she battled what must have been her waning self-belief and filled her lungs for the twenty-eighth time.

Whenever possible, the publicity machine stressed the sense of occasion implicit in the bringing together of a great legend with a prestige orchestra. In the early sixties Norman Newell oversaw the recording of *Love For Sale* and *The Romantic Eartha* with Eartha Kitt and the Tony Osborne Orchestra. The sleeve notes for the latter throbbed: 'as the studio red light went up at the recording of this album it whispered a warning to every man and every woman. Eartha Kitt was in a romantic mood.' In the spring of 1964, when every American household had a Beatles wig, it was announced that Ella Fitzgerald was suddenly one of their most devoted fans and she was coming to London to record her version of 'Can't Buy Me Love' in the home of the hits, with George Martin doing the arrangement. Either the queen of the jazz canaries had experienced an epiphany while listening to her well-worn copy of *A Hard Day's Night* or, like everybody else in show business, she and EMI Studios knew a good publicity angle when she saw one.

Thanks to its being owned by a British company and being home to the Beatles, Abbey Road was already by the middle of the 1960s the best-known studio in Britain. A couple of months after Ella's appearance, Shirley Bassey was in Studio One to record 'Goldfinger', the definitive James Bond theme for the definitive James Bond film. One of the musicians who got the call to play in the orchestra John Barry had assembled for that day was guitarist Jimmy Page, who later recalled: 'The full orchestra sounded absolutely amazing, but then Shirley Bassey arrived. When she sang it took her just one take. And at the end of the tape, she collapsed on the floor. She just held this one note and basically ran out of breath and collapsed. I was in the front row of the musicians, so I really had a good view of all of this.'

This is a good story. The fact that there is no trace of 'Goldfinger' having been recorded at EMI does not in any way spoil things. Instead it underlines for the benefit of those of us used to thinking that the past is mapped by the blinding lights of great records that for those who actually laboured on them the work was zipping by at such a pace it was often difficult to remember whether they were working with Otto Klemperer or Freddie and the Dreamers. Whether or not something you played a few bars on turned out to be one of those records that people remember for ever more or just another B-side to be included as ballast on an overpriced box set decades later was a lottery. Most of us don't recall individual days we spent at work forty years ago. There really is no reason for musicians to be any different.

In June 1966 Yehudi Menuhin returned to the studio to record *West Meets East*, the first of three albums he was to make with the Indian sitar genius Ravi Shankar. At this stage the latter musician was unaware of the fact that his instrument had become suddenly familiar in Europe thanks to George Harrison's use of it on 'Norwegian Wood (This Bird Has Flown)', which the Beatles had recorded in the same studio the previous year. There swiftly followed a short period when this instrument became almost as popular as the piano accordion had been in the 1930s. In 1968 EMI brought forth an album called *Lord Sitar* which was an attempt to marry the ethereal texture of the Indian classical instrument with the jaunty vibe of

Herb Alpert's Tijuana Brass. This had again been recorded in the same studio where George Harrison had taken those faltering first steps in 1965. The sleeve notes by producer John Hawkins hailed that moment as 'one of those phenomenons of our day and age' and finished by saying that only one question remained: 'WHO IS LORD SITAR?' The truth was that Lord Sitar was top session guitarist Big Jim Sullivan, who came from Uxbridge.

Light music, like the heavy variety, does not remain still. It is forever moving into new phases, all of which were reflected in the studios' work. Now that the moonlight-and-roses era of Mantovani seemed to have passed and Joe Loss was no longer demonstrating the Twist on the studio floor, it was seeking new worlds to conquer, always on the lookout for that felicitous combination of the familiar and the exotic which finds such favour with the public that it's possible to turn it out by the yard. Some acts had a greater claim to represent these exotic sounds than others. Pepe Jaramillo was an actual Mexican piano player who settled in Europe, where there proved to be a ready market for his recordings of any tune which could be associated, no matter how tenuously, with the land of his birth, and could be delivered in the strict tempo demanded by the many people in sixties Britain who eschewed rock and roll and whose preferred form of leisure was still ballroom dancing. The titles of Pepe's sixties LPs, which ranged from *Mexican Magic* through *Mexican On Broadway* to *Mexican Champagne*, bespeak a truly single-minded determination to provide what the market evidently desired.

Not all the performers could shrug off claims of cultural appropriation as easily as Pepe. The Magic Accordions of Adriano was cover for one Jack Emblow, who actually came from Lincolnshire. *Shades Of Hawaii* by Basil Henriques and the Waikiki Islanders was a flag of convenience for Basil Henrick from Solihull. The titular star of *The Continental Magic Of Judd Solo* could be found at the

Hilton Hotel, where he could apparently sing in eight languages. Among the musicians actually mentioned by name on his *Mediterranean In Perspective* were Ernie Shear, who played the solo on Cliff Richard's 'Move It' in the same studio, and Kenny Baker, the jazz great who took part in the historic First English Public Jam Session Recording at Abbey Road in 1941. Most of the time players like these went entirely uncredited and, given the variable nature of the enterprises they were called upon to take part in, weren't unduly discomposed by the fact. As long as they were paid they would continue to turn up in response to the contractor's call, serenely unbothered whether they would be moonlighting as a member of the Geoff Love Banjos or providing the primeval rhythm of life of which Mandingo and His Orchestra were so proud. In both cases the man with the baton was the same.

Geoff Love, whose father was African-American but whose mother actually came from the border of Yorkshire and Lancashire, spent more time in the studios over the years than Paul McCartney. It was in the course of recording 'The Honeymoon Song' at Abbey Road in 1959 that he happened upon a formula of gently strummed guitar parts, castanet percussion, distant voices and swirling strings which seemed to demand that it be the work of somebody other than a citizen of good standing in the London borough of Enfield. Thus it was necessary to re-present the ensemble as Manuel and the Music of the Mountains. They sold hundreds of thousands of copies of the likes of *Cascade*, *Carnival* and *El Bimbo*. Most of the songs were performed at Abbey Road by men who in real life had come no closer to a border than the business end of a lawnmower. The Manuel business began in 1960, a clear fifteen years before Andrew Sachs and John Cleese made that particular name a comic staple.

All this appeared in the shops on an EMI imprint called Studio 2 Stereo, which was where the company aimed its radiogram music for the comfortably-off and middle-aged. Stereo of any kind was unknown to the mass audience until the following decade. Radio was medium-wave and mono, and the company had no desire to worry the kids who bought the majority of the records by making them think they would have to buy new record players. This was the reason EMI had been so slow to embrace the long player and the 45. The chairman at the time felt that the public would be disturbed by the prospect of records revolving at any speed other than 78. When the Beatles listened to music at home it tended to be on their own jukeboxes. Even when they made *Sgt Pepper's Lonely Hearts Club Band* they had very little interest in hearing the stereo mix, which they left for George Martin and Geoff Emerick to do days later. The breakthrough stereo pop music album, released at the end of 1967, was actually *Days Of Future Passed* by the Moody Blues, which Decca were keen to use to promote their so-called 'Deramic sound' and their 'Phase 4' stereo. EMI were slower to make a fuss about the technology. For years following the introduction of stereo records each new issue would come with a reassuring sleeve message that stereo albums could be played back on mono 'reproducers provided either a compatible or stereo cartridge wired for mono is fitted'. They added that if you were in any doubt you should consult your dealer. Very few bands thought stereo was a priority. It wasn't until the Beatles' White Album came out in 1968 that it suddenly became a requirement for both bands and record buyers.

One of the first groups not signed to EMI to be allowed to work in EMI's studios, the Zombies, were beginning their magnum opus *Odessey And Oracle* just as the Beatles were releasing *Sgt Pepper*, in the summer of 1967. Professional enough to make sure they had all their material rehearsed and ready when they went into the studio, they were also careful enough with their recording budget to deliver their finished version in mono. This was unfortunate for them because it was at that precise moment that all the record companies suddenly began rushing to embrace stereo. Consequently the Zombies had to pay out of their own pockets for a stereo version to be made. By the time it came out they had split up in the face of widespread indifference. This record, which is now a regular in those lists of the greatest albums of all time which have proliferated in the years since people ceased buying albums, could have been saved a lot of trouble if it had been produced by a traditional artists and repertoire man. A George Martin would probably have spotted that 'Time Of The Season' was a hit single and that therefore the singer might be taking a liberty by stamping his foot and arguing that somebody else should sing it. A Brian Epstein would have ensured that if a friend of the band was going to design the sleeve he should at least be a friend who could spell the word 'Odyssey'. Somebody else would have seen the stereo problem coming.

Between the release of *Sgt Pepper* and the break-up of the Beatles, stereo went from being a nice innovation for them as could afford it to in some cases almost a substitute for music. Some of the stereo tracks being created in Abbey Road during that intoxicating period were more theatrical than auditory. Young Jeff Jarratt, who had joined the company in 1966 on a salary of £8 a week, was the engineer in charge in Studio Two one day in 1969 when John and Yoko asked him to record their heartbeats. Jarratt's first thought, that placing standard microphones on the chest would not produce the kind of dramatic, elemental sound which they fondly imagined, proved to be correct. Lennon returned the following night with a proper heart monitoring machine which he had borrowed from a local hospital. 'They took it in turns to lie down on the floor in Studio Two,' recalled Jeff. 'First of all we recorded Yoko's heartbeat for twenty-five minutes. Then we did the same with John. The problem with sensitive machinery like this is you don't just get the heartbeat. You also get all the gurgling noises of the stomach. It was quite amusing.'

There was a fashion for doing the kind of stunts that seemed to

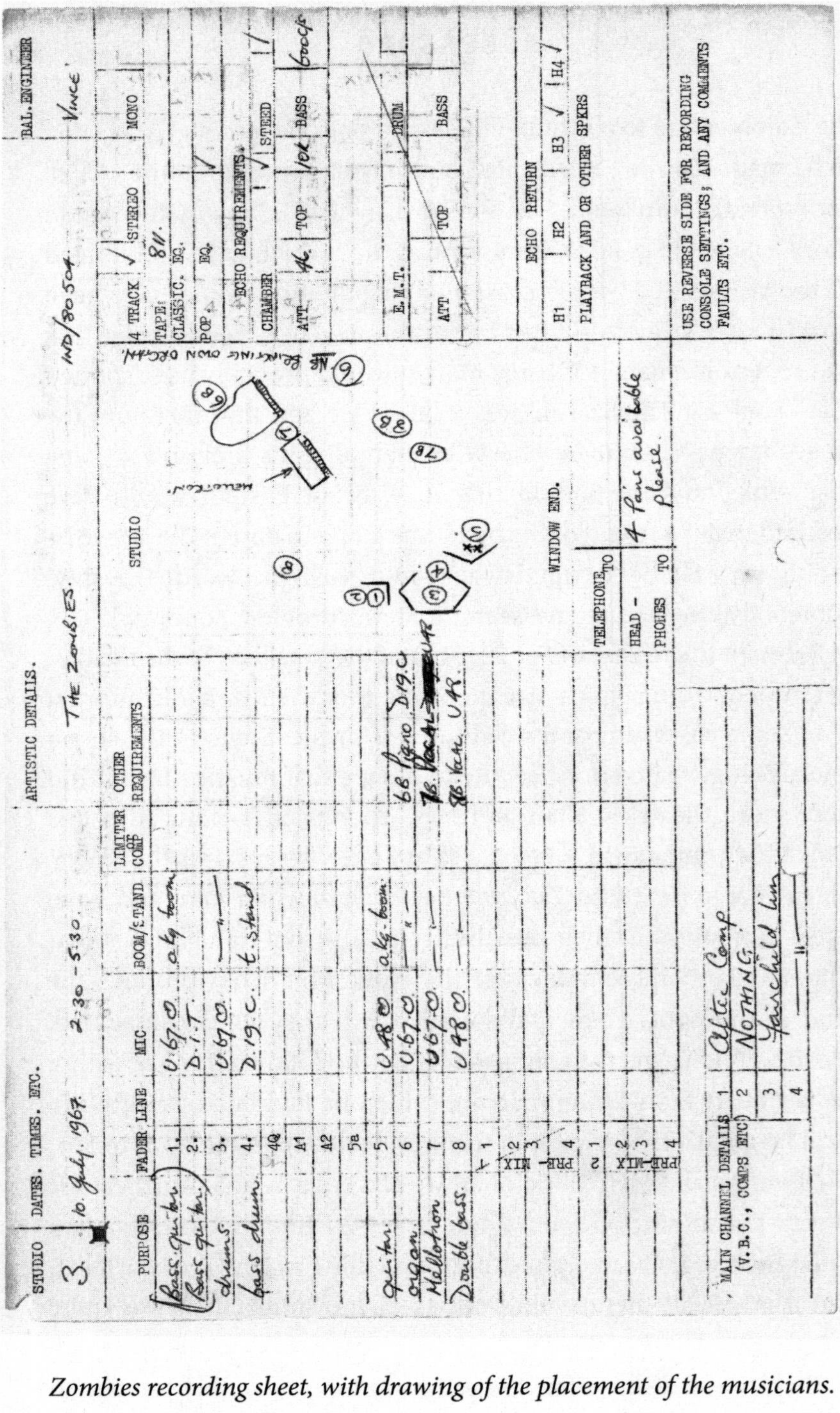
STUDIO 3.
DATES. TIMES. ETC. 10. July. 1967. 2:30 - 5:30.
ARTISTIC DETAILS. THE ZOMBIES.
BAL. ENGINEER Vince
IND/80504.
PURPOSE
FADER LINE
MIC.
BOOM/STAND
LIMITER OR COMP.
OTHER REQUIREMENTS
Bass guitar 1. U.67.O akg boom
Bass guitar 2. D.I.T.
drums 3. U.67.O
bass drum 4. D.19.C. t. stand
4Q
A1
A2
5a
guitar 5 U.48.O akg. boom
organ 6 U.67.O
Mellotron 7 U67.O
Double bass. 8 U48.O
6B Piano D19.C
7B VOCAL U48
8B. Vocal U48.
PRE-MIX 1 2 3 4
PRE-MIX 2 1 2 3 4
MAIN CHANNEL DETAILS (V.B.C., COMPS ETC)
1 Altec Comp
2 NOTHING
3 Fairchild lim.
4
STUDIO
MELLOTRON
6 B
6 MR BLINKINGS OWN ORGAN
WINDOW END.
TELEPHONE TO
HEAD-PHONES TO 4 Pairs available please
4 TRACK ✓ STEREO MONO
TAPE: 811.
CLASSIC. EQ.
POP. EQ.
ECHO REQUIREMENTS. STEED ✓
CHAMBER
ATT 4L TOP 10K BASS 100 c/s
E.M.T. DRUM
ATT TOP BASS
ECHO RETURN
H1 H2 H3 ✓ H4 ✓
PLAYBACK AND OR OTHER SPKRS
USE REVERSE SIDE FOR RECORDING CONSOLE SETTINGS; AND ANY COMMENTS FAULTS ETC.

Zombies recording sheet, with drawing of the placement of the musicians.

belong in a college rag week with the budget of a major company and the technology of a top studio. One of the most talked-about tracks on Pink Floyd's 1970 LP *Atom Heart Mother*, 'Alan's Psychedelic Breakfast', was nothing more than one of their roadies discussing his preferences for breakfast food while noisily marshalling the various courses. The appeal of tracks like this owed something to the sudden popularity of headphones – at the time there seemed no higher recommendation than 'you've got to hear it on cans' – and the childish thrill of seeing something listed on the running order of an LP which you had never seen before.

The sleeve notes of Procol Harum's 1969 album *A Salty Dog*, which was made at Abbey Road, take a sixth-former's delight in listing all the toys they were able to take out from the cupboard and use: celeste, marimba, tabla, sleigh tambourine, three-stringed guitar and bosun's whistle. This last was played on the title track by the band's roadie, known far and wide in the music business as Kellogs. Years later he recalled to the band's biographer how he stood on a chair at Abbey Road up close to a microphone to supply the only two notes a bosun's whistle can supply. And this being 1969, he was credited as such: 'Kellogs – Bosun's Whistle and Refreshments'. Once your name was listed among the credits on an LP in the days when people went into shops and read the credits, you were a legend for life. When the band went on tour in the United States, Procol Harum fans assumed 'refreshments' had been referring to smokeables when, he said, 'what I'd really done was go across the road from Abbey Road to a nearby stall to get them plates of egg and chips'.

Records like these would increasingly be displayed in the shops in browsers marked 'underground' or 'progressive', which said less about the qualities of the music on the albums than the fragile self-images of the people who bought them. The EMI studios had to keep those sections supplied, as well as 'classical', 'comedy', 'light music' and 'children's'. Even in the unpretentious latter precincts there was a demand for specialist input that only engineers could provide. These were as much a part of the studios' work as the Beatles and Pink Floyd.

In the fifties and sixties every business of any size in Britain had a typing pool in which unmarried young women laboured, generally under the basilisk eye of a den mother. Gladys Mills was one such typing pool supervisor. She was running things in the office of the Paymaster General when she was discovered in the early sixties. Mrs Mills, as she became, specialized in relentlessly cheerful honky tonk versions of old favourites bashed out on an old upright piano with lacquer-hardened hammers. This was maintained slightly out of tune so that it sounded like a party taking place in a distant room. Beginning in 1961, Mrs Mills turned out a few albums a year, again under the baton of Geoff Love, none of which strayed far from the initial promise of a knees-up, as could be detected from their titles: *Come To My Party*, *Everybody's Welcome At Mrs Mills' Party*, *Let's Have Another Party*, *Another Party With Mrs Mills*, *Party Pieces*, *Summer Party*, *What A Wonderful Party*, *It's Party Time Again* and, inevitably, *Another Flippin' Party*. When Paul McCartney recorded his piano part for 'Lady Madonna' in 1968, history has decided he turned to the very same Vertegrand upright piano, vintage 1905, which was Gladys's weapon of choice, though engineer Ken Scott, who worked on the basic track, thinks it was a baby grand that was in Studio Three, played so hard that it merely sounded agreeably out of tune.

Finally there was Pinky and Perky, a pair of allegedly porcine children's entertainers who were Britain's answer to the Chipmunks. They prided themselves on delivering everything from 'When The Saints Go Marching In' to 'Those Magnificent Men In Their Flying Machines' at a giddy high pitch such as might be produced by a piglet whose voice was yet to break. Alan Parsons, who joined the studio as a junior eager to work with rock bands but, like all his kind, had first to be content to submit to the authority of the rota, remembers supervising Pinky and Perky recordings at which a bunch of session players and the Mike Sammes Singers would deliver artfully slowed-down versions of the tunes. The vocals would be recorded on a tape running at half-speed which could then be played at double-speed while still remaining intelligible. In 1965, when the studio was turning out hit after hit by the Beatles it was also the birthplace of *Pinky And Perky's Beat Party*, an EP which featured the piglets' versions of 'She Loves You', 'All My Loving' and 'Can't Buy Me Love'. Everybody in the studio knew how to do Pinky and Perky, Parsons recalls.

At the time he came to Abbey Road a host of smaller studios were opening elsewhere in London to cater to the sudden boom in demand for all kinds of things. Some were hipper, more specialized and less dominated by 'bods' with a top pocket full of different-coloured pens. Compared to them, EMI was like a long-established department store. Here a little trustworthiness, a willingness to go the extra mile and a dedication to delivering high-end recording services to everyone from Jacqueline du Pré to Pinky and Perky would prove to be worth any amount of hip. It was Alan Parsons' grounding in these and a thousand other arcane skills which was to lead, albeit indirectly, to *The Dark Side Of The Moon*.

15

The Dark Side Of The Moon, *a record replete with the sounds of the very fabric of Abbey Road, reset the expectations of the record business.*

PINK FLOYD THE DARK SIDE OF THE MOON
THE RECORD THAT ATE THE WORLD AND PLAYED THE WHOLE BUILDING

It so happened that the members of Pink Floyd were filmed at Abbey Road in 1972, as they were beginning to work on *The Dark Side Of The Moon*. They don't say much, which is what generally happens when the members of a band are interviewed in the presence of each other. Behind the actual smokescreen sent up by the cigarettes they all smoke is a secondary curtain of self-conscious evasiveness. Their way of playing to the camera is to pretend that this is a rather tiresome distraction from more important labours. They don't look like people engaged in the business of pop music at all. On the studio floor they present more like men operating heavy industrial equipment than a beat band throwing shapes. Every instrument they play seems connected by plugs and cables to a massive switchboard such as could be found at the heart of every corporate HQ in those pre-digital days. The most telling sequence of all takes place in the Abbey Road canteen, where Nick Mason orders egg, sausage, chips and beans and a tea. Somebody wants apple pie without the crust. Dave Gilmour drinks milk. Watching this film is a salutary reminder that this record, which goes on selling and streaming and syncing fifty years later, was actually made in a world most of today's rock musicians would have difficulty operating in. This is decidedly the land before latte.

The Dark Side Of The Moon would emerge into a world that couldn't imagine anything better. In the year 1972 the living arrangements of Pink Floyd's Baby Boomer fans were increasingly organized around record players. These component set-ups, which could be easily bought in everyone's high street, were no longer known as record players. They were now referred to as 'stereos'. This indicated they were most definitely a cut above the previous decade's Dansettes. The new name also honoured a method of capturing, mixing and reproducing recorded sound which had been largely unfamiliar ten years before but was now considered crucial to listening to music. Just as nobody would have dreamed of watching *Kojak* on anything but a colour TV, the heads of the early seventies would not have countenanced listening to records on anything other than a stereo system. Once people had bought a stereo and installed it in the room where it might be seen and admired by the largest possible number of visitors, they relegated their old mono LPs to the loft and went out and bought records which demonstrated the stereo nature of the sound to the flashiest possible effect. In the 1960s people had wanted records that were direct and punchy. In the 1970s they started to want recorded sounds that enveloped them. This seemed to be the way things would continue to go. In 1972 many took it for granted that the next step would be to a player capable of reproducing the quadraphonic sound, the four-speaker system which was being lined up as the inevitable next stage of development. When *The Dark Side Of The Moon* was launched in the spring of 1973 the plan was to unveil it in quadraphonic at a reception at London's Planetarium. When that proved impossible to arrange in time, the band refused to turn up at all. They effectively boycotted their own party. It apparently didn't make any difference. If anything, it helped cement their reputation as artists who had little use for the tawdry world of commerce in which everybody else laboured.

These new sonic possibilities presented the people in the studio with a new dilemma: were they trying to record the music that was actually occurring in the room or were they trying to produce records that sounded like nothing else on earth once they were in the customers' living rooms? People like Suvi Raj Grubb, who was responsible for recording classical music, were still wrestling with the power stereo gave them to position different instruments and voices in the aural picture devised at the mixing stage for that man in the middle of row 15. Grubb particularly turned up his nose at what he called the 'ping pong effect' in which the sound seemed to come from the extreme left or right, leaving a gap in the middle. He was not like the early pop engineers who seemed only too keen on having trains travel from one speaker to the other because they knew that when people bought stereos they liked nothing more than to be able to show them off. Instead Grubb seized upon stereo as a means to accommodate what he referred to as 'more information' on the record. When he recorded opera he was keen to use the sound picture to reflect where the singer might be in the action at any particular point and how she might be picked up by the right microphone. Recording opera in stereo increased the amount of paperwork needed to accompany every session, with the studio floor often divided into squares to mark where the singers stood at given moments in the action. The other quality he welcomed in stereo, which was to become an even more important ingredient of the big rock records that were beginning to sell and sell in the early seventies, was a sense of space. Whereas so many of the key records of the sixties had sounded like too many people in too small a room – Jane Austen's definition of a successful party – some of the most popular of the next decade were designed to sound like huge empty spaces. Pink Floyd came to the recording of *The Dark Side Of The Moon* straight from shooting a film in the ancient amphitheatre of Pompeii, where they were playing to nobody at all. Once he had more than eight tracks at his disposal when recording a symphony orchestra, Grubb would have two tracks not allocated to any particular instrument. They were there simply to record the ambience of the room. They were there, in effect, to record the very air.

In the early seventies the rock recording industry was hell-bent on complexity. It seemed a given that the more tools the studios had at their disposal the better the records would be. In the summer of 1972, when Pink Floyd began recording their new album, they were delighted that Abbey Road could, belatedly in their view, finally offer them the facility of being able to record on sixteen tracks. This called for a bigger tape – two inches for sixteen tracks whereas mono had required only half an inch – which in turn demanded new machines. Human nature being what it is, sixteen tracks were soon to beget twenty-four tracks and then ultimately forty-eight tracks, which could be achieved by synchronizing two twenty-four-track machines. At the time this proliferation of further ways of adding more and more sounds was scarcely ever questioned. It was assumed that more options had to beget more control, which in turn had to result in better and more popular records. Recording consoles would keep on getting bigger and stereos would keep getting better because what the world presumably wanted was a richer, more detailed soundscape and a more expansive and expensive experience.

The growth in the number of tracks lent itself to what Brian Eno of Roxy Music, who first entered the studio in the new decade and never had any experience of working the old way, called 'the additive approach to recording'. Just as tape had freed producers to manipulate the recorded sound, the increased number of tracks meant there was always room to add to or take away something from the sound picture. In Pink Floyd's case this was often something which summoned a very specific visual image. Whereas their early records seemed to be animated by the desire to take the listeners out there into space with tunes like 'Set The Controls For The Heart Of The Sun' and 'Astronomy Domine', this new one, which was largely written by the band's lugubrious bassist Roger Waters and sung by its figurehead David Gilmour, seemed to concern itself with the space within us and the space between us. It was also, some whispered, about the mental illness that had overtaken their erstwhile leader and glamour boy Syd Barrett, who had slowly disqualified himself from the band four years earlier.

Describing his theory of additive recording, Eno said that in this new dispensation acts no longer came into the studio with a conception of the finished piece as represented by some home demo; they either came in with nothing at all or with a skeleton of the finished piece. By 1972 Pink Floyd had gone through their stage of coming in with nothing at all, other than the aspiration to make an entire album using only standard household implements, and started work on *The Dark Side Of The Moon* (which was almost abandoned as a name when another band got there first) with a skeleton which they had arrived at when playing live at the Rainbow a few months earlier. The drama of the resulting LP was achieved through what they laid over the top of their performances of songs like 'Us And Them', 'Money' and 'Brain Damage'. Some of those contributions were musical and came from outside the band. Dick Parry was an old friend of the band from Cambridge who played saxophone on 'Money' and 'Brain Damage'. Clare Torry was a session singer who was brought in to extemporize in a soulful fashion over 'The Great Gig In The Sky'.

Torry was the kind of person who came in the door of Abbey Road many times, sometimes to sing on the most bread-and-butter sort of cover version albums. Alan Parsons, who was engineering these sessions, had noted her. Pink Floyd wanted Torry to come in on a Saturday night but she declined, saying she had tickets to see Chuck Berry at the Hammersmith Odeon. She came in the following day instead. They played her the track and asked her to sing over the top of it. They were happy with the first take, except in one respect: they would really prefer it if she didn't sing the word 'baby'. Faintly embarrassed, she did it again without using any identifiable words. They pronounced themselves satisfied. She left, and in time got her £30 session fee, which included overtime because it had been a Sunday. She had no firm expectation that this would ever come to anything. Session singers were perfectly accustomed to giving something their all and then hearing years later that it had been left on the cutting room floor or buried in the mix. It wasn't until months later that Torry was in a record shop on King's Road, heard her voice coming over the speakers and realized that this Sunday morning session had actually resulted in something. Over time she came to appreciate that it had resulted in something with the power to be life-changing for her. Pursuant to the unwritten law that where there is a hit there will most assuredly be a writ, in the twenty-first century she took legal action to ensure that she was recognized as a co-composer on that tune. Her participation was eventually worth far more than the £30 she had earned for the hour's work. Sing over the top of it, they had asked. So she had done.

Further underpinning the parallels between *The Dark Side Of The Moon* and the kind of films people would go and see repeatedly because they offered an experience were the sound effects. Back in 1972, when the average home couldn't boast the means of recording even the most ubiquitous noises, these were difficult to source. The BBC had made a point of building up an archive of sounds and sound effects that could be taken out for regular use. The people at Abbey Road started doing the same thing. Studio employees were sometimes sent out on spec to capture the sounds of traffic or geese rising from a lake, so that they might be available if they were needed. Alan Parsons had originally visited a clock shop around the corner from the studio with a mobile recorder, recorded every clock in isolation and then persuaded the owner to get them all to strike in unison. This was done with a view to demonstrating quadraphonic sound, which was threatening to happen at the time. He showed Pink Floyd a way in which his sound effects and the track could be married, and they approved it. What had once been gimmickry was now artistry.

The sound of cash registers that was used as the rhythm track for 'Money', which became a hit single in the United States, was originally developed in Dave Gilmour's garden shed. It wound up being re-recorded at Abbey Road. The racing footsteps apparently trying to get to the plane in 'On The Run' were captured by the simple expedient of having assistant engineer Peter James run round and round on the parquet floor of Studio Two while Alan Parsons recorded him. The voice of the airport announcer was supplied by Hazel Yarwood, the doyenne of the cutting department, a former actress with an appropriately imperious voice who was occasionally called upon to mimic the sound of unseen authority. In the course of making the album they placed everybody they could persuade in front of a microphone to answer a bunch of apparently random questions. Paul and Linda McCartney, who were recording in the studio at the time, were interviewed, but their responses were rejected on the grounds of being too arch. Henry McCullough, who was in Wings at the time, is heard talking about a night when he was very, very drunk. Chris Adamson, at the time one of their road crew, is heard saying that he's always been mad. At the very end a gentle Irish voice states that 'there is no dark side of the moon, really; matter of fact it's all dark'. That voice belonged to Gerry O'Driscoll, who was a doorman at the studio.

Every track had some noteworthy touch, some little detail that people like the friends of mine who listened while reclining on their Kensington Market scatter cushions in their designated 'sounds room' could greet with the knowing smirk of initiates passing through key stages in some unfolding ceremony. *The Dark Side Of The Moon* came out in March 1973. The launch event rather misfired but it didn't matter. In the event it turned out that the album was impervious to any kind of glitch in the first few weeks. It went in the chart and it stayed in the chart, which is always the thing that matters. It wasn't reliant on whether Pink Floyd were on tour at the time or had a hit single. Beyond a certain point it was selling because it had sold. Beyond a certain point the decreasing proportion of the population who hadn't heard it bought it to find out what the rest of the population were so enthusiastic about.

Like those friends of mine, the way people played *The Dark Side Of The Moon* said a lot about the changing role of the long-playing record in their lives. They didn't play individual tracks. They put it on at the beginning of side one, lay back on their Habitat sofas with their head positioned between the speakers of their Laskys hi-fi, and submitted to the itinerary of the record. In the years following *The Dark Side Of The Moon* many's the band who would come along and claim that the most important instrument on their record was the studio itself. Only Pink Floyd could claim with some justification that their instrument was not just the studio but one studio in particular. It was Abbey Road. It was this one very particular establishment, with its Irish doorman, its grand lady in the office, its clock shop round the corner, its drums discovered in a cupboard beneath the stairs, its manifold sources of rattle and hum. Any old house has its noises. They are part of its character. No. 3 Abbey Road was an old house. The cover of the last Beatles album celebrated Abbey Road. The sound of *The Dark Side Of The Moon* is the sound of Abbey Road the studio.

They had begun recording it in the summer of 1972 and didn't complete it until February the following year. It was decided that they should bring in Chris Thomas, who was by then known for his work with Procol Harum and Roxy Music, to mix it. They made this move because they wanted a fresh pair of ears. They didn't want him named as the producer because they were adamant that they produced their own records. He couldn't be named as the engineer because Alan Parsons had that role. The good thing about having Thomas as 'mixing supervisor', the audio equivalent of the editor who oversees the final cut of a movie, was that while the whole band might have been in the studio as they did it, he was the one who was sitting at the desk and it was his fingers on the faders. Parsons supervised the quadraphonic mix, which came out everywhere except the USA. The whole format failed to get any traction beyond the tiny sub-group of hi-fi enthusiasts who had been successful in persuading their significant other to remodel their living quarters to make space for speakers behind as well as in front of the listener – or, as the people who tried to sell the equipment frequently noted, had settled for living alone. By the late 1970s the format had disappeared. In 2010 a collector paid almost $1,000 for a copy of Parsons' quad version of *The Dark Side Of The Moon* on eight-track.

The members of Pink Floyd had originally come together at school or college and the studio had always felt a little like an educational institution. People left; from time to time old boys came back. On 5 June 1975 the four members, by now Nick Mason, Roger Waters, David Gilmour and Rick Wright, happened to be in Studio Three. They were there to listen to a final mix of a new song called 'Shine On You Crazy Diamond'. This song was openly about their former leading light Syd Barrett. They hadn't seen him since the night they'd decided it was no longer worth picking him up on the way to a gig and had just missed him out – a classic case of how bands always leave it to somebody else to deal with the human side. That was seven years earlier and since then there had been scarcely any contact. They knew he was living with family in Cambridge. They didn't dare think about him too much, but they could write a song about him. 'When you were young, you shone like the sun' was the opening line of that song. The album was going to be called *Wish You Were Here*, which was about the same thing.

As they were listening to the playback the various individual members of the band became aware that there was somebody at the back of the room. At first they assumed the interloper must be someone who worked for the studio. Then each assumed he must be a friend of another member of the band. Whichever was the case, he looked slightly strange. He appeared to have shaved his head rather clumsily, and also his eyebrows. It was only slowly that the realization stole over each of them that this unfamiliar, overweight, determinedly ungroomed figure was their erstwhile leading light, their former boy genius Syd Barrett.

He had somehow come down from Cambridge. He had somehow found his way to Abbey Road. He had somehow gained entrance to the studios. He had somehow ended up in the control room at the very moment when they were listening to a song that was all about him. There was some awkward small talk, such as groups revert to at the remotest sign of stress. After a while the visitor slipped out of the control room, never to be seen by his old friends again.

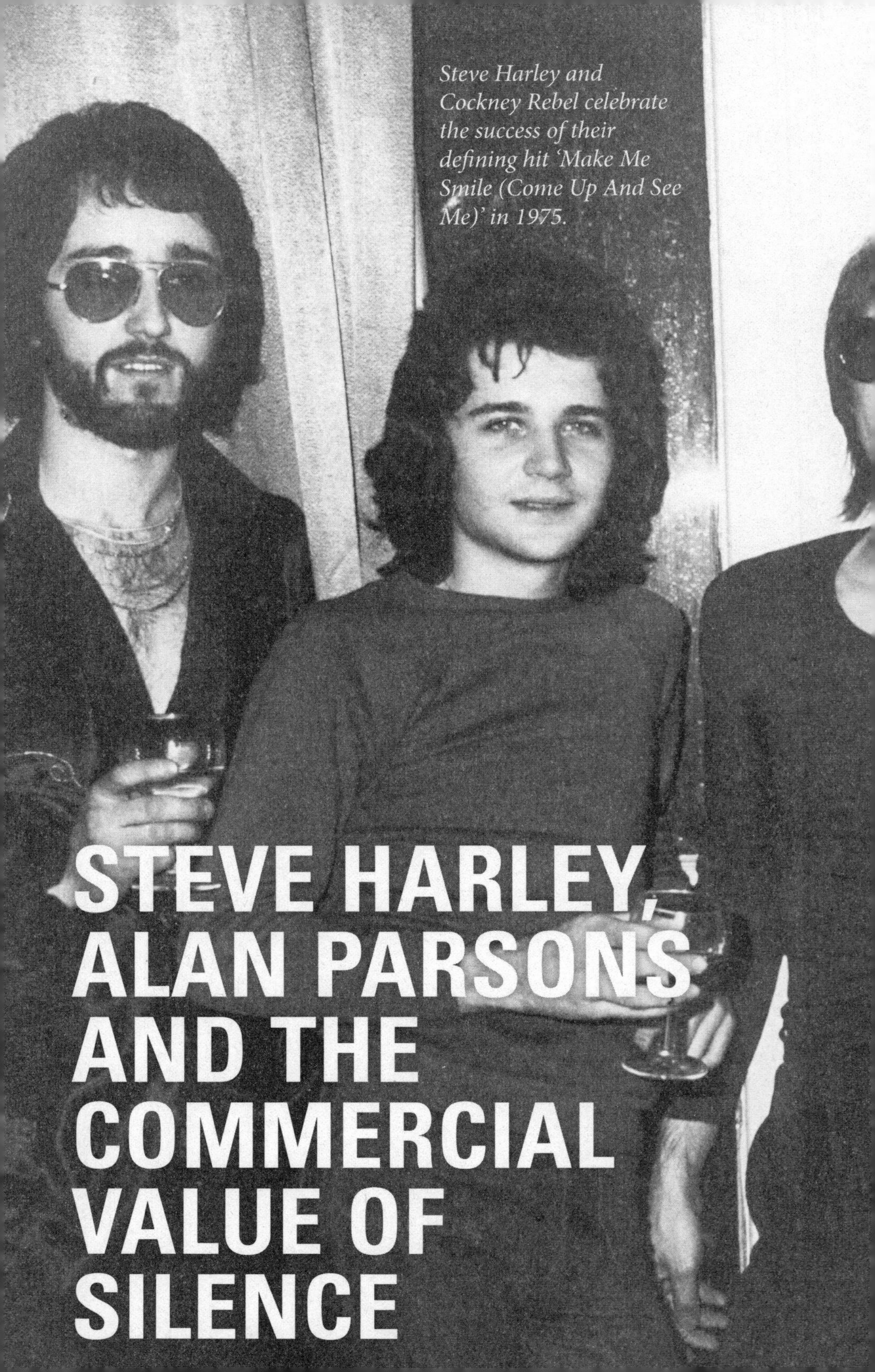

Steve Harley and Cockney Rebel celebrate the success of their defining hit 'Make Me Smile (Come Up And See Me)' in 1975.

STEVE HARLEY, ALAN PARSONS AND THE COMMERCIAL VALUE OF SILENCE

16

'We don't hear a single.'

Of all the thousands of words commonly exchanged between artists and record companies in the course of the often tense and nervous times during which their destinies are intertwined, these five have always been the only ones that matter. Recording artists can talk all they like about making an album that grows on the public. They may carry around with them favourable reviews from publications few people read. The fact remains that their destiny is always in the hands of people out there in the dark, people who neither know nor care who they are, what reviews they have had or what they might have done before. These people simply like the sound of a particular tune out of the many the artist has recorded, so much so that they reach for the volume whenever that tune comes on the radio. That tune will be the single. That single is the only thing that might ensure there is a chance of a recording contract being renewed. The fact that this single is far more popular than the rest of an act's songs put together is clear to everybody except the act. The act are very often the last to recognize this. In some cases in the early seventies they actively disliked the one thing that might have made them likeable.

Whereas the groups of the sixties rarely questioned the fact that hit singles were the price of remaining solvent, the bands of the new decade, who were beginning to see themselves as artists rather than entertainers and to think of the LP record as being their standard unit of artistic currency, preferred to view hits as blessings which might happen along once in a while. They would tell themselves they were going into the studio to make an album. That may have been the way they looked at it, but as far as the record company was concerned they were there to come up with a couple of hit singles. Once they'd done that they could fill up the rest of the record with whatever self-indulgence they felt like. Over time the producers and engineers had been witness to enough self-indulgence to be able to spot the things that were different. Theirs were the first ears that pricked up. Norman Smith, who engineered the Beatles, always claimed he could tell from the first run-through. He was lucky enough to be working with a group whose aims were aligned with his. The Beatles knew they had to come up with a certain number of blockbusters a year. They never questioned it, possibly because they never struggled with it. Not everyone found it similarly easy. In the seventies, hit singles often had to be got out of groups by stealth.

Steve Harley was a former news reporter who had been signed to EMI in 1972 as a member of Cockney Rebel. Like Roxy Music and other groups of that time, Cockney Rebel initially presented themselves as a cross between a pop group and an art project. Like Roxy Music, they shed a number of members early on, re-emerging as a vehicle for the singular ambitions and sometimes overdone vision of one very opinionated lead singer. By the time they came to Abbey Road to record their third LP in 1974, the point in their career where it would be decided whether they would continue to have one, the musicians in Cockney Rebel were simply hired hands serving at the pleasure of top-billed Steve Harley, who wrote the songs, sang them and set the direction.

The producer was Alan Parsons, the Abbey Road employee who had joined the studio as a teenager at the end of the previous decade, serving the usual apprenticeship. The youngsters sent on errands in those days could easily find themselves face to face with people they had grown up regarding as gods. Early on in Parsons' employment he was sent to deliver a package to the studio the Beatles had recently established at their office in Savile Row. After making himself known at reception, he was directed towards a door. As he opened the door, nine heads craned to see who this teenager was who had dared enter, those of Glyn Johns, George Martin, Yoko Ono, Linda Eastman, John Lennon, Paul McCartney, George Harrison, Ringo Starr and the legendary Alexis Mardas, the man who had designed a very impractical recording studio for the Beatles in the basement of their new company. Later that same year he had got even closer to royalty when he worked as a tape operator on *Abbey Road*. Parsons it was who stood poised with a pair of scissors ready to respond to John Lennon's hand signal and cut the tape which provided the abrupt end of 'I Want You (She's So Heavy)'.

New acts coming into the studio were superstitiously keen to have their own efforts recorded at the scene of earlier triumphs. Jeff Jarratt was a young engineer in 1969 when he was booked to work on a session during which Billy Preston and Eric Clapton would put organ and guitar on 'That's The Way God Planned It'. His biggest fear was that he would do something wrong that would make them sound not as good as they had sounded on earlier records. Thus he was relieved when, after putting one microphone in front of Eric's amp, a couple more in front of the Hammond organ, and pulling up the faders, 'it sounded amazing. It sounded amazing because the guys created the sound and the magic in the studio.' The early take was all that was needed but they did repeated takes in the hope of doing something better. 'George Harrison, who was producing, was quite happy to let them go on but he knew we had it in the bag from almost take one. About three months later I was engineering another session for another band who had a couple of hits. The guy was playing Hammond organ and he wasn't very pleasant to me about the sound. He said, "Why can't you get it to sound like that guy who recorded the Billy Preston track?" It was lovely to be able to say to him, "Actually I recorded that, and you're playing the same Hammond that Billy played."'

These kinds of war stories – and more in Alan Parsons' case since he had gone on to work with Pink Floyd – could always be used to impress whoever an engineer or producer was called upon to work with next. Young producers happily took the tricks of one session along to the next. 'The first time I went into Studio Two with Alan Parsons it was to record "Judy Teen",' Steve Harley recalled in an interview for the Abbey Road archives. 'I wanted more of a sound on the off-beat. I told Alan, "I want thunder." He said, "We'll do what Roy Wood showed me on some Wizzard tracks."' This involved him lining up three members of Cockney Rebel at three-step intervals down the stairs which led from Studio Two's control room to the studio floor and having an assistant engineer dangle a microphone on a boom in mid-air alongside them. Because hardboard had been placed over the banister rails at some point in the sixties it had been found that the staircase made a suitably impressive sound when struck hard with the flats of three human hands. 'What you hear on "Judy Teen" is three young lads smashing their hands red raw on the hardboard take after take,' Harley said. 'It's just a gimmick, but hey, it's a hit record.'

At this time, when sales of both singles and LPs were growing year upon year but inflation was also raging, the record business had settled into a way of dealing with talent. They encouraged them to spend more and more time in the studio, mixing up the medicine in the hope that they could come up with the hit single that would make money in itself and would also encourage a growing market to buy the LP. Under this arrangement the band were given an advance from their record company, out of which they would have to pay whatever it cost to make their record. If an EMI act was using an EMI studio, which they generally were, this meant the company was paying out with one hand and taking in with the other.

The only thing that could get the band out from under the burden of debt which would inevitably build up under such a system was a massive hit. Therefore they kept rolling the dice in the studio in the hope of coming up with a double six. Cost was immaterial. The idea of spending less on the record never figured in Harley's calculations. 'Budgeting? What was that? I don't do money, had no interest in the budget.' In this he was no different from anyone else who had a contract with a major label. There wasn't a masterplan. The third album would have to be born and made in the studio. Most sessions would start with the musicians assembling in the studio to learn one of Steve Harley's new songs. There was no rehearsal off-site. There was no trying material out on a crowd. Most days they were going in cold. The studio was now both workshop and factory.

One day in November 1974 he arrived with a new composition called 'Come Up And See Me'. He had been finishing the words in the taxi on the way from his flat near Marble Arch. The musicians started the song in the usual way. 'I would sit them in a semi-circle round the grand piano and we would play the song. The drummer would sit there with a tambourine to get the rhythm.' This particular song was a thinly disguised attack on the guys who had left the group because he wouldn't let them contribute their own songs to the band. Played at a funereal pace, as it was when they first gathered around the piano, it discharged every ounce of the bitterness that only bands and recently divorced couples can harbour for each other.

Producers come from all kinds of different backgrounds. They all work in different ways. Mickie Most, for instance, was one of the first independent producers allowed to work in EMI's studios. Mickie, who had almost been a pop star himself, was known for being able to turn a hit song into a hit record, even if it meant working with artists who considered themselves above such tawdry commercial considerations. It was thanks to Mickie Most that performers as resistant to compromise as the Animals, as doggedly alternative as Donovan and as all-fired awkward as Jeff Beck found themselves in the hit parade. Most was well known for keeping his nose in the business pages of the paper when bands were working on their album tracks – he was prepared to accept they had to get this kind of thing out of their system – but snapped to attention when they came to a song he knew could be made into a hit. Then he would be out on the studio floor working on and among the musicians much as a theatre director would work with actors, smoothing the curves and sharpening the corners of a performance in the manner he knew would make the ears of radio producers prick up. Different producers bring differing strengths, but the one thing they should all have in common is to advise on the basis of what they hear rather than what they know to be the case.

Alan Parsons was a different kind of personality but he had already been around studios long enough to know when to make an intervention. This time with Steve Harley his suggestion was a simple one, but no less valuable for that. 'Alan came down from the control room, listened, and said, "You might want to try that a bit quicker,"' recalled Harley. A basic adjustment to the tempo is so often the first thing a producer says that it's surprising it isn't enshrined on a sign on the studio wall. 'So we did. The drummer picked it up into this mid-tempo backbeat and we loved it, it really started to swing. And of course this diverted attention from the finger-pointing words. It gave it a lighter atmosphere.'

This is where Parsons' responding to what he heard rather than what he knew to be the case paid off. His suggestion to inject a bit more pace was a standard producer's remedy, along the same lines as 'Why not start with the chorus?', which always occurs to the person listening and never seems to occur to the person playing. It strongly suggests that artists feel better about producing songs which are downers while producers know that the more optimistic a song seems the more appealing it's likely to be. The idea that it was a finger-pointing song in the tradition of Bob Dylan's 'Positively 4th Street' or John Lennon's 'How Do You Sleep?' had simply never occurred to Alan Parsons. He heard it as a catchy twist on the old Mae West line.

It was also Parsons who suggested putting the emphasis on the second line of the chorus rather than the first, which is how the song came to be known as 'Make Me Smile (Come Up And See Me)'. By changing the emphasis in this way Parsons effectively changed the name of the song. The mood-enhancing effect of these changes was so appealing that it was decided that the record would benefit from the further lightening which could only be provided by proper backing vocals, the kind that could only be delivered by the sort of people who lend their pipes to everyone from the stars of Saturday night television to the marketing of detergent. By that point everybody had forgotten about the baleful lyrical content of the dirge they had begun with and become enchanted by the pop appeal of this most whistle-worthy of records they were now attempting to finish. Suddenly everyone was trying to make a pop record

'We said, "Let's get some girls in," and Alan knew who to get. We had five of them, including Linda Lewis and Tina Charles, who were hit makers in their own right. Then I wanted a sax solo. Jim Cregan, the guitar player, said, "You haven't got a sax. Let me try it on acoustic guitar." Why not? And there you are. It turned out to be one of the most famous guitar solos in pop history and it only came from him being in the room and overhearing the plan. We made a composite of three different solos, which took ages in those days, muting faders and taking a bit from this take and a bit from that take. Jim can take all the credit in the world but the truth is he didn't actually play that solo.

'You can't give anyone credit for a hit. You've got to say it was a combination of ideas. The other thing that made the record were those dead stops, which are called tacets. I said to Alan I wanted it to stop completely and then restart every time. It happens four times. Today you can just cut and paste. What he did back then was masterful. He put in the length of that gap on tape running at thirty inches per second. That's fast, that's spinning. It may be only a bar of silence but crikey, that's a lot of tape. He said, "Well, that will take two days." I said, "Well, I have to pay the money back to EMI so it's my money. Just do it."'

There then followed these two expensive days in the most prestigious recording facility in the world, labouring over multiple tape machines with scissors and leader, twisting the spools by hand back and forth over the machine's heads, ignoring the crude pre-digital read-out, purporting to identify which point of the tape you had reached, just listening back for the slur that announced the re-entry of the vocal and then making an incision which might well turn out to be at the incorrect juncture. All to put what on a record? Uniquely in this case, to put nothing on a record. The sound of silence. A gap with which radio DJs have been amusing themselves ever since.

The most crucial few minutes in the life of a hit record are the minutes when you first play it to the boss of your record company. Steve Harley had been around long enough to know that you never get a second chance to make a first impression. 'Bob Mercer at the time was the managing director of EMI. He was going through a divorce, so he was living in a block right next to Abbey Road. He came in that night after a dinner at which he'd had a couple of drinks. Alan did a rough mix and played it to him through these massive studio monitors in Studio Two.'

Such a ceremonial unveiling of a hopefully killer track in front of the handful of people who could be said to decide its fate is, like a first kiss, something that can only happen once. The people playing the track traditionally take out insurance by increasing the volume to such a point that conversation of any kind is bootless. The people listening are meanwhile frantically searching for a form of words the others will find acceptable without constituting a legally binding contract. Bob Mercer, who had dined well, was on this occasion in no shape to resist.

'I said, "What do you think?" and he said, "Number one." In those days there were five or six massive record companies. In those days they could move mountains. They couldn't guarantee a number one but they could guarantee a big hit. They would get all these guys in their company cars out there, hitting the record stores and really pushing them, getting copies into the shops. If you got a Record of the Week on Radio One it changed your life. When "Make Me Smile (Come Up And See Me)" came out in March 1975 we sold fifty thousand copies a day. It went to number one. It had sold about seven hundred thousand by the time it came out of the charts. It ultimately did a couple of million. They call it my pension. That's absolutely right.'

Since then it has attracted over a hundred cover versions, from the likes of Erasure and Duran Duran. The overwhelming majority of those cover versions don't refer much to the original song, that philippic which had been aimed at the former boys in the band. Instead the thing they seek to emulate is the final record with its brisk pace, the hit record with its blithe ooh-la-las. For the average listener, who's paying even less attention to the words than Alan Parsons did in 1974, it conjures blue skies, wedding discos and the clinching power of a great chorus. Musicians like Harley may have gone into the studio to record a dark, bitter song, but once it became clear that, with a tweak to the tempo and a sunny chorus, they were suddenly dealing with a hit, they forgot their previous agenda and chased it. Steve Harley had arrived with a sour dirge. He went home with a hit for the ages. In 2015, when he was in the newspapers after having incurred a £1,000 speeding fine, the presenters of the BBC motoring programme *Top Gear* encouraged their viewers to download the song because, they said, 'he's been making a meagre living out of that one hit single'. This was an appeal which betrayed their naivety about just how much wealth can be derived from one hit single and how little of it comes from the traditional sources.

Fifty years on, Steve Harley still tours. That's the song that people come to hear him play. His other passion is horse racing. Horse racing is another world in which success is just as difficult to achieve, owes more to teamwork and dumb luck than conventional wisdom likes to concede, and can be similarly impossible to replicate in the fallow years which follow.

Ken Townsend took over as studio boss in 1974, making the momentous decision to rename the business Abbey Road.

17

KEN TOWNSEND CHANGES THE TOILET PAPER, THE NAME AND THE BUSINESS

Ken Townsend had started work at the studios in 1954. He didn't leave until his retirement in 1995. Having been witness to the dawn of the long-playing record, the arrival of stereo, the delirium of the swinging sixties, the unconstrained experimentation of the seventies, the eclipsing of classical music by pop, the false dawn of quadraphonic, the comeback of Hollywood and the Eldorado that was the age of the compact disc, few knew better than Ken the difficulties of introducing new technology or, for that matter, new anything to such a place. This didn't just relate to the business of the studio.

'The canteen had the first microwave oven in the country,' Ken recalled when long retired. 'We had a security man called Len Moss. He put two eggs in it on the first day and they exploded. There was a hell of a mess inside.'

When Ken joined, there were almost no recording studios in the country. EMI ran theirs as a service centre. They were not looking to make a profit. The fact that it was dominated by the classical side of the company meant it behaved more like an arm of an arts organization than a business. The fact that it was dominated by men meant in other respects it was much like a division of the armed services.

From his position in the engineering department, among the technicians who wore the white coats and set up the recording equipment on the studio floor, the people who roamed free between Otto Klemperer, Cliff Richard and Joe Loss, Ken had always been ideally placed to observe the way the place operated as a business and as a social unit. 'There was an extreme divide between pop and classical. All the equipment ever bought, everything was designed for classical first,' he recalls. From early on he noted how some of the ex-public school producers working on the classical side sometimes put on airs which they had borrowed from the ennobled maestros whom they served. Ken felt his grammar school background equipped him to deal with people equally at all levels. He noted that neither Sir Adrian Boult nor the young Cliff Richard had any problem taking the teas round. It was one of the unique features of Ken's long period of service that by the time he retired the latter had also been knighted. This was just one of many features of the world of recording that would have been inconceivable in 1954.

Chick Fowler retired in 1967. He was replaced as studio boss by Allen Stagg, who was not an EMI insider. Stagg was reputedly as abrasive and interventionist as Fowler had been near invisible. Ken is far too diplomatic to go into details about what made the reign of Stagg one of the less happy periods in the studio's history. Stagg seems to have put up the backs of the classical side by making the place available to non-EMI artists, to have irritated the people on the pop side by trying to maintain what he saw as standards, and to have gone looking for disagreements over what contemporary politics would call wedge issues. The memoirs of engineers Geoff Emerick and Ken Scott describe his lack of simpatico. One employee, when required by Stagg to get his hair cut, said that he would only do so when Stagg compelled Sir John Barbirolli to do the same.

The decision to appoint a classical specialist at the time when the bulk of the studio's work was coming from pop could be seen as a mistake. It was becoming increasingly clear that the changing nature of the work being undertaken in the studios could not be managed from the executive floor. It was no longer possible to imagine quite so many innovations coming out of the laboratory at Hayes. Things were moving too quickly, often in response to the demands of a generation of impatient young men who had hardly seen the inside of a studio a handful of years before.

An example of this was Ken Townsend's invention in 1966 of what became known as automatic double tracking. This was the kind of project which could only be done by someone who understood not only how the machines worked but also, more importantly, how they might be made to work. 'Paul McCartney would be putting his voice on track three and then again on track four. I thought there must be simpler ways of doing this, and I came up with the idea of using some of the equipment we have to put the voice on again when we were remixing,' Ken recalls. 'We fixed up a four-track machine, and I put this rack of equipment in, and we took the vocal track off one track of the J37, put it into the BTR2, on to the input of the BTR2, and I worked out the distance between the record head and the replay head on the J37 was half the distance almost of that on the BTR2. And if I put the other one on frequency control, put the BTR2 on frequency control so you can vary the speed of it, you could then add the voice again, off the delay signal, at the same time as you take it off the replay head of the J37. And it worked.'

It was as a result of this very boffin-like arrangement that *Revolver*, the record the Beatles were making at the time, achieved the other-worldly fuzziness that the world came to regard as psychedelic. Thanks to the efforts of a man of sober habits who knew every machine in the building by its acronym, John Lennon, a man of less sober habits, a man who would make up new names for things to save himself the trouble of having to learn the proper ones, was saved the tedium of having to double up his vocal in the normal way and thereby tripped into a whole world of weird.

That which the Beatles had one day, the rest of the world would be wanting the next. Things were moving too fast for management's liking. Ken was called in.

'After we'd been using it a month, I was called up into the office by Mr Fowler. The chief engineer was there and he said, "I hear you've come up with some scheme – can you explain it to us?" I was told we mustn't use it until it's been technically approved. I was working on a Beatles session that night. I wasn't going to tell them they couldn't use it because it's got to be technically assessed.'

In the middle of the sixties the idea that an effect in a recording studio had to be technically approved by the men upstairs seemed particularly beside the point. Out there on the circuit, bands were deliberately pushing guitars and amplifiers beyond the limits they had been manufactured within in order to achieve exciting effects. Who at EMI was to say that the Beatles couldn't do something similar in Studio Two? Technicians like Ken Townsend were keen to offer them refinements they would never have happened upon themselves.

'I later found out that if you put a hundred-and-eighty-degree phase shift in, you could wobble it as well to get effects like on "Lucy In The Sky With Diamonds" for drums. But if you wobbled it as well, put it out of phase, you could actually get phasing, *shwooa* sort of sounds. There was quite a lot of that on *Sgt Pepper*. When George Martin was explaining it to them he was using one of his Peter Sellers jokes about bifurcated splanging and John Lennon called it a flanger. He used to say, "Can we flange this?"'

This was the kind of happy outcome that could only be brought about within a company where the technicians and the artists worked under one roof and reported to the same place day after day. It could also only happen in a building where the utterly undirected working methods of a John Lennon could intersect so productively with the dogged patience of a Ken Townsend, where the self-styled Working Class Hero could owe so much to the fixtures secretary of Wooburn Park Cricket Club in the county of Buckinghamshire.

Ken is not one to seek the limelight but in 2001 he did modestly assert the following: 'I tried throughout my life to do things differently to the way they have been done. When I became fixtures secretary of the cricket club I changed the whole concept of cricket fixtures by not playing people twice a year. I found being in the control room with the Beatles and listening to the comments I could come up with answers. I suppose if I was brought into the world to do something, that's it.

'When I was promoted to be manager of technical operations the Beatles heard about it and I got a phone call from [road manager and PA] Mal Evans saying the Beatles wanted me to come along to the studios because they had a complaint to make. I was shaking because they'd never complained about anything. Two hundred and ten songs we recorded. Or was it two hundred and eleven? I went into the control room of Studio Two and there were the Beatles stood behind the mixing desk. John says, "Mr Townsend, we have a complaint to make. This toilet paper is too hard and shiny and it's got EMI Ltd written on it. Unless we get it changed, we're going to go and see Sir Joseph Lockwood." I charged upstairs to see Allen Stagg, the new boss, and told him, and we changed all the rolls of toilet paper in the whole building. I didn't realize at the time, but it was obviously a wind-up.'

When Stagg left in 1974 he was replaced by Ken Townsend. This was an understandable effort to reconnect the management with the culture of the place and also to introduce somebody with the requisite people skills to steer them through what were bound to be troubled times. Townsend understood that in show business, if you don't look after the business somebody else will soon be running the show. 'I'm not an accountant but I can do the maths and I know that in the end the only thing that matters is whether you make a profit. When I started, there had been fewer than ten studios in the country. By the time I was in charge there were over two hundred. We had to change from being a service centre to being a profit centre. Suddenly we've got to make money.'

In retrospect it seems amazing that the most consequential decision taken in those years of uncertainty, the one that would ultimately do most to leverage the studio's heritage for the future they were bound to enjoy, the one that would invoke the ghost armies of the musicians who had passed through its portals over the years to witness just what a special thing a recording can be, and the one that would place Robin Hood's arrow in the essentially sentimental heart of popular music, was taken not by an imagineer or a visionary head of marketing, but by Ken Townsend from the Amp Room.

It was Ken who changed the name of the business from EMI Recording Studios to Abbey Road Studios, thereby making it at a stroke an institution and ensuring it would still be there for decades to come.

The Beatles' last album in 1969 had been planned to be named *Everest*, in honour of the famous peak and also of the brand of menthol cigarettes favoured by Geoff Emerick, the engineer on the later recordings they made at the studio. There had been marijuana fantasies of having their pictures taken on the mountain. Clearly that was never going to happen. In the event they chose the less ambitious alternative of stepping outside on an August morning to have their pictures taken on the zebra in the road. Three times they crossed. The photographer took six exposures, only one of which was usable. That was the last day the four of them worked together at the studio. In the shot used they were walking away, as though from their final day at work. The outside world would prove to be far quicker to spot the significance of this than the people at EMI.

The Beatles' final album had been done at Abbey Road because the members of the group had found *Let It Be*, their experiment in seeing whether they could make their magic just anywhere, interesting but unsatisfactory. They had aborted work at Twickenham Film Studios in January 1969 and repaired to their studio at Savile Row, and had only managed to get that working by calling up EMI to dispatch men with screwdrivers to finish what hippies had begun. Following that project, which was predominantly shelved, they called George Martin and said they would like to make a record in the old way, which meant that he would be in charge and it would be done at the old studio. The decision to call the record *Abbey Road* was, hilariously in retrospect, consistent with their desire to make clear it was just another piece of work, this time named after their actual place of work. It was part of the Beatles' ongoing effort to convince everyone that they were only human. The effect achieved would, as in all the other cases involving the Beatles, be entirely the opposite.

By the middle of the following year the only Abbey Road street sign still remaining in the area was the one which had survived because it was placed too high up on the wall of a pub to be got at by thieves. Eighteen-year-old Graham Pratchett from nearby Cricklewood was one of three schoolboys 'of previously good character' who found themselves up in court for being nabbed in Abbey Road at night with a screwdriver, intent on making off with their own souvenir. In the same year Booker T. & the M.G.s put out *McLemore Avenue*, an instrumental tribute to the Beatles record, on the cover of which they were crossing the street in front of their recording studio in Memphis, Tennessee. This was the first of hundreds of tributes, pastiches and desperate bids for magic-by-association which have employed the same idea down the years, all of which have only served to underline the majesty of the original.

Then there were the people. Slowly, fans began to come to the scene of this photograph and to inscribe their tributes on the bricks of the wall outside. This took time. Throughout most of the 1970s it was still possible to drive down Abbey Road without having to stop at the zebra crossing to permit a crocodile of fans to perform a ritual enactment for the benefit of a friend's camera. It was only gradually that this street in north-west London became one of the capital's most popular visitor attractions. The process of it being recognized as an historic site did not happen overnight. Following the death of John Lennon in 1980 it became one of those places where fans could gather in the expectation of being in the company of kindred spirits. In 1983, when the installation of a new mixing desk in Studio Two necessitated the studio being closed for business for a few weeks, Ken, who was the manager of the studio at the time, decided to open the place to the general public for the first time. The event was called 'The Beatles at Abbey Road' and the studio was set up with some of the equipment which would have been there when the Beatles made their records. Twenty-two thousand visitors flocked in on those days to watch two videos outlining the band's history with the studio. Once the event was over, people's curiosity about the place increased, encouraged by the anniversaries of various Beatle events, most of which seemed to lead back there.

As it turned out, this opening was somewhat ahead of the curve. At the beginning of rock's third decade, nobody saw classic rock coming. At this point it was still difficult to take seriously the idea that the usual nostalgic interest in what had happened with music in the past was starting to shade into a fascination which would be at first historical and then almost mystical. It was years before the people at Abbey Road appreciated this. It took a while before employees of the studio realized that when young acts expressed a desire to have a look inside Studio Two there was little point telling them it was just a room which looked like a school gymnasium. Even they, who might have been expected to guess, did not suspect that one day the equipment which they were getting rid of at the time in order to keep up with what seemed like a ceaseless race towards the future would one day be discussed in tones of reverence, as though dealing with fragments of the true cross in the Middle Ages. In October 1980 they held a sale in which they disposed of the four-track recorder on which *Sgt Pepper* had been recorded, alongside the actual Mellotron the Beatles had used for 'Strawberry Fields Forever', with many of its original tapes intact. The company was proud to state it was clearing away all this clutter to make room for a new sixteen-channel digital mixer.

This was not the first time they had cleared out the heirlooms. When the recording console was replaced in Studio Two in 1973 the old one eventually found its way into the possession of former Abbey Road employee Mike Hedges, who installed it at his studio in rural Normandy, one of the many recording facilities which was luring bands who wanted to combine recording with a change of scene. Known as the Dark Side of the Moon desk, it was last sold in 2017 for almost $2 million. The buyer preferred to keep their name secret.

It wasn't just the technical and musical equipment which attracted this kind of interest. Over the years any fixture and fitting which could be proven to have had a role in the studio's fabled past has been at one time or another seized upon by the retailers of the past. In 2017 the auctioneers Bonhams announced that they had just sold for £2,000 one of the items which had first been flogged in the so-called Sale of the Century of 1980. This was accompanied by a letter of provenance from Ken Townsend, assuring the buyer that this item had been placed in the studio by the staff in brown coats prior to sessions involving many different artists, but primarily it had been placed at the disposal of Ringo Starr during Beatles sessions. It was into this cast brass ashtray with its circular tray and large cigarette lip supported on a tripod stand with a lion's head above each

EMI RECORDS (UK)
20 MANCHESTER SQUARE LONDON W1A 1ES
TELEPHONE 01-486 4488
TELEX 22643
CABLES EMIRECORD LONDON W1

NEWS

ABBEY ROAD SALE

Recording equipment used by the Beatles, Dave Clark Five, Mike Oldfield, Tornadoes, Elton John, Moody Blues and a whole host of pop stars during the past 20 years goes on sale in London this month.

The sale - billed as "The Sale of the Century" - is being organised by Jackson Music Ltd. and EMI Records' Abbey Road studios and takes place at Abbey Road studios on October 15 and 16.

Equipment, both new and old, valued at over half a million pounds has been gathered from studios around the world and includes mixing consoles, multitrack recorders, mastering and dubbing machines, monitors, microphones, cutting lathes plus tapes and videocassettes. In addition, two 24-track mobile recording studios are on offer and will be parked in the Abbey Road car park.

Also on sale will be the Studer J37 4-track used by the Beatles on their legendary "Sgt. Pepper" album; the Fairchild Limiter used by producer Joe Meek on the million-selling Tornadoes single "Telstar"; a Mellotron tape organ used by the Beatles; an echo plate used by Mike Oldfield and a 1967 Neve Console used by the Dave Clark Five, Elton John, Tom Jones and the Moody Blues.

The sale was prompted by the building of a new penthouse studio at Abbey Road which caused storage problems. It was then decided to add, to the EMI stock, equipment from other studios and the search for sale items has proved so successful that two days have been set aside for the sale.

Beginning on each day at 10 a.m., the sale is scheduled to run through until 9 p.m. and has been organised into three stages.

On the first day - Wednesday, October 15 - all the equipment on sale will be available until 1 p.m. that day at a marked price. From then until 3 p.m. the following day, offers for sale items will be taken on the condition that a reserve price is met. The auction of specialised items and memorabilia will begin at 2 p.m. on October 16.

Ken Townsend, general manager of Abbey Road studios, said today; "The quality of the equipment being sold is very high indeed. We, in fact, have some items that have only just been taken out of their factory wrappings and will be of great interest to prospective buyers."

For further information please contact:

Brian Southall
Publicity Executive
EMI Records (UK)
Telephone 01-486 4488 Ext. 285

October 1, 1980

EMI

THE GREATEST MUSIC COMPANY IN THE WORLD

1980 press release announcing the sale of vintage studio equipment.

foot that Ringo had cast over the years the butt-ends of what must have been thousands of cigarettes as he waited for the other three to get their guitars in tune.

If the remains of those cigarettes had also been retrieved there would presumably have been a market for them as well.

18

As the classical business shrank, blockbuster franchises like George Lucas's Star Wars *cam to the rescue of Studio One with renewed demand for large-scale orchestra dates.*

STAR WARS SETS DOWN IN GOD'S AIRCRAFT HANGAR

On 31 January 1980 a memo was presented to Ramon Lopez, at the time the head of EMI. It was headed 'Abbey Road – Studio One'.

The thrust of the memo was that the downturn in the recorded music market that had come at the end of the seventies had been so steep that neither EMI nor its clients in the other record companies was booking the large orchestral studio which had been opened in 1931. It appeared that the recording of classical music was in terminal decline. Everything in the canon had been recorded once in mono and then again in stereo. There seemed no earthly reason why anyone would wish to do any more. All the services that the studios offered were under pressure from increased competition. Rock bands now had many other places to go. EMI's marquee names like Pink Floyd and Queen were now signed to other companies outside the United Kingdom, had built their own studios or fled to countries where they could record more tax-efficiently. They were certainly no longer grateful to be allowed to use the company's own facilities.

This was most serious for EMI when it came to the giant Studio One. It was now running at 60 per cent capacity, which meant that it was losing money. Bookings could be so few and far between that it was known to be occasionally used as a five-a-side pitch for matches between Pink Floyd and the studio staff. Engineer Peter

Mew remembers they would get out the booms which held the microphones, placing them at each end of the studio to make goals. 'It was a break. Game of football for half an hour about midnight. We had Kevin Ayers and the Whole World against the Greatest Show on Earth. That's the one I remember because of the names.' All this kind of thing had taken place at night when the grown-ups were at home. Some studio staff had even been known to repair their cars in there.

The document on Lopez's desk outlined the alternative courses of action for this space. The most drastic involved replacing the giant studio with smaller rooms more suited for pop music and using the space beneath for storage or even a car park. The counter argument was that there was now so much standard studio capacity in London even smaller new studios would have to scrap for market share against a background of declining rates for hire. There was talk about turning the place into a space suitable for audio-visual work.

At the end of 1979 Ken Townsend had gone looking for ways to ensure the survival of Studio One. He spoke to the facilities company Molinaire about the place's future, possibly as a TV studio. He contacted the people who ran EMI Films, which was soon to be sold. Most significantly he spoke to a company called Anvil. The people at Anvil had been specialists in film sound since the early fifties. The redevelopment of the studio at Denham in Buckinghamshire where they were based meant that they would soon be homeless. It would also mean there would be one fewer studio large enough to accommodate the giant orchestras which were required to record film scores the way they had been recorded in the days of Bernard Herrmann and Dimitri Tiomkin. To do that required a room vast enough for a fifty-piece orchestra, it called for a surface on which it was possible to project a love scene or a car chase, and there had to be some provision of a vantage point from which

EMI

EMI RECORDS Recording Studios
3 Abbey Road
St. John's Wood
London NW8 9AY
Telephone 01-286 1161
Telegrams Emistudios London NW8

Mr. R Lopez S
Manchester Square

31st January, 1980

ABBEY ROAD

FUTURE PLANS FOR STUDIO ONE

The utilization figures for Studio One for the period July - December 1979 are a very clear indication of the cut-back in recording budgets by ICD and CBS, both of whom cancelled booked time for economic reasons. Previously figures for a similar six-month period have been in the order of 1000 hours, representing 60% of maximum availability time.

It therefore becomes a matter of extreme urgency to take remedial action. Apart from the obvious solution of doubling the price there are four options open to us at the present time to increase utilization and therefore revenue:-

1) Subdivide the studio into two or more smaller pop studios, with either a basement storage or a car park.

2) Attempt to obtain more work from independent clients of a classical or classic rock nature.

3) Combine the facility with sound recording for films.

4) Convert the studio into an audio-visual or video studio.

Each of these options is analysed in more detail.

1) Two years ago this solution would have been the obvious choice. The recording industry is now in an over-capacity situation regarding pop studios in London; with the result that charges are unable to reflect satisfactory returns against investment. If this major scheme were undertaken Abbey Road would have the finest pop complex in the world but the capital outlay for building work and equipment would be well in excess of £1M. Much smaller sums are required to expand the pop facilities within the building, and also modernise existing areas.

EMI Records Limited
Registered Office: Blyth Road, Hayes, Middlesex. Registered in England, No.68172

A member of the EMI Group of companies
International leaders in music, electronics and leisure.

1980: the EMI boss is presented with the alternatives to turning Studio One into a car park.

studio executives might make their views known at the end of every bar.

The good news was that by 1980 the old-fashioned way seemed to be back in vogue once more. The cinema was making a comeback. On 5 March 1977 a recording had been made for a film which was to dramatically change the destiny of more than one studio. This time it was made not in St John's Wood but out at Denham Studios in Buckinghamshire. The eighty-six musicians assembled that day were from the London Symphony Orchestra. The score they were faced with was no fewer than eight hundred pages long. After eight days they had still only recorded eighty-eight minutes of the hundred and twenty the score called for. The man with the baton, who was also the composer of the piece, was John Williams. The film, which had been shot on sound stages in the UK, was *Star Wars*.

When *Star Wars* opened in cinemas a couple of months later it had begun with the full Cinemascope version of the famous Twentieth Century Fox fanfare. This had been composed in 1933 by Alfred Newman, the head of Fox's music department and uncle to Randy Newman. It hadn't been used for years. For film purists, particularly those who care deeply about the music which accompanies and helps shape the experience of film, the return of the fanfare was a signal that this film's maker, George Lucas, was in some senses harking back to the golden years of a night at the cinema and a time when the big beasts of film music were as important to the making of a film as Alfred Hitchcock or John Ford. For the ten years before *Star Wars*, film and film music had been in retreat in the face of television. At the time, those who were hired to score big new movies were warned that their key priority was to come up with a hit record which might be associated with the film. It wasn't always necessary that these pop records be in the finished film, just so long as they did their job of promoting it. (Matt Monro's 'Born Free', a ballad recorded at Abbey Road under the baton of John Barry in 1966, suffered the indignity of being chopped out of the print of the film of the same name immediately prior to its royal premiere because the producers didn't care for it. However, it went on to be a hit and helped make the movie better known.)

The music of *Star Wars* was in a very different tradition. Its style was orchestral but the delivery was on a grander scale than ever before. Whereas fifty musicians had previously been thought to make a big band, Williams preferred to use as many as eighty. When the double LP, which was seventy-four minutes of straight orchestral music, came out, it sold almost a million copies in no time. It was to become the best-selling symphonic album of all time. The large orchestra became the sound de rigueur of the blockbuster film. While special effects might lose their impact over time and any soundtrack too smitten with a voguish pop sound would quickly date, the sound of an eighty-piece orchestra swelling to the rescue of a beleaguered hero had the effect of instantly reconnecting a cinema audience with the way they felt when they first went to the movies. With the benefit of hindsight it's possible to see that the element that keeps fans wedded to the *Star Wars* franchise after nearly fifty years, much as it does with the James Bond franchise after an even longer period of time, is not the action or the stories or the actors but the sound of the music. The less that music sounds like the pop music of the time, the more it's likely to endure.

At the time, people were being drawn away from their televisions by the promise of movies with scale. The sound of a vast orchestra helped bolster that grand illusion. Music was similarly at the core of the branding campaign which would bring people back to watch the sequels and thus it was important to get the details of performance exactly right and to be able to repeat them. The music had been initially recorded in London for the unsentimental reason that British players cost a third of their Hollywood counterparts, but Williams also loved the way the local musicians, particularly the brass, played. The first sound we hear in *Star Wars* was provided by Maurice Murphy, who had grown up playing in colliery bands in the north of England and was on his first day as the LSO's principal trumpeter. Williams was so impressed by what he called the 'heraldic spirit' of Murphy's playing that he made sure he used him on everything he did subsequently, from *Superman* to *Harry Potter*, even bringing him out of retirement to play on the later additions to the *Star Wars* franchise when they were made in the twenty-first century.

Executives who were there recall that *Star Wars* was the first movie where the actual quality of the sound seemed to matter. If a cinema wanted to show it, it had to have a stereo system. The first time they screened it, without the effects or the music, Lucas's supporters and backers were convinced it was an utter disaster. A few weeks later they screened it again, with the music as well as the action – the sizzle as well as the steak – and they found the audience were standing up and cheering. Critics said it was a cheap amusement park ride. They were wrong in one respect. It was anything but cheap.

It was against this background, which was promising a revival in demand for Studio One, that Ken Townsend proposed the formation of a company between Anvil and Abbey Road. It came in the nick of time for both parties. For Abbey Road, the structural changes required at the outset were minimal: they needed to drill a small hole in the wall for the 35mm projector and to place a pull-down screen at the other end. But the arrangement wasn't ideal. At the time the recording engineers sat side-on to the orchestra, which meant that if they could hear the speakers they couldn't see the screen. Subsequently they relocated the control room so that the people who were in it, ranging from the recording engineers to the film's directors and producers, could look directly at both the musicians and the images on the screen. Improvements were made to satisfy the exacting standards of Anvil's Eric Tomlinson, the best engineer in his field, one of the first being to establish a direct voice link between the control room and the projectionist's booth, thus ensuring they no longer had to dial an extension to ask him to stop the film.

The first session in Studio One under this arrangement was for the 1981 British spy film *Eye of the Needle*. In this case the music was conducted by Miklós Rózsa, a genuine Hollywood aristocrat who had won Oscars for his music on *Ben Hur* and *Spellbound*. Other distinguished composers followed, such as Jerry Goldsmith with *Outland* and *First Blood* and James Horner with *Brainstorm* and *The Dresser*, but the most significant booking was for John Williams to conduct the London Symphony Orchestra on the later pictures in the *Star Wars* series. Films like these and the Indiana Jones series (when Kate Capshaw sang the Mandarin version of Cole Porter's 'Anything Goes', which opened *Indiana Jones and the Temple of Doom* in 1984, it was at Abbey Road) weren't merely films. They were blockbusters, which became franchises; and over time these franchises would be exploited on new channels undreamed of when the Anvil deal was done. It could not have been a better time for a recording studio to raise its profile and burnish its prestige within the moving pictures industry.

There were considerable practical advantages for both the musicians and their movie paymasters in the location of the new company alone. They didn't have to trek out to anywhere as distant as Denham or as insalubrious as Wembley to add the music that became such a vital part of their films. The music seemed to have an earthing effect on the movie. The further the action might stray in time and space, the more comfort audiences seemed to derive from the fact that the heartbeat of the action was being provided by a hundred musicians playing nineteenth-century acoustic instruments. It also helped that these seemed to have been captured in a room commensurate with their dignity. As John Williams put it, Studio One at Abbey Road 'has fine acoustics so we can capture specific close-up aspects of the orchestra but we still get the full bloom of the room itself'. As Andy Partridge of XTC later described it, Studio One is 'God's musical aircraft hangar'.

Not everyone within Abbey Road saw the coming of the movies as an obviously good thing. Ken Townsend had to deal with a lot of politics. 'I had a lot of hassle from the classical engineers, who thought it was sacrilege to destroy their studio. The people in the classical department didn't like it because it wasn't as easy for them to get bookings. I nearly got the sack from it but it was quickly justified by the results.' There were also demarcation disputes. When Neville Marriner recorded the score to the 1984 Oscar winner *Amadeus* there were those in the company who felt this should be taken care of by the classical side of the business rather than the soundtrack people. The soundtrack people won, and Eric Tomlinson won an award for his engineering of the resulting soundtrack. By then, however, he felt that the arrangement between Anvil and Abbey Road had run its course and there was an amicable parting. The joint company had played a key role in the story of the studio by rescuing it from one of those tight corners which occur in the entertainment business at intervals between one tide going out and the next one coming in.

It had been the lack of demand for classical recording time at the end of the 1970s which had opened the door to soundtrack work. Three short years later the introduction of the compact disc triggered a boom where there had previously been a bust. Suddenly the classical departments of all the companies couldn't wait to re-record the repertoire of the major composers digitally and market the resulting CDs under the banner 'perfect sound for ever'. Now the classical people were clamouring to get 'their' studio back. Eric Tomlinson, the master engineer who had brought his business from

Denham just four years earlier, realized he would have to go freelance and be able to take his work to different studios.

At the same time the business of recording rock bands was coping with different challenges. In the last few years of the 1970s Abbey Road hosted its share of bands that were, for good or ill, associated with the New Wave, bands such as Magazine, Gang of Four, Simple Minds and XTC, for whom this was the first studio of any kind they had ever known. These were still recorded in much the same way as the Edgar Broughton Band or Deep Purple had been a few years earlier. The sound of the record had to be achieved by the sum total of the musicians in the room when it was recorded. These would prove to be the last days when this was the case.

In 1980 EMI's new star artist Kate Bush spent months in Studio Two recording songs for what would become her LP *Never For Ever*. Bush had enjoyed a number one with her first single and had just completed a tour that made her front-page news. Since she was her own producer, nobody was going to object when she took days recording and re-recording her new song 'Babooshka' with a succession of different bass players. In Graeme Thomson's biography of the artist, guitarist Brian Bath recalls as many as twelve. They were summoned, they played, they were thanked for their contributions and then somebody else was called, as though the fingerprint of a particular musician could be the key to unlocking some distantly apprehended form of magic. Sometimes it seemed that the best results could be achieved by withdrawing the players of standard instruments altogether. If it was Kate's view that something wasn't working, individual players would be invited to climb the stairs to the control room to sit this one out for a while. This went down as well with the musicians as it does with footballers substituted for the good of the team.

Although the recording process was traditional in most respects there were glimmers of the coming of the machines which would shape recorded music in the rest of the decade. At the time, they were anything but accessible. The first of them appeared at the very top end of the market. In 1980 all musicians had heard of the Fairlight CMI, an instrument which promised the power to take any non-musical sounds that could be 'sampled' from the outside world and transform them into music. These musicians hadn't got their hands on one because they were being developed in Australia and would cost more than the price of a home in London. The producer and musician Richard Burgess was so fascinated that he flew to Sydney in 1981 to investigate. Thus he became the first person in Britain, apart from Peter Gabriel, actually to take delivery of this magic box. This was on the understanding that he would enthuse key people in the industry with its capabilities. The first performer he enthused was Kate Bush.

To do this he loaded the component parts of the Fairlight into the back of his car and drove them to Abbey Road, where they were assembled in the control room of Studio Two. Once put together it looked more like an item of recording equipment than an instrument. It had a keyboard, a computer drive which took large floppy disks, and a green screen. It seemed more like a medical scanner than the kind of instrument which might fire the blood of an adolescent. The musicians, who are always in the market for a toy, gathered round to see what it could do. Burgess's partner John Walters, who was there, remembers them being so enthralled that they tried to give it a role on every track on the album. They borrowed items of glassware from the Abbey Road canteen, took them to the control room and sampled the sounds of them being smashed. These sounds could then be speeded up, slowed down, played high or played low until a place was found for them in the resulting soundscape. The sound at the end of 'Babooshka', the album's first track, is Richard Burgess playing a slow arpeggio of smashing glass on a Fairlight keyboard. It's said they went through so much of the canteen's glassware in the course of making this record that they had to buy Belgian chocolates as a peace offering to the ladies who worked there.

During the *Never For Ever* sessions there were early glimpses of a future in which the makers of records would have every possible sound at their fingertips and would have to steel themselves against the temptation to use them all. This was the point when, as Richard Burgess was to write later, 'manipulative power became integral to our creative processes'. That manipulative power was in the hands of the chief recording artist, who might feel the sound she wanted was as likely to arise in response to the pushing of a button as it was from calling up the right musician. There was inevitable tension between the people who desired control and the musicians, some of whom could never understand why you didn't simply get a musician to play something. This came into focus for Max Middleton, a veteran of the Jeff Beck Group, when he heard sounds of a penny whistle being put into the Fairlight and then being played back via the keyboard. His question was, why not simply get a penny whistle player? For Ian Bairnson, who also played on the sessions, it was one of the first times when he felt the equipment may have been in danger of taking over, with four or five multi-track machines all loaded up with options. 'She had God knows how many tracks. She kept overdubbing things. You can have too much choice.'

The same technology that was to transform recording studios as they moved from analogue to digital in the early part of the 1980s was also changing the way people worked in the worlds of film and journalism. Whereas the old craft skills depended on people making early decisions and then living with their consequences, the possibility of an unlimited number of tracks on which it was possible to line up options and the coming of an 'undo' button meant that they could always put off the moment when they had to make the final cut. The two most significant albums made at Abbey Road,

Sgt Pepper and *The Dark Side Of The Moon*, seemed to advertise the place's attractions as somewhere where it was possible to escape from all the tiresome aspects of a musical career and just lose yourself in a massive game of trial and error with the help of the latest mind-boggling toys. It was the way Stevie Wonder worked, and for many musicians it was very alluring in that it placed almost as much emphasis on the journey as on the arrival. Many of Kate Bush's best records came out of this way of working, so there is no indication that she was any more a victim of this than anybody else. In 1993, when she recorded 'Moments Of Pleasure', a song which celebrates her happiest musical memories, one of them was 'spinning in the chair at Abbey Road'.

Tina

T U

When Tina Turner arrived to start work on Private Dancer she asked, 'Where's the band?'

TINA TURNER, THE CD GOLD RUSH AND THE APPLIANCE OF SCIENCE

R N E R
19

In 1980 Steely Dan released the last word in studio finesse, an album called *Gaucho*. The record had been two years in the making, which seemed a long time. However, according to Roger Nichols, that was quick. With *Gaucho*, Nichols became one of the first recording engineers to get his picture featured on the back of an album cover alongside those of the musicians. The musicians didn't mind at all. The musicians knew that without Nichols the record couldn't have been made. They knew that his contribution was as important as any of theirs. Roger said that if they had carried on doing it the old way, with Steely Dan's Donald Fagen rejecting drummer after drummer in his quest for the perfect timekeeper, they would likely never have finished it. To save all that time and trouble, Nichols invented a digital drum replacement system. He called it Wendell. For those whose job it was to engineer and produce pop records in the post-disco age, where the beat was increasingly the most important thing, this offered the chance to play with the rhythm long after even the most metronomically reliable timekeeper had departed for the golf course. Wendell was just another step in the transfer of power from the studio floor to the control room. This transfer of power was to change pop for ever.

For the bands who had been swept up in the punk rock scare of the late 1970s this was unfortunate timing. Most of them never managed to capture the raw fury of their in-person appearances in the studio. To hear them talk they had no apparent use at all for the blandishments of the higher end of the recording process. It was assumed that all they had to do to create an exciting album was repeat what they played on stage in the studio. All too often the results were too shrill and hollow to appeal to people who listened to the radio. The first Clash album gave a decent account of their rawness but it was clearly never going to get played on American radio stations. Not only were its lyrics all about England but the sound of the record meant it could never be played alongside Blue Öyster Cult. Hence for their second album the Clash brought in the latter's producers and wound up with a record even the producers admitted was the most overdubbed in history. For a band that had pinned everything on their pureness of heart this was a bitter pill. It was only with their third album, *London Calling*, that they found a way of producing in the studio a simulacrum of what their fans were hearing in their heads when they went to a live show. In the modern studio it was increasingly the case that authenticity, like anything else, sometimes has to be faked.

The eighties saw an unprecedented arms race in studio technology and recording facilities. An increasing number of suppliers vied with each other to provide the clients with kit that made them feel in control and the surroundings in which they would be happy to pass the months it took to finish a new CD. It was to this end that Ken Townsend ordered the conversion of a number of post-production rooms at the top of the building into the Penthouse Suite, which had access to natural light. This was an attractive idea to A Flock of Seagulls, who became its first users in 1981. However, it was unlikely to save them from the condition known as 'studio tan', which afflicted all those fated to spend sanity-endangering amounts of time listening to the same few seconds of a record again and again and again. Twenty years earlier, when the Beatles had made their test recording for EMI, they were allowed two tracks. In

1981, when A Flock of Seagulls made their test recording for EMI, the Penthouse's new Neve desk offered them as many as forty-eight inputs. Whether this increased facility made their music twenty-four times better history does not record.

When Studio Three was demolished and rebuilt at the end of 1987 it was according to the design of the Japanese studio designer Sam Toyoshima. The new facility offered a sixty-four-input Caltec/IMS console plus the latest Solid State Logic console through which mixes could be automated, stored and recalled at the push of a button, thereby dispensing with the need for the old system, whereby all the studio staff and all available musicians might be called upon to adjust faders during a mix, their arms snaking around each other as though in some strange game of Twister. The new studio also had a live drum room with mirrored walls – a nod to the so-called Stone Room at the Townhouse Studios in west London wherein engineer Hugh Padgham had discovered that if you recorded Phil Collins' drums with the maximum reverberation and then used 'gating' to artificially abbreviate the reverb you got a new sound that sold tens of millions of CDs.

In every direction the business was scaling. MTV had made it possible for even the least likely performers to hit the mainstream. CD was making it possible for them to earn more money than ever if they did so. Recorded music was changing. It was now a business, like the movie business, where the bets were fewer but bigger and nobody was going to argue about a few thousand pounds spent on a picture disc, a ludicrous video or another remix. Freed from the need to tour all the time to pay their bills, bands spent more and more time in the studio. Pink Floyd were the first band to grace the new Abbey Road studio in 1988, but they weren't making new music. Instead they were mixing their live album *The Delicate Sound Of Thunder*. Mixing was a process which in the new decade could take just as long as recording an album of new material had taken in the

EMI

Memorandum

To Mr. Colin Miles

Date 28th November, 1980

Tel Ext

From Ken Townsend

Div/Co. Abbey Road Studios

Dear Colin,

This is to confirm my conversation with you regarding the use of the 'penthouse' at Abbey Road on Friday 5th December 1980 for 'The Flock of Seagulls'.

Providing they do not fly too high over the 24 track machine or mixing console thereby leaving a deposite there will be no charge for recording time; only for any tape materials used. We will also make available this facility for one day the following week if required.

Engineer will be Pete James

Regards,

Ken Townsend

c.c Ms. C Brownhill

File
KT
1/12/80

Distribution

Ken Townsend welcomes A Flock of Seagulls in characteristically jaunty fashion.

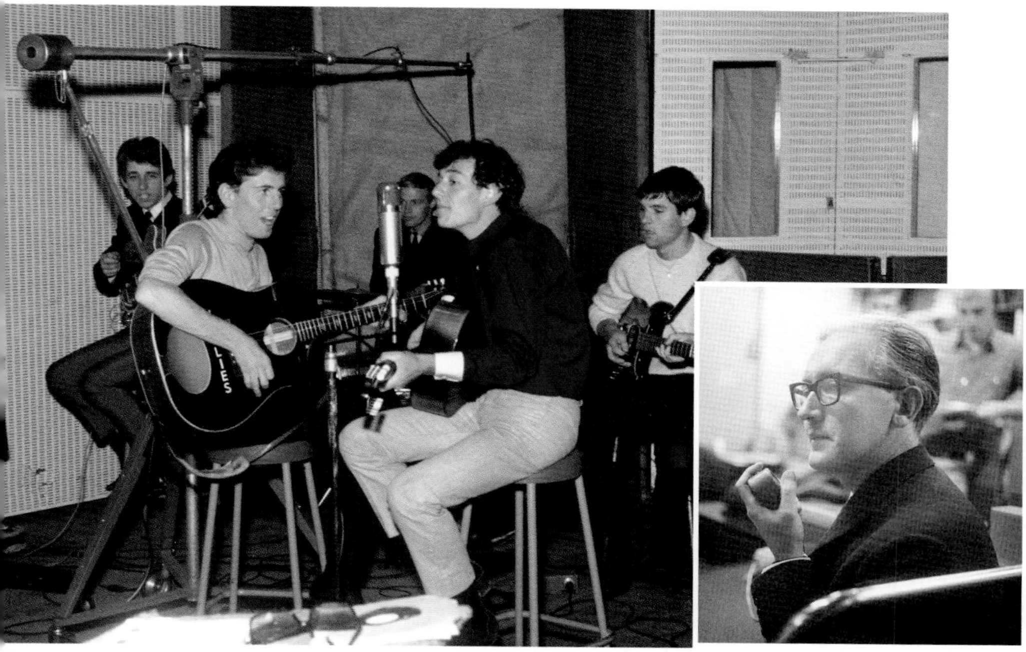

Above: *The Hollies cranked out a series of hits at Abbey Road during the 1960s under the command of Ron 'Don't stop' Richards (***inset***), who liked to be finished for opening time.*

*The Beatles' groundbreaking 'Strawberry Fields Forever'/'Penny Lane' (***above***) came out of the same Studio Two as the more conservative sixties hits of fellow Liverpudlian Ken Dodd.*

Above: *John Lennon with George Martin and the inventor of 'flanging' Ken Townsend, two of the team who laboured long and hard to make 'Strawberry Fields Forever' possible.*

Left: *Jacqueline du Pré and Daniel Barenboim in Studio One the same year.*

*Engineers dealt with everything the rota sent their way, whether it was Eric Morecambe and Ernie Wise doing a routine in Studio Two (***above left***) or John Lennon and Yoko Ono deciding they wanted to record their heartbeats (***above right***).*

Classical producer Suvi Raj Grubb, pictured here with pipe-wielding maestro Otto Klemperer, divided Studio One into squares in the early days of stereo so that he knew where each voice in his sound picture came from.

Above: *From the earliest days Pink Floyd used the studio as a place to experiment as well as record.*

Right: The Dark Side Of The Moon *seemed to sample the entire building and its staff.*

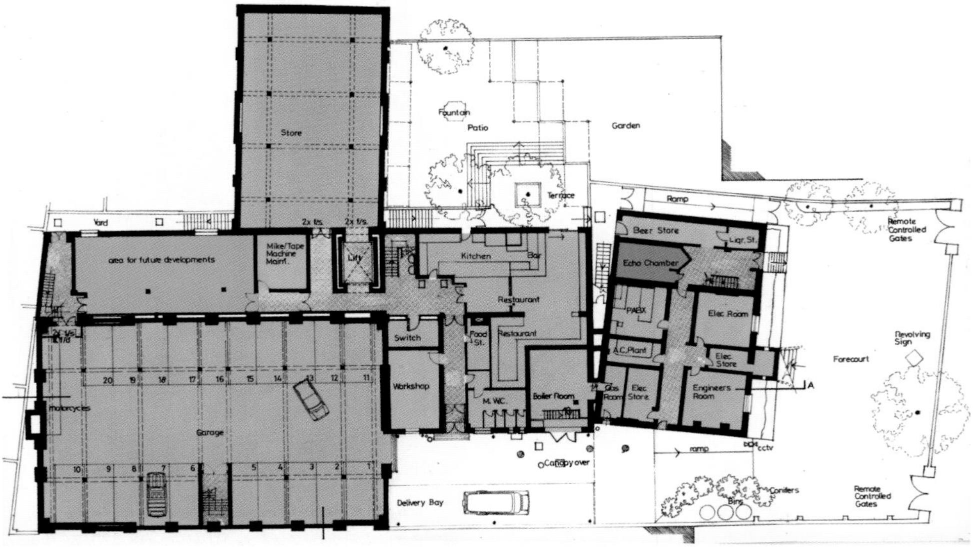

The 1980 ultimatum that reached the desk of EMI boss Ramon Lopez led to these plans to turn Studio One into a car park.

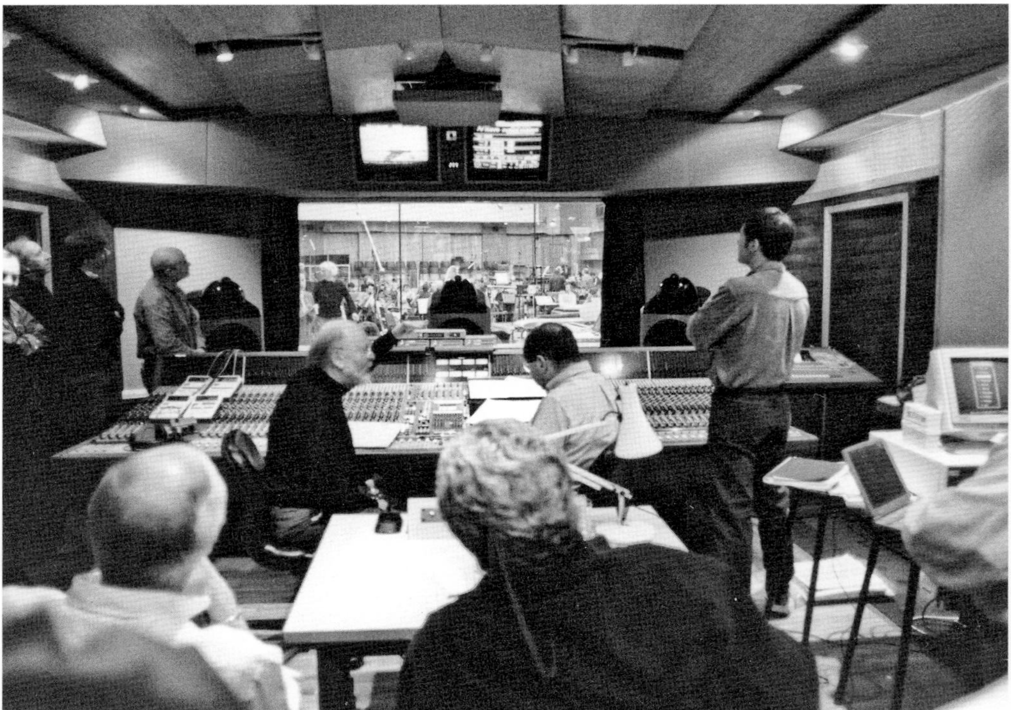

John Williams supervises the music for Star Wars: Episode 1 – The Phantom Menace *in Studio One as George Lucas (***centre foreground***) looks on.*

Kate Bush shoots the video for 'Sat In Your Lap' in Studio Two in 1982.

Left: *At 1980's so-called Sale Of The Century equipment such as the Mellotron* (**above in background**) *used by the Beatles went under the hammer.*

Below: *Queues formed when the studio was thrown open in 1983 for 'Abbey Road Presents The Beatles'.*

Above: *The 'Threatles' plus George Martin pull together on the nineties archive project* Anthology.

Left: *The four-piece Spice Girls assemble in the back garden while recording tracks for* Spiceworld *in 1997.*

Below: *'Lara Croft' helps conduct the soundtrack to* Lara Croft: Tomb Raider *in Studio One in 2002.*

When Travis arrived in Studio Two in 1998 to record The Man Who *they were, they later recalled, 'almost too excited' to work where the Beatles had played.*

Amy Winehouse recorded a duet on 'Body and Soul' with her idol Tony Bennett at Abbey Road in March 2011. It would turn out to be her last session.

Above: *When US hip hop group Brockhampton moved into the studio in 2018, sleeping on couches as they recorded their* Iridescence, *it was Abbey Road's associations with Kanye West and Frank Ocean which had attracted them.*

Below: *On 8 August 2019 an estimated ten thousand tourists and alleged lookalikes celebrated the fiftieth anniversary of that first, most consequential crossing of the fabled thoroughfare.*

previous decade. The same Pink Floyd record was given a further mix thirty years later, by which time it had become clear that there was no longer such a thing as a finished record, merely a mix that had been temporarily abandoned.

Ken Townsend had made sure that the new self-contained studio incorporated its own lounge, kitchen and bathroom facilities. This was particularly welcome for those bands who wished to maintain the illusion that they were the only people in the building. Studios like Abbey Road were facing new competition from facilities based in distant beauty spots, such as George Martin's outpost of AIR on the Caribbean island of Montserrat. Here bands could get away from record companies, family members and unfortunate connections. In such surroundings they could pad barefoot to the studio in the morning and enjoy spectacular sunsets over dinner in the evening. This was a luxury which could only be afforded by those bands that probably weren't in a tearing hurry to make a record at all. Paul McCartney, Stevie Wonder, Dire Straits and the Police were among the clientele. Nobody used it more than the Rolling Stones, Mick Jagger having learned a decade earlier that the first priority was to lessen the distance between the bed Keith Richards slept in and the studio where he was expected to report the following morning. The place suited the latter's less than Stakhanovite approach to work. 'Everything is there,' he enthused in a speech that would have made an accountant blench. 'A great bar, great restaurant, great cook. The studio itself is like a plus.' It was shortly after the Rolling Stones completed *Steel Wheels* at the end of the eighties that a hurricane devastated the island. At around the same time record companies were beginning to question the benefit of allowing their superstars to 'work' quite so far from their supervision, and George Martin decided that particular game was up.

A survey of cultural trends undertaken by the Policy Studies Institute in 1990 found that classical music was enjoying a boom on the back of the compact disc, a carrier which was if anything more popular with the older, more conservative fans of orchestral music than it was with younger fans of pop music. There were mutterings about the format in some quarters but the overwhelming majority of customers seemed to be sold on the eerie quiet between tracks where previously scratches and pops had made themselves felt, and soothed by the fact that there didn't appear to be anything they might do which could make that state of affairs any worse. Everybody who bought their first CD player bought at least one classical CD to place next to it. A televised performance of Vivaldi's *Four Seasons* in 1990 had resulted in Nigel Kennedy selling six hundred and fifty thousand copies by September, while the success of the Three Tenors at the World Cup in Italy in the summer made Italian opera the preferred kitchen soundtrack of the young urban professionals who bought CD players. In response to this demand the major companies embarked on a major programme of new recordings of the major composers. For the first time the marketing of classical music was reaching out beyond the retired headmasters who read magazines like *The Gramophone*. During this time Abbey Road lent its name to the Abbey Road Collection, a compilation of extracts from the works of the big beasts which was done in collaboration with a brand of speakers, using the famous name even though not all of them were recorded at the studio. Such was the demand for studio time that Kennedy's recording of Vivaldi had to be farmed out to a church in Hackney.

Compact disc meant a catalogue-rich company like EMI had the golden chance to sell in a new format what it had already sold in the old format, this time at a far higher price. Suddenly reissues of all kinds, which had previously been the Cinderella wing of the record business, became a priority. Even run-of-the-mill albums from the past which had been forgotten by everyone but the people who made them could be 'rediscovered', thanks to this new, reputedly future-proof format. Getting these old recordings ready for this rebirth provided a whole new branch of the studio business, one which called for people who understood how things had once been done and also how they might be done in the future. Peter Mew, who had joined Abbey Road in the 1960s and been a recording engineer in the 1970s, moved into the reissue business full time in 1988, preparing recordings which had been made with vinyl in mind for a new medium in which they would be subject to a different kind of scrutiny.

At first they simply took the original tapes out of the library and put them on CD. This was only the beginning. Then they introduced a digital editing work station, which meant that it was possible to take the original tape, turn it into digital information and then improve the sound, if only you could decide what constituted improvement. This was the beginning of a wider transformation in the way the whole studio worked, one as far-reaching as the arrival of magnetic tape just after the war. A few years earlier there had not been a single computer in Abbey Road. Now they were springing up everywhere. Once it was digitized you could certainly manipulate sound in a way that had not been possible on an analogue tape. You could do seamless edits, remove clicks, reduce background noise, take a bit out of this section and use it to cover a problem in another section, and produce any number of copies without degradation. Peter Mew was now doing a lot of his work looking at information on a screen.

Because it was still the early days of CD the artists were happy to leave the remastering to the back-room boys. Mew's philosophy was always to try to be true to the original. Because he'd been there back then he was aware that even the original had been a compromise and the new one would be a different kind of compromise. He began remastering old recordings for CD release at a time when fans were just delighted to be able to hear their old favourites with what seemed like the muck of ages cleaned from them. However, the illusion that CD was the final frontier for the reproduction of recorded sound didn't hold very long. He was still working on remasters when the same people decided that CD might be just a bit too hard-edged and bright for their tastes and that they might be more exhausting to listen to than vinyl.

Peter Mew was still in place a decade later when new equipment came along which could make CDs sound louder than ever before. This was in time seized upon by new acts, record companies and anyone else who lived in fear of their CDs not sounding as loud as their competitors', particularly if they were being played in a club. The temptation for remastered versions of records which had been made three decades earlier to reach for the same gear was all but irresistible. 'Fashions in sound change people's expectations,' Peter observed. 'If you listen to a modern record compared with its equivalent of twenty years ago it will be at least twice as loud.' It is also a fact insufficiently noted that compared to the teenagers who bought their copies of *Revolver* in 1966, the middle-aged man spending £13 on a CD reissue thirty years later was, thanks to years of travelling through an increasingly noisy world with headphones jammed in his ears, to all intents and purposes hard of hearing. What had sounded loud to him in 1972 would barely register twenty years later. The idea of 'perfect sound for ever', one of the promises of CD when it was first introduced, was clearly one of those mirages which tended to recede the moment it seemed to be within reach.

However, that ship had sailed. Punk rock may have grabbed the headlines but the most profound changes to the way music was being made were technological, and these made themselves felt right across the board. They also brought together the most unlikely bedfellows. In 1982 the recording career of Tina Turner, recently split from her husband and controlling influence Ike Turner, had been at a low ebb. Thanks to her name, her act, her wig and her legs she could always get work as a well-paid live act. However, she and her new manager Roger Davies still yearned for the kind of transfusion which only a hit record could provide. At the same time Martyn Ware and Ian Craig Marsh, recently departed from the Sheffield group Human League and not much more than beginners at the recording game, were keen to establish themselves at the forefront of a new generation of hit makers capable of marrying the old-world virtues of the well-made song with the purposely pre-fabricated sound that might make a record appealing in the one place it seemed to matter, which was the dance floor. Their plan was an album called *Music Of Quality And Distinction*, which would match well-known singers with well-known songs in a new way. Their lead track was going to be the Temptations' 'Ball Of Confusion' sung by James Brown. But when Brown turned round at the last minute and demanded all the proceeds they offered it instead to Tina, who jumped at it. It's said that when she and Davies turned up in the studio on the first day they said 'Where's the band?' and Ware pointed at the Fairlight CMI. 'That's the band,' he replied. This then led to the same team producing further tracks with her at Abbey Road. The resulting album, *Private Dancer*, had a list of credits longer than the scroll at the end of a major Hollywood movie, to reflect the many songwriters, producers and musicians who had been involved in its making. This was the way things were going. If albums were going to be like blockbusters it was worth going the extra mile to secure the perfect shot that might make the difference.

A perfect example was Paul Simon's 1986 release *Graceland*. This was recorded in half a dozen different studios on three different continents and involved musicians from different traditions from all over the world, an expense of effort which would have been inconceivable in any earlier decade. It was more like a field trip than a recording session for an album, since Simon had no songs written down. He simply believed that once he got into the studio with musicians from different cultures he admired, they would be able to bring something forth between them.

Simon had heard the South African twelve-man singing ensemble Ladysmith Black Mambazo and wanted to work with them. He had nothing more than a fragment of a song called 'Homeless'. St John's Wood was settled on as the location of their rendezvous. The group and the singer assembled in Studio Two of Abbey Road, where the microphones had been placed as though the group were going to give a concert. Their performances naturally involved a certain amount of bodily movement, which in its way contributed to their sound. Expecting to record as many as twelve songs in a day, which was their standard rate of progress, they were genuinely worried when it got to six o'clock on the first day and they still hadn't captured what they thought they were capable of doing.

They came from such different musical traditions it wasn't obvious to see how they might be married. The music which Ladysmith Black Mambazo performed was so bound up with the realities of life among the Zulu people it was difficult to hear how it might co-exist with Western pop song. Since nothing was written down it was impossible to point to particular passages which might work. Fortunately they were on Paul Simon's recording budget rather than their own, which meant they could come back the following day and try again. They didn't waste any of the additional time. 'We went back to our hotel very disappointed,' said Joseph Shabalala. 'When we get in the hotel we had dinner, and we got together, we pray. Our prayer was very deep that day. I was so concerned. I've never failed in anything. This is no time to fail now. We practised the song until midnight, and then the song was together.'

The following day they started to sing their number, which was based on a traditional Zulu wedding song. It had been rewritten in the light of Paul Simon's title, meant to reflect the idea that the Zulu men who went from their villages to the big city in search of work often had to sleep on their clenched fists. Simon had it explained to him what their song was about but obviously didn't understand the words. What they were groping for lived in the region of pure sound and would only step into the light when it came tumbling into the air. Thus when he got on the studio floor, faced them and came in with the single sung word 'homeless' he was simply reacting to the moment, the company he found himself in and the surroundings of the studio in a manner which was more like an actor in an improvisation than a playwright at his desk. However it was done, it just seemed to work. Some kind of sweet spot had been arrived at. The fact that it just worked was written on the faces of everyone in the room.

'When Paul comes in with "homeless" I nearly fainted,' remembered Joseph Shabalala.

They completed it in two takes.

20

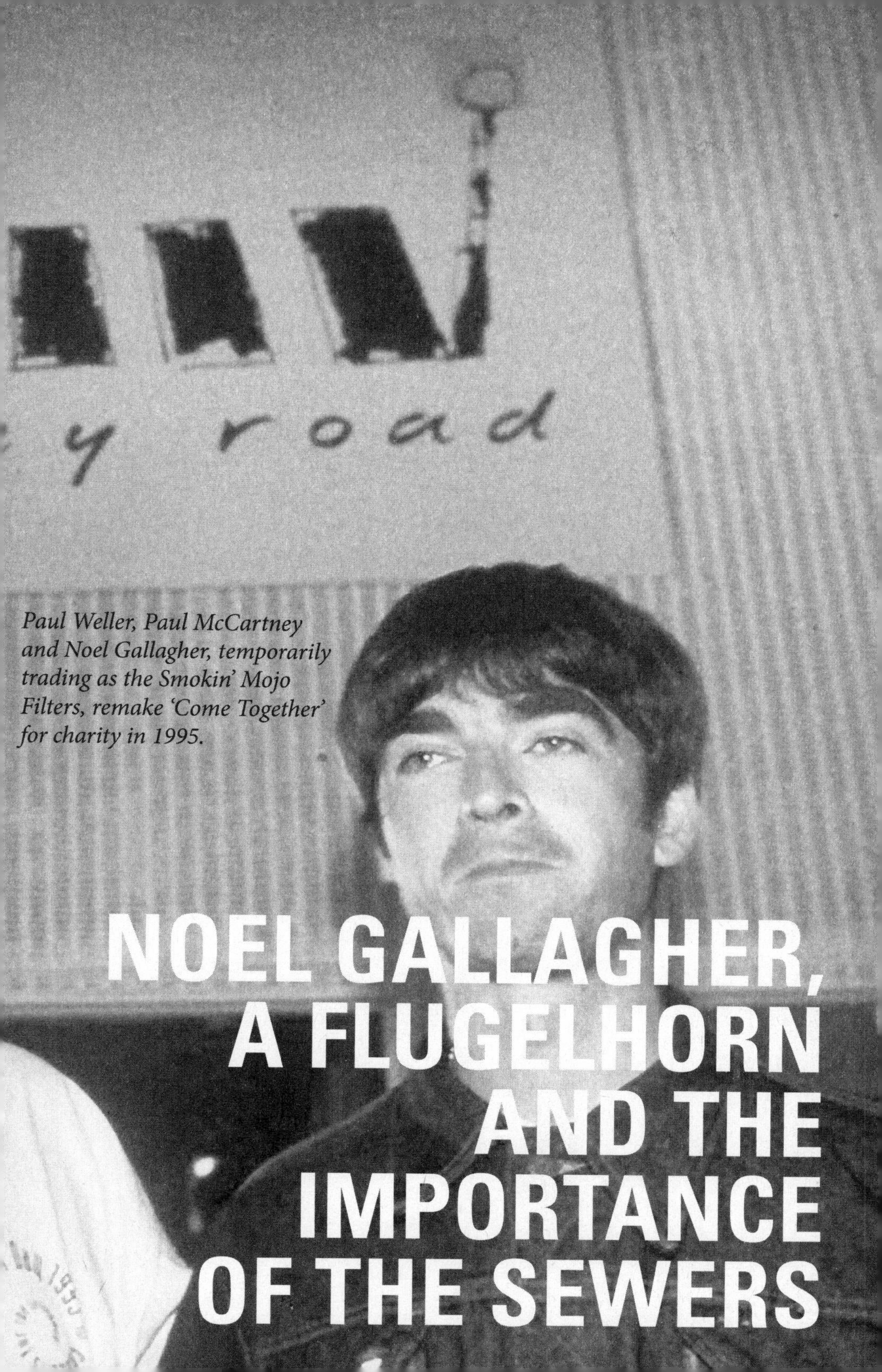

Paul Weller, Paul McCartney and Noel Gallagher, temporarily trading as the Smokin' Mojo Filters, remake 'Come Together' for charity in 1995.

NOEL GALLAGHER, A FLUGELHORN AND THE IMPORTANCE OF THE SEWERS

In March 1993 George Martin gave an interview to *The Times*. On this occasion he was keen to publicize his new AIR studio, which had recently opened in a converted church in Hampstead large enough to be able to accommodate orchestral recordings. When the inevitable questions came, he was no less keen to pull focus away from any talk of his erstwhile clients in NW8. At the time there didn't seem to be any sign of a revival in public interest in the Beatles, nor was there anything which might pique such an interest. He confirmed he had been to Abbey Road and listened to all the unreleased Beatles songs, and while 'there were one or two interesting variations, it's all junk. Couldn't possibly release it.'

Within two years the Beatles would once more be the biggest story in pop. Within two years they would be EMI's biggest money-spinner all over again. Within two years that 'junk' that George had said couldn't possibly be released would be alchemized. This entirely unforeseen gold rush came about thanks to a new generation of Beatles fans who were, if anything, far more energetic collectors than their forerunners and certainly spent more money; thanks to the seventy-four minutes a CD could accommodate, which made it twice as long as an LP; thanks to the media's twitch on the thread, which seemed to be all it took to reawaken pop's love affair with its Greatest Story Ever Told; thanks to the market's willingness to listen around the imperfections of recordings made long ago, providing they were by people they happened to really admire; thanks to their happiness to regard material which had been previously considered of no commercial appeal as a unique and fascinating new branch of archaeology; and most crucially of all, thanks to those alchemical abilities of the technicians at Abbey Road.

For record buyers old enough to recall the days when it had only been possible to obtain bootleg records by shopping way off the beaten track and making appointments, often through trusted intermediaries, with the sketchiest of characters, this was a turn-up they hadn't seen coming. Suddenly the people out there talking up the album of out-takes would be the very musicians who forty years earlier had claimed these should never see the light of day because their release would be injurious to their reputation. Suddenly the heads who had devoted years to building up their collections of vinyl bootlegs, with their variable production standards and sometimes hilariously cheapskate packaging, would find their prized hoards valueless. Suddenly highly paid designers would be labouring long in the offices of chic packaging companies to come up with a look suggestive of an illicit purchase made from a Portobello market stall in 1972.

George Martin may not have been aware of it at the time, but by 1993 there were already people at EMI and Apple, where the Beatles' original roadie Neil Aspinall continued to clock in every day to keep an eye on the band's – now brand's – interests, who had noted the success CBS had enjoyed putting out on CD expensively packaged collections of unreleased Bob Dylan material. They had even called them 'the Bootleg series' because nothing made them seem so desirable as the fact that in an earlier time people had been prepared to risk prosecution to put them out. This was in many cases the same material which the artist's lawyers had always claimed in the past was not up to the artist's high standards. Apple had further noted that the bootlegging industry was enjoying an Indian summer, recycling out-takes and live recordings of classic acts on the new, apparently indestructible format of the compact disc.

There were other straws in the wind. In that same year I was involved in the launch of a new music magazine called *Mojo*, which focused on the more canonical rock bands and didn't bother taking too much note of whoever was going to be the next big thing. It was quickly apparent that the readership we had originally aimed at, who were Baby Boomers, was being swelled by a younger generation of new traditionalists who had come to the bands of the sixties and seventies long after they had split up but who were nonetheless eager to relive something they had never lived through in the first place. These people were far hungrier for detail and if anything far more knowledgeable about the big acts than the people who had grown up with them.

Many of these people had arrived at the feet of the Beatles, Kinks and Small Faces, having been directed there by stars of Britpop such as Oasis, Blur and Pulp, many of whom had gone to great lengths to talk about how this was where their own inspiration had come from. Whereas the big names of punk rock had grown up listening to progressive bands but denied it under questioning, the big names of Britpop probably exaggerated how much they had grown up under the spell of *The Kinks Are The Village Green Preservation Society* or *A Saucerful Of Secrets*. They seized upon any route that might get them into the magic garden of the sixties, one of which inevitably led them to the studio which was most associated with that place.

In September 1995 when the charity War Child were making an album to benefit victims of war in the Balkans, it seemed inescapable that this had to culminate in a version of the Beatles' 'Come Together' performed by a group which comprised members of Paul Weller's band and Oasis. If you were going to do such a thing, there was clearly no better place to do it than Studio Two at Abbey Road.

This was no longer the simple business of making a record. This was now more in the nature of a pilgrimage. The hipsters of the moment all duly turned out, but even Kate Moss and Johnny Depp were forced to take a step backwards when Paul McCartney turned up as though by magic to bless the proceedings (and some said to make sure he didn't slip too far from the public eye). Even in the highly evolved firmament of celebrity in the nineties it was increasingly clear that musical fame aced all other varieties of fame, musical fame earned in the sixties trumped everything, and Abbey Road was starting to enjoy some of that magic by association. On the 'Come Together' session the studio time was donated for charity; nonetheless signage promoting Abbey Road, now represented by an illustration of the famous zebra crossing, was prominently displayed.

At the same time, the New Labour establishment and Britpop were cosying up with each other for their mutual benefit and it seemed that the thing they could agree on was the fact that the Beatles had been Britain's miraculous gift to the world and that Noel Gallagher was their only begotten son. When Gallagher first visited London as a roadie for the Inspiral Carpets he was enthralled simply to drive past. When he came back as the leader of the platinum-selling Oasis he was to tell his management that he wanted to live down the same road just to be close by. Happily for the management of EMI's recording studio, No. 3 Abbey Road was now more than just a place you made records. It was a place you went to in the hope that miraculous things might also happen for you. It was a locus of dreams.

The greatest beneficiary of this nostalgia for a golden age turned out to be the act which had given that age its golden quality. The Beatles had been talking about doing a retrospective film since the 1970s, and to this end their man Neil Aspinall had been quietly making sure that they controlled all the materials they would require to do it. Nobody in the business of popular music played a longer game than Aspinall. No courtier ever knew his masters better. This business did not get any easier with time. Like the wise old shepherd he was, he knew he had to pick his moment to gently usher the three remaining Beatles and the heirs of the fourth through the gate that would lead to a decision about the film. By 1992 George Harrison, who had been personally liable for his company Hand Made's adventures in the film business, was badly in need of the advance such a project would inevitably attract and therefore he suppressed any reluctance. Paul McCartney, who had always been the Beatles' biggest fan and also the one realistic enough to understand their importance in his continued prominence, had always been keen. Ringo would go along with the majority decision.

By 1992 the project was labouring under the unlovely and not very descriptive title *Anthology*, which sounded dry. An anthology might have excited the hardcore fans, but the newspapers and TV stations could only get excited by the prospect of something they could bill as a Beatles reunion, even though such a thing was, as the survivors pointed out, an impossibility, even if it had been desirable. Around this time Yoko Ono, showing the flair for timing which has been the mark of the conceptual artist down the ages, handed the other three some demos John had made long after the group broke up. This gave them a news story. It also gave them something to sell. Paul, George and Ringo got together with producer Jeff Lynne (insisted on by George, presumably to stop Paul taking charge) down at Paul's studio in Sussex and worked on trying to make something of 'Real Love' and 'Free As A Bird'.

Nothing could have been less like the old days than this attempt to make something out of these ancient fragments. Nothing could have better illustrated the changed relationship between inspiration and perspiration involved in making a record thirty years after they first began. For a start they had to spend a week working on the original tape, which had been done on a machine scarcely more sophisticated than a Dictaphone, a machine which moreover was some yards away from the singer at his piano and was further blighted by a mains hum. The manner in which Jeff Lynne now layered his allegedly simple pop records was by then so dense that even this, the slightest of songs, had to be constructed out of no fewer than forty-eight different tracks. There was one track for the stand-up bass that Bill Black had played on those early Elvis sides at Sun Studios in Union Avenue, Memphis, which was now owned by Paul McCartney, because what else do you get the bass player who has everything? There was another track containing a single snare drum. There was a further one on which a drum synth was recorded. This was the ultimate demonstration of the absurd lengths to which recording technology was now prepared to go to give the impression of not having gone to much trouble at all. What John Lennon would have made of it we can only guess.

The Lennon tracks would provide the hit singles which would lead the marketing campaign. But what would make up the rest? It was now apparent that the previously unreleased material, which according to George Martin in 1993 wouldn't even make a single CD, was now miraculously good enough to justify three double CDs because now they were trying to be near-comprehensive rather than carefully selective. They might be able to spice the mix with ancient home recordings, tapings of TV performances at the height of Beatlemania and snatches of live performance from overseas tours, but the bulk of it would comprise unfinished recordings made over the years at Abbey Road – the very stuff the original producer had said they couldn't possibly release. Of course if your criterion was whether something was likely to be of interest to a hardcore fan rather than whether it would go on to a radio station playlist, your net could be cast a lot wider. The truth is that fans would not wish to hear an allegedly better version of a much-loved record, because such a thing cannot exist. They would rather hear a version which peters out halfway and eavesdrop on the ensuing conversation about whether the suitcases are in the hotel or in the van, because it gives them the thrilling feeling of being a fly on the wall at a point when history is about to be made.

The job of going through everything Abbey Road had in the vault went to George Martin and engineer Geoff Emerick, who proved himself a stickler for authenticity, or at least the semblance of authenticity. The studio's archivist, Alan Rouse, had already copied all the studio tapes which were held at Abbey Road on to digital tape as a safety measure in 1988. Not caring for the way these sounded, Emerick then asked for everything to be mixed down to quarter-inch tape and then played on an old Studer tape machine at thirty inches per second. To mix them down, he ordered up a vintage EMI mixing desk with the kind of crude outboard equipment they would have had at the time of the original recordings. The only modern thing he allowed himself was the speakers over which he listened.

He didn't actually instruct the canteen to go back to serving Nescafé and margarine, but in every other respect he seemed to take a former employee's pleasure in putting things back the way he remembered them. He demanded the reopening of the old echo chamber, which had fallen into disuse. This room, which was next to Studio Two, had been a key part of how records were made in the days before engineers had a button for everything. The space, which looked like a cross between a cellar and the ruins of a Greek temple, was used for its dramatically reverberant qualities. A signal would be relayed to a speaker in the chamber, and the sound would ping off the chamber's various surfaces and then be recaptured. This Heath Robinson arrangement, which had been a key part of the sound of early rockers such as Elvis Presley and the Beatles, had fallen into disuse once the recording console offered acts a way of synthesizing the same effect at the flick of a switch. The team at Abbey Road did their best to get this back in working shape for Emerick's work on *Anthology* but, as engineer Peter Vince later commented, 'with the best will in the world there was no way to totally replicate Studio Two's echo chamber because you couldn't get the sewer pipes as they were'.

Interest in the way the Beatles had made their records in the sixties was enjoying a new birth at the precise point when the march of scientific progress seemed to have obliterated the conditions that made it possible, in many cases consigning the equipment on which it had been done to the scrapheap of history. Everybody sensed that an attractive rawness and spontaneity had been lost and they were prepared to do everything they could to rediscover it, as long as it didn't involve being raw and spontaneous.

Records are made for and by the technology available at the time and it's impossible to reimagine them for anything that comes later. A Fats Domino 78 from the fifties didn't sound quite right on the Dansettes of the sixties. Play a Motown 45 from the sixties, at its best on a jukebox with a lead weight for a tone arm, on a seventies music centre and it seemed strangely reduced. Would Dickens have written differently had he had a laptop? Would the films of Hitchcock have been different if he had been able to edit them digitally? Beginning with the Beatles *Anthology* series of the nineties, remastering became a whole new line of work for studios like Abbey Road, as record companies found they could make more money out of what they had already recorded than those things they were about to record. There was a new record buyer out there, a person who, given a choice, liked nothing more than the idea of laying their money down for an apparently enhanced version of something they had long ago satisfied themselves that they loved, a person who was no longer a teenager or even a twentysomething.

By the nineties the market for recorded music was no longer dominated by teenagers. There was gold in the past. Record companies were starting to do research into the salience of the acts they had signed thirty years earlier, trying to judge when would be the best time to bring them back into the forefront. EMI made more money out of the three Beatles *Anthology* sets than they did out of anything else they released that year, thus ensuring that in the future bands signed to major labels would have to hand over every last hard drive containing all the mixes and session recordings just in case some George Martin of the mid- to late twenty-first century should decide that they were worth releasing.

It was also no longer a question of producing music for records. In 1997, three decades after the Beatles' animated film *Yellow Submarine* had been first released for the cinema, an Abbey Road engineering team led by Peter Cobbin remixed its music soundtrack for 5.1 Surround Sound, using the multi-tracks of the original recordings and putting them through a combination of vintage equipment and 24-bit digital audio technology. One can only imagine how much more take-up there would have been for all these new ways of reproducing sound if they had only been given names like stereo or quad, the sort of names to which the general public could ascribe some meaning. Nobody realized that the next revolution was to involve the distribution of music rather than the perfecting of its sound. At the time the future they were envisaging still looked in most respects rather like the past, except bigger and more profitable. That was not to last.

The mid-nineties turned out to be the high point of the record business. Because CDs were still selling, and selling at retail prices which produced an awful lot of fat, much of which could be spent on hype and hoopla, it turned out to be quite a party. In terms of wealth, decadence and even ostentatious drug use in the music business the nineties was the decade the seventies has the reputation for being. It was a time of excess on all fronts, particularly on recording. It was a time when people of otherwise sound mind actually queued up all night outside one of London's megastores to be the first to buy a new album by one of the feted names. It was a time when recorded music, particularly in Britain, was even more popular than it had been in the sixties. Buying it and making a fuss about buying it was very nearly a civic duty. The apotheosis of this mad moment was the 1997 release of the Oasis record *Be Here Now*, which gained a subsequent reputation as a disaster that perfectly mirrored its predecessors' reputations as masterpieces.

The band had begun work on it in Mick Jagger's house in Mustique, which is rarely a good start. They then moved into Abbey Road and did two tracks there before moving out. Accounts as to why they moved out vary. There's a school which holds that the studio was a bit too near their homes and the sources of their distraction. They themselves said they were making too much noise for the neighbours, which is the kind of explanation that chimed with the Gallaghers' self-image. This reached such a pitch that John Fraser of EMI Classics, who was supervising a recording in Studio One, came in and asked if they could turn it down. The way Noel Gallagher told it in one of the interviews through which they energetically inflated their own mystique, they were playing in one studio at their usual volume when somebody came from one of the other studios and asked if they could turn it down while they recorded a flugelhorn part. 'We were like, take your flugelhorn and stick it up your arse, mate.' In fact, as Noel told me when contacted for this book, they were all sitting in a circle on the floor of Studio Two, reverently listening to all the Beatles albums in strict chronological order, albeit at deafening volume. 'It was agreed we would be better off going somewhere else.'

Eventually it took them weeks to finish the record at a remote studio in Cornwall. They overdubbed and overdubbed and mixed and remixed, which should have been a sign that there was something inert about the basic performances. By this time they could no longer hear the music for the tramp-tramp-tramp of the cocaine in their ears and their overarching desire for this record to be their 'top of the world, Ma' moment.

They did everything in their power to make the release as auspicious as possible. The title *Be Here Now* came from an interview with John Lennon; the Rolls-Royce which appeared on the cover partially submerged in a swimming pool even had the same registration number as the van on the cover of *Abbey Road*. The record came out to reviews which were almost as overblown as the record itself, reviews which were gradually withdrawn over the succeeding months as *Be Here Now* earned the sardonic alternate title *Played Just Once*. Years later, after the mad euphoria of the record's release had been followed by the greatest outbreak of buyer's remorse in the history of the record business, even the band admitted that they should probably have stuck with the demos. The bands of Britpop had been keen to copy all the tried-and-tested techniques which had shaped the recordings of the sixties, apart from what was probably the most significant one. This was the clock. The one aspect of old-school record-making that none of them seemed interested in embracing was the speed with which records used to be made, the willingness to abandon an idea early when it wasn't working and a belief that if the initial performance didn't have the requisite magic, all the mixes and remixes in the world would never produce it. Like many albums which follow up unexpected hits, *Be Here Now* was the kind of mistake you can only make very slowly, very deliberately and very expensively.

21

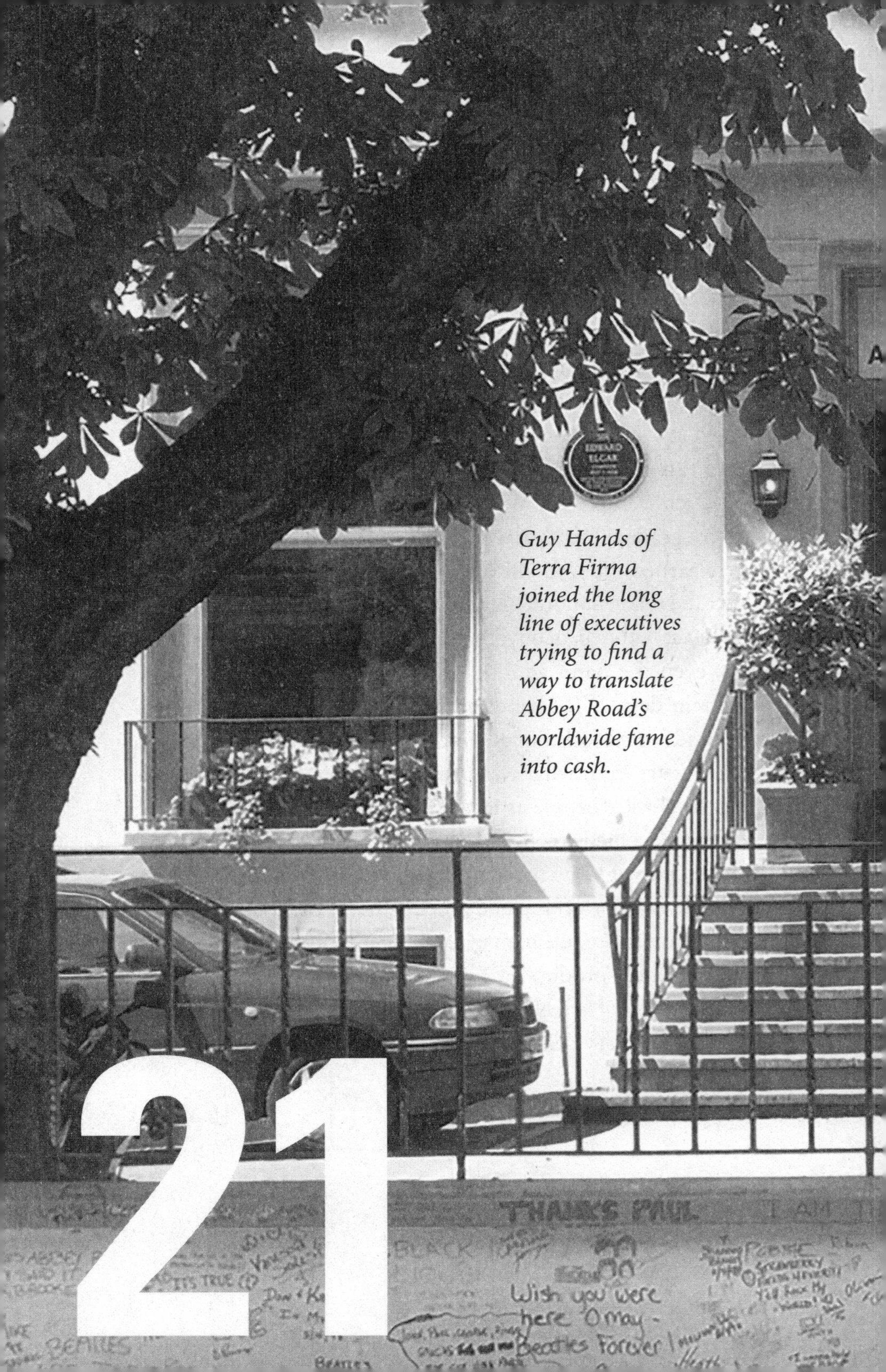

Guy Hands of Terra Firma joined the long line of executives trying to find a way to translate Abbey Road's worldwide fame into cash.

GUY HANDS, ENGLISH HERITAGE AND MONETIZING THE BRAND

By the turn of the century the excitement around the music business, which had traditionally been about the music, was increasingly about the ways in which music found its way to people. The same digital technology which had made CD such a profitable format also meant that ripping and burning your own CDs was the work of a moment. The arrival of Napster in 1999 meant that tens of thousands of other people could download your music without needing to do even that. When Apple launched the iPod in 2001 they would not have dared to predict that within a couple of years their inscrutable toy would prove more exciting than any of the thousands of tunes it could house, and that distribution rather than content would turn out to be king, with catastrophic consequences for the revenues of record companies.

Of course every journalist, business consultant, corporate raider and poverty-stricken musician claimed to know exactly what the record companies ought to do when faced with such an existential threat. Being both a public company and a part of the British establishment, EMI came in for more of this free advice than most. Having tried and failed to ensure its survival by buying Warner Music, burdened with debt and with a shrinking market share the company was eventually delivered up to Guy Hands' private equity firm Terra Firma in 2007 for over £4 billion. At the time Hands probably knew less than most about the precise extent of what he was buying.

David Holley happened to be the executive responsible for running all of EMI's studios, at the time a small empire which included, in addition to Abbey Road, Olympic in Barnes, where the Stones and Led Zeppelin had made many of their most famous records, together with Capitol in Hollywood, where Sinatra and Peggy Lee had done their most memorable work. In addition to this responsibility Holley happened to be on the board of the EMI Archive Trust, which was an organization established in 1996 'to foster and promote the study and appreciation of the art, techniques and development of sound recording and the history of the sound recording industry'.

It was in this latter capacity that Hands phoned him one day early in the new regime. At the close of the conversation, Hands lightly enquired what was the reason for Holley being based at the famous Abbey Road Studios. It was gently explained to the mogul that Abbey Road was in fact an EMI studio and thus one of the facilities which the company he now headed actually owned. To the hard-pressed tycoon, already fully occupied with trying to impose what he saw as best practice on the idiosyncratic ways of a record company – many of whose employees secretly regarded him and his gang of corporate planners as barbarians bent on the sack of Rome, few things more reliably bringing out the patrician side of record company people than interlopers threatening to instruct them in the sucking of eggs – this evidently came as fresh information. However, swiftly calculating that where there lay an asset with such powerful worldwide brand recognition that even his investors would have heard of it there must surely be a closely adjacent seam full of cash, he dispatched a posse of his myrmidons to Abbey Road to help work out how the latter could be mined and extracted.

What happened next would have been familiar to anyone with experience of what so often happens when business consultants alight on what they perceive to be a greenfield site. All manner of monetizing schemes came bubbling up from corporate brainstorming sessions. There were those within the new company who talked of turning it into luxury apartments. After all, Abbey Road was clearly one of the most famous addresses in the world and therefore to imagine prestige-conscious oligarchs wishing to give theirs as 'Abbey Road Studios' did not require a real-estate visionary. It was also a huge tourist attraction and a site of major historical interest, and therefore there was further talk of turning at least part of it into some kind of visitor centre.

They quickly realized there were two major stumbling blocks to such a course of action. Before developing the home of the late Elvis Presley into an attraction, the Presley estate had bought most of the surrounding sites and turned them into parking lots. In a residential area like St John's Wood, on the other hand, it would be impossible to establish an infrastructure such as the one Graceland used for efficiently processing the maximum number of visitors and separating them from their cash. The other was the central dilemma of running the studio in the twenty-first century. Simply put, this meant that as soon as Abbey Road attracted visitors it would no longer attract clients. And as soon as it ceased to attract clients, the visitors would quickly lose interest. People flock there because it's a working studio. At the very core of the enduring mystique of Abbey Road lies one fact. You can't get in.

In *The Final Days of EMI*, Eamonn Forde's book about the Hands era, people who were there or thereabouts at the time, and whose recollections are unsurprisingly coloured by what side of the argument they happened to be on, talk about the various proposals which were made for getting round this problem. Hands himself believed it would be possible to open some kind of visitor centre without interrupting the studio's normal work – there was talk of two-way mirrors behind which visitors could stand and watch artists in the middle of recording – and there was even a plan to sell a

VIP version of a Robbie Williams CD in which there would be a golden ticket entitling the winner to a helicopter ride to Lord's Cricket Ground from which they would be conducted into the studio by the artist himself. Whoever ran this particular proposal up the flagpole had clearly never had any dealings with either a rock star or the MCC. Among the armies of sharp young people who descended on EMI at the time – people accustomed to being parachuted into underperforming businesses and seeking out additional value they might unlock – there may even have been the odd good idea which might have worked; however, most of them fell upon stony ground because, as they were to discover, the music business is not one that goes in for revolutions, unless forced by dire economic circumstance, and in the path of absolutely every plan are the same five words: the acts won't like it. If the acts don't like it, this line of reasoning goes, they will either refuse to cooperate altogether or will do it in such a surly fashion that you will wish you hadn't asked.

The other aspect of the music business that would come as an unpleasant surprise to the proposers was that music companies do not exert the same level of control over their products as did the grocers and chemists they might have been accustomed to dealing with. That's because they have to deal with the artists in order to be able to do anything with the art. If you wished to do something with an item in the catalogue of an act, even if it was an item that had been done and dusted decades before, there was no alternative to going and talking to the members of that act, each of whom might have a different manager and at least two of whom probably couldn't bear to be in the same room as each other. One of the major challenges for anybody charged with managing EMI over the years was that they had to be able to tell their investors how much money they would make the following year. This would depend on whether albums by their big money-spinning names were ready for release.

This in turn depended on which side of the bed said money-spinning names had made their egress earlier that day. Compared to this, the biscuit business is straightforward.

Hands wasn't the only one looking to see what could be done with the studio. During the period of Terra Firma's stewardship there was a funded proposal for a management buyout. Eminent people in the film industry, some of whom had spent happy times watching their movies being scored there, were among the backers. Eminent people in the music business, who tend to be slightly longer on sentiment but shorter on cash, were vocal in their support for keeping it in the studio business but less keen on putting their hands in their pockets. The valuation put on it was almost £30 million. In February 2010 the headline in the *FT* read 'EMI to Sell Abbey Road'. Sources in the management buyout team think Terra Firma may have leaked this story in order to smoke out further bids. At this point the great and the good pitched in and suddenly it was no longer about buying and selling a recording studio. Suddenly everyone had a view on the future of the business. Suddenly it was about dividing up a precious piece of the national heritage. This wasn't just another studio. This was Abbey Road.

The same technological storm which was coming for record shops and record companies had not spared recording studios. Many of the biggest chart hits of the twenty-first century had been made in an entirely new way. This was what John Seabrook in his book *The Song Machine* termed the 'track and hook method'. Under this method, all records began with a producer. That producer worked at home and probably wouldn't even need a studio. The producer would begin by developing a rhythm track. Once he had got that to the requisite pitch of catchiness he would send that out to a number of specialists who would come up with 'top lines' or hooks to be sung over the top of the rhythm track. When he found a match he liked he would put the two together and then go looking for a well-known singer to record it. This meant that many of the traditional customers of studios could now do without them. It was becoming plain that the widespread adoption of technologies such as Pro Tools and the dominance of records which were made 'in the box' meant that an increasing number of acts had neither the budget nor the inclination to pay for time in an expensive studio.

The same recording technology made it possible to record musicians playing anything but concurrently; if they did wish to do so they could even jam across continents using ISDN connections. One of the last projects to bear the name of Frank Sinatra was an album of duets in which he never met any of the people he purportedly sang with. This fresh wave of recording technology dramatically reduced the need for spaces in which musicians could gather and collaborate at the very moment an influx of overseas capital in search of a West End address meant that the spaces in which they had formerly communed could be turned into apartments, many of which would never be occupied and could be used as nest eggs for wealthy foreigners. All over London, recording studios in which legendary records had been made were being turned into luxury flats, and it didn't seem to cause anyone a moment's concern. Many of them were in areas which had once been cheap and cheerful parts of the city in which to operate and were now enclaves of wealth. Sarm Studios in Basing Street, Notting Hill, where Band Aid had recorded 'Do They Know It's Christmas?' and Bob Marley *Exodus*, was shrunk down to a space in the basement so that the rest of the building could be turned into bijou residences. The same fate awaited Britannia Row, the space in Islington where Pink Floyd had made *The Wall*. The Townhouse in Goldhawk Road, the place where Phil Collins made 'In The Air Tonight', which had been latterly owned by EMI, was destined to be turned into a dozen four-bedroom homes valued at over £2 million each. Sometimes the space could be worth more if it was merely used once a fortnight. Maison Rouge, where Blur made *Parklife*, became a car park for Chelsea Football Club.

All this had happened without exciting much comment in the media for the simple reason that the media hadn't noticed. Fearing the attentions of fans, most studios had done everything in their power not to advertise their presence during their lifetimes and therefore it would have seemed perverse indeed to draw attention to their moving away. Things were not the same with Abbey Road for the simple reason that it was the only recording studio most people knew the name of. That fame reached all over the world and went far beyond the circles of those who read the credits on album sleeves. Furthermore, it was picked up by the antennae of those who detect an opportunity to stake a claim on behalf of the nation. The National Trust said that they would consider buying it for said nation, in much the same way that they had acquired stately homes following the Second World War. The scarcely less savvy Radio Two DJ Chris Evans, sensing the potential for a campaign based on pop sentiment and beleaguered patriotism, started his own campaign to save Abbey Road, rattling a notional tin in the direction of Paul McCartney, Richard Branson and Philip Green. None of them actually put their hand in their pocket, though McCartney did appear on television saying how his sympathies lay with the people who wished to preserve it as a working studio. He still had the house round the corner at Cavendish Avenue, which he had bought in 1965 for £40,000 because it was close to his place of work.

At this point English Heritage, who had long fancied No. 3 as a target for preservation, jumped in and accorded Abbey Road Grade II listed status, to the annoyance of both the people keen on turning it into residential accommodation and the Abbey Road management, who wished to know what exactly they were supposed to be preserving and how. Preservation organizations, always alive to the value of column inches, were newly keen to put their brand on anything that could be considered hip, and Abbey Road was in this respect a perfect target. Behind the Victorian facade the building had been reconfigured at regular intervals over the years. Identifying what exactly is the true Abbey Road is as difficult an undertaking as ring-fencing the original features of a glamour model. Although the building appears largely the same from the road and the three main studios are in the same places as they were in 1931, control rooms have been rebuilt and expanded over the years, staircases have been put in, rooms repurposed to reflect the changing functions of the business, and support services shuffled up, down and sideways until, like Downing Street, the White House and a handful of other famous old dwellings that house entirely unsuitable businesses, its calm, classic exterior belies a warren-like interior which has clearly been knocked about quite a bit.

By 2011 this was no longer the problem of Guy Hands and Terra Firma because they were no longer in the picture, though there were traces of their efforts to monetize the magic of the brand in the establishment of an office through which companies and even private individuals with enough cash could hire the previously inviolable spaces of the big studios for their product launches or grand celebrations.

Meanwhile, recording technology continued to advance at such a pace that there seemed no division between present and future. The digital revolution, like all revolutions, quickly turned out to have been overestimated in the short term and then underestimated in the long term. When it fully kicked in it left no part of the music business unaffected. Record shops were closing their doors all over the country as the public decided it preferred to download and then stream its favourite music one tune at a time rather than in the form of long-playing records presented like novels or movies. This meant there was less call for making these records in the old way, no matter how noisily the performers might pine for its passing dignity. In

2008, Andrew Leyshon of the University of Nottingham authored a paper about the decline of the recording studio sector. In it he described a business wherein a diminishing pool of suppliers had difficulty keeping up their rates because they were dealing with such a small pool of buyers, the major record companies, any one of whom could say, with some justification, that they could get their album recorded round the corner for less money. At the end of his research he concluded there was no point looking at a studio's published day rate, which had long since replaced the hourly rate in which studio time was once calculated, because that would not bear much resemblance to what people actually ended up paying. The studio business is much like the hotel business in the sense that even the Ritz will do you a deal if the alternative is leaving a room empty. Leyshon concluded that what people actually paid for studio time in the first decade of the new century wouldn't be much more than they might have paid twenty years earlier. This is not what any finance director wishes to hear.

People in such positions don't wish to hear about the soft benefits. Acts such as Oasis and Mark Ronson had continued to be attracted to the studios by their high standards of engineering, their historical associations and the fact that they felt like studios should feel and that going there felt like going to do a job of work. Florence Welch went so far as to describe its atmosphere as 'semi-devotional'. Interestingly, Leyshon found that in addition to space to record in, as well as the best technology and expert staff, the other thing that studios offered was what he termed 'emotional labour'. Following many interviews with people who worked in recording studios he was surprised, he wrote, 'just how "nice" – there is just no other word for it – everyone in recording studios seemed to be'. Considering that studios tend to attract staff whose only desire is to work in studios, this shouldn't have come as a huge surprise, but it could be something people only miss when it's no longer available. Despite such intangible benefits the increasing popularity of computer desktop technology like Pro Tools, Logic and Cubase had made it possible for the next generation of musicians to make their new album – a product which, it would appear, they were determined to keep on producing even though there was not much indication that the public had an appetite for same – in their spare room or their garage. This was not simply a question of budget. When Todd Rundgren had overdubbed himself playing all the instruments on his 1973 album *A Wizard, A True Star* and then engineered and overseen every element, he was clearly taking on a job which 99 per cent of his peers would not have known how to begin doing. Music recording, mixing and editing software changed all that at a stroke, making it possible for anyone to make a record which at least sounded as though it had been made in a professional studio. Because, like all software, it had an 'undo' button, there was a limit to how far you could go wrong and no limit to how much time you could take over it; it was the work of a moment to keep a copy and the person making the record could come back upstairs after dinner and keep on noodling around. The records they made would always be works in progress.

Once a craft skill is demystified by being turned into a computer program it becomes as much a way of passing the time as a means of getting things done. Thus it was with film editing and the manipulation of words and pictures, so it was with the internet, and so it became with the recording of music. Whereas in 1967 the only people in the UK in the act of making a record were people who were on some level getting paid for it, by 2007 recordings of some kind were being made in an attic in every street in the kingdom. They were made using equipment which the operator had paid for themselves. They were a hobby, a toy, in some cases a reason for living. Having invested in this kit, which was available at an affordable price, they would quite happily pay for any refinement which promised to introduce even the tiniest sprinkling of magic fairy dust such as that which a proper studio might impart.

This gamification of recording was a threat to the old established studios but it could also be an opportunity. In the early days of the new century the Abbey Road staff would be invited from time to time to get out the flip-chart and brainstorm potential money-making ideas which were consistent with the name of Abbey Road. It was following one of these meetings that an engineer suggested an idea. He didn't want to offer it up in public during the meeting for fear that the other engineers would shout him down. The engineers knew that the thousands of people sitting in their attics working/playing with Pro Tools were already buying additional pieces of software known as 'plug-ins', which were sold on the promise that they would introduce some quality associated with a record or an era that was considered cool. 'Cool' was now the all-purpose adjective of approval. 'Legendary' was the other one. These plug-ins sold better if they were associated with the cool and legendary name of either a producer or a studio. This employee's suggestion was that Abbey Road could develop and sell plug-ins under the name of what was surely the coolest and most legendary studio in the world.

Thus was born the Abbey Road Collection of plug-ins for your computer, which started by modelling the RS 124 compressor with which Norman Smith had squeezed the sound of the Beatles in 1965 and grew to include scores of different products, from the Studio 3 NX, which promised to bring the acoustics of the famed control room to your headphones, to something called Vinyl, which would make sure your new recordings had 'the vintage warmth of vinyl records played on classic turntables and needles'. These products and others like them promised to add qualities to your essentially digital recording – qualities such as 'pumpiness', 'realism' and 'grit' – that derived from that vanished physical world whence in many cases successive generations of engineers had done everything in their powers to exclude them. The long march of sound recording, which had once seemed to be heading towards a future where all would be smooth and easy, which had once been about overcoming the limitations of machines that had been big, expensive and hot to the touch, now seemed to be thrown into reverse as all the musicians in the world sat at exactly the same keyboards and vied with each other to conjure the illusion of edginess from the same machines their accountants used to do their taxes; they sought to forget for a moment the fact that they were all in their own bedrooms, from Malmö to Macclesfield, and to experience some distant echo of a sense of place in a world where it was increasingly the case that everything sounded as though it could have been done anywhere. For most of its history the music business had been about manufacturing that which you could hold in your hand. Now it was about that which you could send down a line.

There now appeared to be an additional premium on the past. During the making of the 2010 film *The King's Speech*, which concerned King George VI's efforts to conquer his stammer for the time it took to deliver the words expected of a wartime sovereign, while looking round the EMI Archive at Hayes, Abbey Road's director of engineering Peter Cobbin uncovered the actual microphones which had been used to record the King's 1939 announcement as it came down a telephone line from Windsor Castle. These were then taken to Abbey Road and painstakingly restored to working order by microphone custodian Lester Smith so that when the film's original score was recorded in Studio One it could be via one of the original microphones that had been used for the royal broadcasts. The King's Microphones inevitably began another life as digital toys in the Abbey Road Collection, where they could be used to achieve all kinds of effects, not all of them pre-war. It was even claimed that engineers loved using them to create unique guitar and synth layers. As with everything else in the collection, graphic designers were employed to make them display on a screen as though they had been ported from a Jules Verne steampunk fantasy. On the computer screen they showed up via graphics that emulated the municipal colour schemes, reassuring heft and grippable switches of the old machines, pictures that summoned vistas of vanished control rooms with walls of speakers, refinements that called up the spinning spools of entirely fictional tape recorders, an array of virtual knobs and faders which promised to put the owner at the controls of the original Abbey Road echo chambers – every element of the sometimes dangerous world of tape and solder and razors and overload reimagined as an escape from the real, the entire pulsating hyper-reality of the gaming industry brought to bear for a generation of home producers who wished to travel without ever arriving; the world of recording reborn as something you could see and live in as well as hear.

Despite all the promises to the contrary, technology rarely actually makes anything quicker. Instead it makes things more accessible, which gives the user unlimited options. One of the easiest things to access is the past. Digital photo technology allows the possibility of making the picture you take today look as though it was actually snapped on a box Brownie during the Korean War. Hip hop records which were made entirely on an Apple Mac use the surface noise from ancient shellac to lend themselves a feeling of being from a vanished world, a world moreover which the same products have, to all intents and purposes, obliterated. Now that we expect anything which might be developed in the future to be here already, the patina of the past is the one thing that bestows credibility. In the sixties there was no greater compliment you could pay than to say something was up to the minute. Now there appears to be no greater compliment you can pay anything than to describe it as 'old school'.

As in the world, so in recording. In 2007, BBC Radio Two, increasingly keen to map out a world in which both Razorlight and the Beatles could be encompassed, decided it would be an idea to get a bunch of bands like Oasis, Travis and the Kaiser Chiefs to re-record numbers from *Sgt Pepper's Lonely Hearts Club Band* using the nearest thing they could find to the original equipment (borrowed from twenty-first-century owners Mark Knopfler and Lenny Kravitz) and engaging the help of original engineers like Geoff Emerick and Richard Lush. In the present century there's a brisk trade in any vintage gear which can claim an association with the Beatles or Pink Floyd. Most of it is snapped up by wealthy musicians who like showing it to other musicians. Knowing how much of the equipment was built by EMI at Hayes in the sixties and seventies and how much of it was shipped for use in EMI-owned studios overseas, Abbey Road insiders are often sceptical of how likely it is that these faders were actually touched by those hands at this or that special time. Following decades when it seemed impossible to imagine that anyone would ever have any interest in old recording machinery there came this period when every last example of it was preserved and fetishized. However, as this episode proved, doing things the old way is rarely about the equipment.

The fact that most of the members of the bands taking part in this exercise were already considerably older than the Beatles had been at the time they made this record only served to underline how glacially slowly the world of pop moved in the twenty-first century. The Kaiser Chiefs were startled when they saw that they were going to do this on four-track. This would require a level of discipline which nothing in their recording career had prepared them for. Undaunted, they went into the studio and played 'Getting Better', which was the straw they had drawn. To their ears it sounded fine. The long faces in the control room suggested this opinion was not shared. They came back in and listened to the playback and were forced to agree. They eventually asked the film crew covering the proceedings to turn their cameras off, called a band meeting lasting two hours, then came back and spent the rest of the day working on it until they had something they were happy with. The original, unsurprisingly, sounds like the Beatles. It has the unique vocal blend of those four people. It also has some of the magic which comes from musicians trying to do something that hadn't been done. That was bound to sound better than musicians trying to do all over again something that had already been done.

The Kaiser Chiefs on this occasion just sounded like one in a million bands doing an acceptable job of sounding like the Beatles. Furthermore, they had to face the fact that when the Beatles had done it, it had been far more difficult. It was like the old line about what made Ginger Rogers a better dancer than Fred Astaire: because she had to do the same as he did but backwards and in high heels. The Kaiser Chiefs found the experience somewhat chastening. 'It's like having an elder brother,' complained their singer, not entirely jokingly. 'It's all been done.'

22

UPMIXING THE PAST AND REMIXING THE FUTURE

Kanye West was filmed at Abbey Road in 2007 with a full orchestra for his Late Registration *project.*

When time was called on Terra Firma's custody of EMI, the company which had once been proudly trumpeted as 'The Greatest Recording Organisation in the World', which had once been one of the brightest jewels in what was then known as British industry, it was not the most seemly spectacle. The end came, as ends are wont to do, slowly at first and then very, very quickly. Guy Hands had to sign EMI over to Citibank, the company that had lent him the money to buy it, and they disposed of it largely to Universal, who were by now the biggest of the handful of dogs dominating the business. European competition law meant that they in turn had to divest themselves of certain parts of the business. Therefore labels such as Parlophone and Columbia were sold on to other companies. By now record labels no longer meant what they used to mean because there were no records and hence no need for labels. Labels only meant something to people old enough to have watched those same labels revolve on a turntable.

Streaming is only the most recent of a series of technological revolutions to have been roiling the music business ever since there was a business worthy of that name. Gadgets such as the player piano, the phonograph, the radio, the jukebox, the long player, the unbreakable 45, the cassette, the Walkman, the iPhone and the MP3 have all come along in their time to briefly upset the apple cart. At each stage the apple cart has been reassembled in a slightly different shape with the emphasis in a different place. At each stage the business has taken up the new way of doing things while retaining an anachronistic attachment to the old.

In the case of EMI, a lot of the outward manifestation of the old was already passing away. One by one the features of this most archetypal of British firms, which had in its time followed the flag, set up its outposts and established its way of doing things all over the globe, were removed from view. The factory at Hayes, which at one time had provided thousands of people with jobs, was inevitably repurposed to provide almost as many with homes. The unlovely corporate HQ in Manchester Square had long gone. Its only feature of historical interest, the staircase over which the Beatles had peered in 1963 as photographer Angus McBean lay on the floor in reception, had been removed and taken to a new HQ in Hammersmith and now even that had yielded to the march of time. At the time of writing the old HMV Shop in Oxford Street, whose proud boast was once that it was the biggest record shop in the world, is dedicated to the bulk retail of candy.

In the absence of all these, the building at No. 3 Abbey Road is now the only indication of the fact that there once was such a company as EMI. And all because of a decision taken in 1969 by four young millionaires who couldn't be bothered to do anything more than step on to the zebra outside long enough for six frames to be exposed.

When the Beatles had first turned up at EMI in 1962 the one thought they would never have entertained was the notion that within the lifetime of two of them that massive company would only be remembered because of them. When they stepped on to that zebra in August 1969 even they, who had seen the world lose its sense of proportion before their very eyes, could not possibly have imagined that over fifty years later teenagers who were not born during Britpop, never mind the sixties, would make a pilgrimage to this spot to follow in their footsteps. Those seeking support for the theory that the Beatles are the exception to all the rules governing show business in general and pop music in particular are left to ponder the fact that the zebra on Abbey Road may be the most famous music-related location in the world partly because it's the only one that has not been ploughed under by the developers or placed off limits by new owners. History has not been similarly kind to the street in Greenwich Village where Bob Dylan posed with his girlfriend Suze Rotolo for the cover of *The Freewheelin' Bob Dylan*. Nobody stepped in to preserve the phone box in Heddon Street where David Bowie stood for his *Ziggy Stardust* cover picture. There isn't a classic picture of the Rolling Stones or Led Zeppelin or Queen or T. Rex or the Kinks which so confidently puts them in such a specific place and time. And yet every year, thanks to the Beatles, millions of visitors send home a snap of them and their friends or family posing in this most prosaic but comforting of English scenes, something which to them has shades of the not-quite-real London of Mary Poppins or Sherlock Holmes. The survival of Abbey Road, which appears to the casual visitor pretty much the way it looked in 1969, is a miraculous deliverance. Developers have vandalized much of London but this they have been unable to lay so much as a glove on.

When in November 2011 it was announced that EMI's recorded music interests would be sold to the French-owned company Universal it happened to be the eightieth anniversary of the opening of Abbey Road. Therefore Lucian Grainge of Universal parried the inevitable questions about its future by assuring the world 'it's very much our intention to keep the Abbey Road Studios. It is a symbol of EMI, it is a symbol of British culture, and I think it's a symbol of the creative community.'

Words like 'culture', 'creative' and 'community', which were once the domain of politicians, academics and faith leaders, were now part of the way the British music business, which was owned by overseas conglomerates, preferred to think of itself. With its illustrious history and unique standing, Abbey Road was perfectly placed to be the church where this new establishment went to enact its rituals. It was certainly the place where they placed their big bets. Recording at Abbey Road was a token of solemnity. *Ceremonials*, the second album by Florence + the Machine, Universal's great white hope, had been recorded in Studio Three in 2011 and was presented with great seriousness; parallels were drawn with not just Kate Bush but also William Shakespeare. Nobody sounded as though they were making music for a lark any more.

Producer Paul Epworth was also responsible for recording the theme for the new James Bond film *Skyfall* the following year. This was a classic case of how such projects had over the years become grave responsibilities. Adele was flattered by the invitation to be associated with a great British brand but felt that her autobiographical approach to songwriting wouldn't suit. She was reassured that this wouldn't be a problem. It took the best part of a year for this song to reach fruition. Epworth watched thirteen Bond films in an effort to crack the code of what made a successful Bond song and made a demo using Logic, which used every instrument that would be involved in the finished recording up to and including the gong. This was not a rough idea of how things would work. This was like an architectural plan. They even knew at precisely what second in the film's action the opening chord of the finished record would come in. When they recorded it in Studio One a seventy-seven-piece orchestra was conducted by American J. A. C. Redford. If you were going to do something portentous, it seemed that Abbey Road was as good a place as any to do it. Lady Gaga had made her own manifesto record 'Born This Way' in 2010. The song only took her ten minutes to come up with. The recording of that one song, however, which credits four different producers, was made in a variety of locations, one of which was Abbey Road.

As the music business continued to be roiled by forces beyond its control, the unsymbolic, doggedly practical work carried on inside. People continued to turn up and make records because that's what they loved doing. Bands came in to do the things they couldn't do in their smaller local studios. Even for those acts that worked in non-traditional ways, there had always been times when they needed to open up. Forty-two string players had been required to play the string charts Wil Malone had written for 'Unfinished Sympathy' on Massive Attack's 1991 debut album *Blue Lines*. To record them required a space big enough to house them and central enough for them all to turn up on time. The record, with its subterranean bass, its distant sampled female vocal, its oddly up-front strings and deliberately askew title, is an example of the way in which records that came out of club culture played with the listeners' expectations, mixing the rough with the smooth and always seeking to play with the focus. Bands from all kinds of traditions continued to work at Abbey Road. The French duo Air may have made the majority of their 1998 hit *Moon Safari* in Paris but they came to Abbey Road to record the strings with British veteran David Whitaker. Where there had formerly been a vogue for always using the hot new talent, there was now an increasing fondness for finding somebody from the school they knocked down to build the old school. Whitaker had done the strings on a 1965 arrangement for the Andrew Loog Oldham Orchestra that was eventually to resurface on 'Bitter Sweet Symphony' by the Verve in 1997. The musicians who played on the latter hit were some of the same who had played on Massive Attack's 'Unfinished Sympathy'. It's tempting to speculate that some of them might even have been the offspring of the people who played on the 1965 record. In all these cases they will have drawn their session fees and gone home, never to participate in the life-changing fortunes which would accrue to the people who ended up with their names among the publishing credits. The old adage about the music business, that most people in it are poorer than you might think or richer than you could possibly imagine, continues to hold good. Representatives of both groups will be found in any studio.

However, it was increasingly possible for anybody to sound rich. There had been a time when it was only the records made by the acts signed to the big companies that enjoyed the benefit of a certain level of polish. Bands signed to small indies tended to make records that sounded as though they were signed to small indies – records that seemed to have emanated from damp rooms lined with egg boxes. That had been an important element of their appeal to their core audience. It helped them sound authentic, whatever that meant. But if you needed to reach beyond your core audience it was best to sound slightly more expensive.

The Scottish group Travis, who were still called indie to denote the fact that they were neither a boy band nor a hip hop act, for such were the newly iron-clad categories into which music was being herded as the twentieth century came to a close, were signed to an independent label but recorded part of their 1999 album *The Man Who* at Abbey Road. The foundations of the record had been laid at Mike Hedges' studio in Normandy. When it came to finishing it, the point at which all the really consequential decisions as regards choice of singles, editing, track order and mixing are made, they needed to be somewhere closer to the real world and their record company. Their first surprise on arrival at Abbey Road was to discover that they couldn't smoke on the premises. This would have come as no less of a shock to all the bands who had recorded there in the past. Like every other place of work at the time the studios had had to fall in behind the societal trend towards health and safety. A patio was built outside the canteen to give people somewhere to light up.

The Man Who, with its single 'Why Does It Always Rain On Me?', was one of the last examples of the ways of the twentieth century. It sold almost three million copies in the UK, most of which were bought on CD, which was entering its twilight years as the leading physical format. The record was also done with great deliberation. When they first recorded 'Why Does It Always Rain On Me?', Mike Hedges had to put together the best bits from twenty different performances because, as the group's leader Fran Healy later confessed, 'I could never have sung it that well in one go. The energy of the band recording is four guys looking at each other thinking, "Who's going to fuck up first?"'

The sound of the finished *The Man Who*, which came into full bloom when they entered Abbey Road, with Nigel Godrich as producer, had just enough edge to satisfy the indie purists while being sufficiently gentle to sidle into any radio station playlist. 'Even I think it's one of the best records' is Healy's verdict. 'You have a producer at the top of his game, and you have a songwriter that's just been chucked. Everything coalesced in a nice way. So I'm glad it's that record that got huge.'

Back in 1990 the eighteen-year-old Godrich had written a hundred letters to studios looking for work. Because these were the last days of the old world, these were actual letters on actual paper dispatched with actual stamps. He wrote a hundred of them because that's the number of studios there were in the London area in 1990. He received a polite letter of rejection from Ken Townsend. This didn't hold him back. Within four years he was at Abbey Road working as a lowly engineer on an album called *The Bends* by Radiohead and even getting a production credit on one track. By 1999 he was again at Abbey Road as producer of *The Man Who*.

The Man Who would turn out to be one of the last records actually made on tape. For years it had been possible to arrive in a record studio and immediately set eyes on the most important piece of machinery in the control room. It was the tape operator's job to make sure that they were recording the right thing on the right tape at the right time. Nobody could make or mar a session quite so directly as the tape operator, who was usually young and hadn't had enough sleep. Even the most celebrated record producer will be able to tell the story of how they once messed up a take by pressing a button too early or too late. Back then there was no back-up, no safety net, no second chance. The tape was the final product of everybody's effort. If you wished to take your recording to a new studio you had to haul the tape with you and guard it with your life.

Come the twenty-first century, this began to change. Over the next ten years, whether eagerly or reluctantly, acts would move away from tape and began to record more and more to hard drive. They might do this via the analogue desk in the studio, but at some stage the sound would be put through a digital converter which would turn it into digital information which could be stored on the drives. It was then possible to manipulate that sound via both the desk and a DAW (digital audio workstation) such as Pro Tools. In order to restore any warmth which might be deemed to have gone missing during this somewhat antiseptic process you reached for the digital plug-ins such as those marketed under the reassuring name of Abbey Road.

Many of Abbey Road's activities in the twenty-first century have reflected this foregrounding of the symbolic nature of Abbey Road. After all, such symbols, like land, are valuable because they are no longer being manufactured. The symbolic value of the place counts for a great deal. When in 2005 Kanye West decided he wanted to re-render his album *Late Registration* with an all-female string section to make the point that hip hop deserved parity of esteem with other forms of music, he put on a big show of doing it at Abbey Road. At the time he enthused, 'Being able to spit true, heartfelt rap lyrics in front of an orchestra is juxtaposing what's thought to be two totally different forms of music . . . it shows you that it's all music. We tried to alter people's perception of the music.' On this occasion his only disappointment was that the studio door was not big enough to permit the admittance of the prop he had demanded be present for the taping – one of the world's largest mirror balls.

On another visit West was given a conducted tour, at the end of which he decided he would like Studio Three for the rest of the week. While he was there, Coldplay were recording a show for Radio Two on the premises and so Kanye left the studio and returned with Chris Martin, who ended up contributing to the track 'Homecoming', which appeared on Kanye's *Graduation* album. Mirek Stiles, who happened to be engineering on this occasion, reflected, 'If Studio Three hadn't been available that week none of it would have happened. If Kanye hadn't asked and put in the effort to warm Chris to trying something out, none of it would have happened. I guess I learned that some things are meant to be and if you don't ask you don't get. I found those sessions really inspiring.'

It was Kanye's example which brought the US hip hop collective Brockhampton to the studio in 2018. A thirteen-strong outfit who came from a completely different tradition, having formed around a Kanye online forum and ascended by means of talent contests, artful use of social media and a spirit of digital can-do, they decided that they wanted to write and record a whole album at Abbey Road in no more than ten days. This they thought would be child's play for the self-declared hardest-working boy band in the business. They announced that when in future people talked about Abbey Road they wished to be part of that conversation. 'We want people to say "Brockhampton recorded there – that's so cool".' So thoroughly did they embrace the place that they actually moved in and lived in the studio while they were making the record, sleeping under duvets in the control room and, like airline pilots in the old Soviet Union, remaining on Los Angeles time for the duration of their visit like some strange hip hop combination of the Monkees and the Grateful Dead. The album they recorded there, *Iridescence*, was a success, debuting at number one in the US album charts. It even contained one track, 'Tape', named for the vintage Studer J37 tape machine which was used to record it. The experience of recording Brockhampton was so stimulating for the younger members of the Abbey Road staff who worked with them, including runner Andy Maxwell who operated as engineer, that they rather hoped it would be repeated. Instead, in 2020 Brockhampton announced they would be taking that most modern of things, the indefinite hiatus.

When asked why they chose the place, Brockhampton mentioned the fact that Frank Ocean had recorded there, and that it had also been the place where Amy Winehouse had made her final recording in March 2011. This was a duet on 'Body And Soul' with Tony Bennett, done in the simplest fashion, which was no trouble to the old-school saloon singer but caused her great anxiety. 'She was very nervous to perform, but I said, "You know, it sounds like you're influenced by Dinah Washington." And all of a sudden, her whole life changed,' Bennett said later. 'She said, "How did you know that Dinah Washington is my goddess?" She did some Dinah Washington licks, and from that moment on, she just relaxed. And it came out wonderful. She was like, "Tony understands me, you know?"'

As the other studios were closed down and ploughed over, as many of London's favourite venues took on the alien names of sponsors, Abbey Road answered the need for approved neutral ground on which to enact ceremonies. When TV producer Michael Gleason was looking for an in-concert format for a TV series capable of tempting big-name artists and attracting wider TV distribution, he came up with the idea of *Live from Abbey Road.* This ran between 2007 and 2012 and featured the likes of the Killers, Elbow, Dr John, Dave Matthews, Ed Sheeran and Paul Simon. His plan was to do it without an audience or a presenter because he wanted to mimic, in his words, 'what happens when an artist goes into the studio'. What he should have said was that he planned to mimic what people *think* happens when an artist goes into the studio. For the artists he was offering the reassurance of being able to do TV without the drawback of TV sound. For audiences he was offering an impression of the purity of performance.

When a brand consultancy was engaged in 2015 to 'reimagine' the Abbey Road brand they decided that the studio was best known for two things. One was its being at the forefront of the latest and best in recorded sound. The other was its historic association with a handful of uniquely charismatic albums by the Beatles and Pink Floyd. This may have been underestimating the challenge because the association is deeper and wider than that. Abbey Road is revered because given a choice between magic and science, we tend to take the former every time. We believe in things happening more than we believe in the illusion of something happening. Furthermore, we believe in groups more than we believe in solo artists because we warm to the amity they represent. Our feelings about how things work in a recording studio are similar to our feelings about how things work on the training pitch at an elite football club. In both cases most of us will never be in a position to witness how this particular form of human interaction operates. In the absence of direct experience we combine our feelings about music – that it's a matter of divine spark occurring between human beings with a shared purpose – and our feelings about people – that they are at their best when they are happy and inspired – to create a picture which satisfies our need to be emotionally invested in its making. In that sense, what Abbey Road represents in its position as the best-known and, from certain angles, the last recording studio in the world is a whole way of feeling about music.

Music remains the same thing it always was. It's the records that are always changing. For most of the ninety-plus years since Abbey Road opened its doors, those records were clearly finished with once they were done. In the last twenty years powerful forces – the appetite of the pop market for endless alternative mixes of the tiniest successes, pressure from the producers of movies and video games for music they can play with, the archaeological instincts of the people who crave nothing more than a boxed set of things they have heard a million times before, and the irresistible power of whatever happens to be the latest toy – have combined to change all this.

James Clarke is a New Zealander who started working at Abbey Road as a software engineer. Because he came from this kind of background he was more prepared than most to regard everything he dealt with as scientific rather than emotional information. To that end he was talking to sound engineers in the canteen at Abbey Road one day in 2009 and asked whether it would be at all possible to take mixed recordings and, so to speak, 'demix' them. What he was wondering was whether it would be feasible to take classic records, which had been recorded on two or four tracks and then mixed down into one mono track, and in some way separate them into their constituent parts. They laughed, saying this was the Holy Grail of sound recordings and couldn't possibly be done. Once a multi-track recording had been mixed down to either a mono or stereo version there was no way of unmixing the paints. The best you could hope is that you could go back to the unmixed tapes, if such things still existed and had survived the hurly burly of corporate takeovers, and that was very unlikely. During the seventies and eighties nobody at record companies had ever thought they might be dealing with heritage assets.

James Clarke was not dissuaded. He reasoned that if an acute human ear could hear separate instruments on a recording it ought to be possible to develop a programme which could similarly separate them. He first applied his work on the proposed re-release of *The Beatles At The Hollywood Bowl*. This was a live recording that had been made in 1964 when the screaming was at its height.

Furthermore, American union restrictions meant that George Martin had no role in deciding what got recorded and how. The result was a recording that was high on excitement but low on musical value. Clarke set to work. By looking at the signal as a spectrogram he was able to visually identify the vocals, the different instruments and the screams. He could see where each fell on the spectrum. Then, by treating the screams as though they were just another instrument, he was able to reduce them in the mix. He was able to put them in the background of the mix, bring the group to the front, and change the picture the sound presented.

This was the appliance of science to the suck-it-and-see world of record production. The further he got into this new field the more he began to speak of deep learning, neural networks and non-negative matrix factorization. He set himself the task of isolating the single element that is George Harrison's Gretsch Country Gentleman from the elixir of life that is 'She Loves You'. To do this he modelled hundreds of different performances of the song in order to accurately plot the dynamics. In the course of this he discovered that once the Beatles had recorded a song they didn't stray far from it in performance. He then developed an algorithm which could read these performances and separated the original instruments into tracks, now given the medical-sounding term 'stems'. Once he had Harrison's part it took him nine months to clean it up a few seconds at a time. A piece of Roman marble unearthed on a historical site could not have been more painstakingly brought into the light. Having done this, he played it once more into Studio Two and then recorded the results as though the very air in that by now sacred room would impart some quality to it which nothing else could.

Clarke unveiled the results in the course of a lecture at Abbey Road in 2018. His audience were the kind of people who are drawn to a technical lecture at a recording studio. The reaction underlined that Beatles scholarship is now as schismatic as Judaean politics in *Life of Brian*. Some accused him of having spoiled his case by using a version of George's solo from the German-language version of 'She Loves You'. The muttering continued in a million forums.

Heavy books have been devoted to how Jane Austen wrote her novels and how Alfred Hitchcock made his films but there is seemingly no field of artistic expression which has had as much attention paid to it in the twenty-first century as the work done by the Beatles in Studio Two of the EMI Recording Studios between 1962 and 1969. Some of that attention is musical. When Ian MacDonald published his *Revolution in the Head* in 1994 his analysis of every one of the Beatles' recorded songs seemed as if it would be the last word in how the sausage was made. Given the number of Beatles books that keep on coming and the staggering amount of details they offer, it now almost seems like a primer for beginners.

The interest is not purely musical. For every would-be bass player trying to work out how Paul McCartney played the part on 'Paperback Writer' while singing at the same time it seems there is a would-be recording engineer or gear head spending time on the internet trying to find out more about the EMT 140 plate reverb and wondering how they might be able to introduce some of its qualities into the home recordings they have made in their bedroom using Pro Tools. If you want to understand just how deep and wide this fascination goes it's worth travelling to the nearest library that can afford to buy a copy of the 2006 book *Recording the Beatles*, a massive slab of a volume which comes in its own tape box. Here you will find an entire large page devoted to the EMT 140 plate reverb. Here you will find details of the firm that built the stands on which stood the monitors through which the Beatles heard 'Across The Universe' in 1968. Here, if you are so disposed, you may pore over a full-page, perfectly reproduced photograph of a Levell TG-150M crystal oscillator.

As the number of professional studios has shrunk there seems to have been a worldwide explosion in fascination with what they did. This is driven by semi-professionals through home enthusiasts to people who simply like nothing more than sitting over a laptop pretending they are Mark Ronson; what all these people want to do is come up with a cool twist on something which is old and familiar, if only for the dopamine hit provided by the appreciation of their peers. With the growth of what is now known as 'upmixing' they all get the chance to add their own fingerprint. Now that the ownership of the rights to those masters is increasingly passing into the hands of investors who need to get their money back somehow it seems reasonable to assume that some of this aimless tinkering will find a profitable outlet.

The arrival of sampling, drum machines and associated paraphernalia led to some of the most exciting records ever made, but this way of doing things doesn't have quite so much use for a full service studio. There are nothing like as many groups around today as there were in the sixties and seventies. As soon as people no longer had to have a drummer they decided to dispense with one. As soon as it was proven that you only needed two people to make a pop group, that's what most pop groups became. As soon as it was realized that you could be a solo artist and simply hire people to do your bidding and then dismiss them once that bidding was done, that became the way of the world. Records nowadays are constructed over a period of time, often from fragments of earlier records, mulled over in bedrooms, sent back and forth first on cassettes, then floppy disks and then, eventually, as emails. The romance of record-making is gone. At the same time as records are being made in a way that was unimaginable in the past, the people who are making them yearn for nothing more than the textures of the past. The culture of nostalgia and the love of toys run so deep within each new generation of musicians that, even though nowadays the sounds of all the classic drum machines are available as pieces of software, they still crave old defunct machines because they believe they are possessed of some special mojo. At the back of all this is a feeling that if it were possible to recover the technology of the time it would be possible to recapture the music of the time. To get back to where they once belonged.

At Christmas 2021, as this book was being researched, Peter Jackson's film *Get Back* was released and the world was treated to something it had never been treated to before, a genuine fly-on-the-wall view of a band in a recording studio. It depicted everything: the false starts, the disagreements, the bum notes, the technical glitches, the misunderstandings and the long periods of boredom. The studio wasn't Abbey Road. It was the studio they had commissioned in order no longer to be dependent on Abbey Road. However, in order to use it they had to call in engineers from Abbey Road. The idea of the sessions had been to see if they could make a record the way they had made the first couple of records, the first in a day, the second in not much longer. Even then, in 1969, which was a mere six years since that first record, the moment for recording in such a set-up-and-play fashion appeared to have gone. As the sixties gave way to the seventies there was the beginning of a great divergence. Pink Floyd were beginning their reckless adventures, multi-track technology was being developed that would give artists chances and second chances, drum machines were being invented that would in time replace a lot of drummers, recording projects were being embarked upon which would expand to fill the time available for them, and the simple crackle of a band playing together in the studio would be supplanted by the more deliberative approach where each member would come in, perform their part until it was done to their satisfaction, and then go home. The Beatles found it no longer quite worked to do things in the old way, which was why they shelved the release of the album until after making *Abbey Road*, a record that worked with the grain of the studio rather than against it. They had thought there was one way of recording and they had to get back to it. What turned out to be the case is that there were beginning to be many ways of recording. Now there are even more. In 1931, when Abbey Road was the first and only studio, there was really only one way of recording music. Now that it's the last studio there are a hundred different ways, and under its roof it has to provide every single one.

OUTRO: THE ROAD GOES ON FOR EVER

In his role as Abbey Road's chief creative advisor Nile Rodgers was responsible for bringing in the likes of Bruno Mars and David Guetta and also reminding the wider world of the special magic of the studio experience.

As this book was being researched and written the world was having its normal patterns of behaviour disrupted by Covid. When I visited Abbey Road at the end of April 2022 some of the staff were still working from home on certain days of the week. As was the case with all outposts of big companies – Abbey Road is owned by Universal Music – visits could only take place following a declaration of the visitor's state of health. There is no longer a commissionaire at Abbey Road but there is uniformed security and the signs, prominently displayed, make it clear that you are not encouraged to take pictures.

A hundred people work at the studios these days. The largest group are engineers but there's the inevitable layer of management, many of them with job titles that could have wandered in from any modern business where they speak of mission statements and corporate DNA. There are no longer white coats or brown coats in Abbey Road and the atmosphere is no longer as school-like as it was back in the sixties and seventies. The staff is now 25 per cent female and some of those are engineers. The boss is Isabel Garvey, whose background is in digital. She was appointed in 2014 and charged with overseeing a programme of expansion and investment. This expansion meant continuing to make the most of the studios' unique heritage while also ensuring they don't lose touch with the rising generation of digital natives who have grown up in bedrooms equipped with more firepower than would have been found in Abbey Road in its formative years. The studio had to recognize that the balance of power had tilted. Whereas the likes of the Beatles and the Shadows had to submit to a proficiency test before they could be allowed in and let loose on its expensive toys, Abbey Road now behaves as though it has realized that the boot is on the other foot and it must woo new talent to get it over its threshold. These days they even have an 'Artist Relationship Manager'.

Kohzee are three young men from the Home Counties who are here thanks to a tie-in with a commercial partner. Few things move in the music business nowadays without a sponsor. Having been identified as coming talents, Kohzee's reward is two days at Abbey Road with producer Hannah V. Those two days are not in one of the big rooms. They wouldn't have much use for them. Instead Kohzee are in the Gatehouse, a smaller studio which has been newly constructed alongside the main building, the idea being to provide a small, non-intimidating space more suited to the requirements of modern record-making. This offers what the brochure calls 'a mix of classic analogue gear and cutting edge digital audio workstation integration', which seems to suit them. Their modus operandi involves a similar mix of ancient and modern. Kohzee had brought somebody in to play bass. He plugged in and played alongside them in the control room but the sound was being played back and recorded via an amp in the studio because from there it would sound better. There is a traditional Neve recording console in the control room with a reassuring array of sixteen faders but Hannah, whose website announces her as 'a pioneer in a new generation of entrepreneurial female producer/songwriters', seems to be doing most of the work at a small laptop. As she makes her minute incisions in the waveform that is the song they are working on, the group sit around trying to look involved. She's accustomed to having a group wishing to spend most of their time in the control room rather than on the studio floor because, as she says, 'some people like the privacy of the studio, some people prefer the hang of being in here'.

The second small space opened in recent years is the Front Room, formerly part of Studio Three – and long before that the listening rooms for the classical department, and before that somebody's living room – which has now been designed for smaller-scale set-ups and suits the collaborative writing sessions which are so much a part of the way records are built in an era when it is not uncommon to see as many as half a dozen writers credited on a hit. Some of these sessions were convened by Nile Rodgers during his tenure as Abbey Road's chief creative adviser, a role which was at least partially ambassadorial. Rodgers, whose third age has seen his reinvention as everybody's favourite musician, has been responsible for not only bringing the likes of Bruno Mars and David Guetta into the studio but also letting people know about it. Even the last full service studio in town, even one that cannot go anywhere without being formally preceded by the adjective 'legendary', needs to let a widening world know that it is open for business, and new business is the best business of all.

Studio Three is closed for its first major refurbishment since 1988. At the same time the management have taken steps to make the services the studio provides accessible to those beyond the building and even beyond the mainstream of the professional music business via their Production Hub. This can be accessed online. The services it offers extend from the usual tips and tricks you can adapt to make your recording sound better to channels through which you can have your own recording mastered at Abbey Road.

Mastering is now a bigger part of the business than ever. Mastering is the final stage in the process of recording. Mastering provides the last opportunity to change the sound of something before it goes out into the wider world. Today's customers have included

French Kiwi Juice, Pigs Pigs Pigs Pigs Pigs Pigs Pigs, the Snuts, James Yorkston and Nina Persson, Belle & Sebastian and Cymande. Abbey Road's senior mastering engineer, Geoff Pesche, operates in a room at the top of the building, a room built on a floating floor, a room which has undergone every form of treatment to ensure that it is the very best place to audition music. Over to one side of Geoff's mighty console is the forty-year-old Neumann cutting lathe, the heavy precise machine which was used to master a record when that had to mean vinyl.

Vinyl was the standard way of working when Geoff entered the business. Over time the lathe fell into only occasional use as the CD took over the market. Now the majority of the work Geoff does is in the preparation of mixes for streaming or download. Fewer and fewer people bother having their music mastered for CD. It's only records with a middle-aged market where they still have the players, apparently. However, cutting for vinyl is once again a significant part of the work. If you'd told him this twenty years ago, says Geoff, he would have laughed at you. At the same time he can't help wondering what will happen to vinyl when the last lathe gives up the ghost and the handful of people on the planet who know how to maintain them die off. There is, he tells me, now only one factory in the world making the blanks engineers like him use to cut vinyl records. The Chinese can't do it, he says. They don't think it's worth the investment. 'Vinyl's hanging by a thread' is how he puts it. There's a thought which should send a shiver through Shoreditch.

Sitting in front of speakers so enormous that they will reveal the detail which may not have been apparent elsewhere, and happily untrammelled by the direct experience of having been involved in getting it this far, Geoff auditions the music, which may be thrash metal or Katherine Jenkins, decides whether it needs more bass or more treble, judges whether he can use his forty years of experience to beneficially boost certain elements of the sound picture, and then, having done so, puts it in the proper form to send it down the line to the people who keep the streaming services supplied. His clients used to leave with an acetate disc of their new record. Since this could only be played a few times before it wore out this was the single most exciting thing anyone could ever walk out of a building with. Nowadays they leave with nothing more than Geoff's assurance that he has done his best. Nevertheless, he reckons 50 per cent of his job is technical; the rest is knowing how to strike up relationships with the people who have nervously entrusted to his care work they consider the most important thing they have done in their lives. There's a lot to be said for doing it the new way. On the occasions when he can't do anything about something he might call the person who mixed it, they might fire up their Pro Tools file, adjust the vocal minutely, and then email it back to him. Back in the day, he says, somebody might have had to go back into the studio, having first thrown the Rolling Stones out, and do it again. It could have taken weeks. Now it's ten minutes.

A few years ago, all Geoff's clients were demanding that their track sound louder than everybody else's in the hope it would punch through on the radio. They were wasting their time, he says, because radio stations have limiters to bring the quiet ones up and take the loud ones down. These days the streaming companies impose similar limits. Now clients just want it to sound as good as it can sound. They come to him because, thanks to the old pieces of 1970s kit which sit in slots on Geoff's console, Abbey Road offers the clearest signal path. He doesn't need to boast about the fact that he was the guy who mastered New Order's 'Blue Monday' in 1983, which became the biggest-selling twelve-inch single of all time. Thanks to the internet they already know. Indeed, so febrile is the world of recording nerds on the internet they send him emails asking what was the signal path he used on a particular William Orbit track from 1998.

In the last few years the internet has made it possible for Abbey Road to access a wider customer base, which goes beyond the UK and also beyond the professionals. Geoff's coming in this weekend to do an album that has been sent by somebody in Mumbai. The last job he's got on the day we're speaking is a single for somebody who is probably, he reckons, a singing dentist. Lots of people still want to make a CD to have something to show for their ten thousand hours of practice. They send in their work, pay their £90, and get to say their record was mastered at Abbey Road. What they want, Geoff says, is the interaction with somebody at Abbey Road. If they're not happy with what is sent to them they can ask for it to be done again. That's all priced in. It's a good business. 'They're dropping into the inbox as we speak. It's been an absolute revelation.'

Geoff has been here long enough to have seen people with tears in their eyes because they never believed they would get to be on the inside of Abbey Road. Covid has recently reduced the number of clients accompanying their work to his studio and also finally broken the resistance of those who refused to work remotely. It further accelerated the trend to worldwide working. In 2021 Abbey Road acquired a company called Audiomovers, a startup begun by two Ukrainians who had developed software that promised to facilitate remote audio collaboration in real time and in lossless quality. What this means in practice is that musicians and producers all over the world could be looking at the same mix, hearing it in the same quality, and being able to see and speak to each other without the slight delay known as latency, the little gaps which make the whole experience seem marginally unreal. A hundred dollars a year will get you a subscription. The incubator operation known as Abbey Road Red recognizes the fact that innovation is as likely to come from outside the studio as from within and is always looking to work with the brightest minds in the worldwide community of boffins, the kind of people who might be developing technologies which will one day be standard in the recording business.

The future of Abbey Road is no longer tethered to that of the music business as it might have been in the past. In the summer of 2018 the London Symphony Orchestra and the Bach Choir of London was in Studio One for four whole weeks recording a complex score written by Englishman Stephen Barton and American Gordy Haab. This was not intended for the concert hall. It was not for a movie or television series. It was for the video game *Star Wars Jedi: Fallen Order*. Such games now command retail prices that are far ahead of what most people would spend on recorded music and therefore they increasingly have music budgets matching those of major motion pictures. Because games players are seeking just the same level of immersion that was formerly sought by those people who bought *Meddle* in 1971, the music people who provide the soundscapes for games are in the vanguard of moves to develop technologies such as those that fall under the umbrella of spatial audio. This, as far as Abbey Road is concerned, is 'anything beyond stereo' and can include Dolby Atmos, 5.1 Surround Sound, ambisonics and other technologies that mean little to the person in the street. Maybe this time it will be different. Nobody says it aloud, but there is a feeling that the take-up of wireless technology within the home means that spatial audio may not face the same 'over my dead body' objections as were placed in the way of quadraphonic.

At the moment it's the games people, always keen to enhance the feeling of 'player agency' by having sounds seeming to emanate from particular places, who are leading this charge. They are the ones playing with new microphone arrays, ambisonic microphones, and even shuffling the positioning of different instruments in the orchestra. They are the ones looking to use soundbar and headphone technology to replace the standard stereo idea of recorded music, which is all about width, with an expanded sense of space within a recording. Barton is a member of the Abbey Road Spatial Audio forum so it's not surprising he thinks it's the future of listening. 'When spatial audio is done well, it's like the walls of the listening space, or the headphones, drop away completely – and the emotional effect of that is absurdly powerful.' I can't help thinking they're going to have to come up with a better name.

You can't imagine Noel Gallagher talking about spatial audio. On the day I was there in April 2022 he was in the control room of Studio Two with engineer Paul Pritchard, a fifteen-year veteran of Abbey Road who has worked with Wolf Alice, Elton John and Glass Animals. Down below, a string section were adding their parts to the last of five tracks on his next album. He had done the basic tracks for this record at his own studio but that wasn't big enough to accommodate a string section plus conductor, and besides, as he freely admits, he'll take any excuse to be in Studio Two at Abbey Road. He is a devoted believer in the magic of rooms. 'If you're doing strings in that room, it sounds like the Beatles. I don't care what anyone says. I've recorded at Abbey Road before and it's a good vibe but there's just something about doing strings in there. When you're down there in the room with the players themselves and the sound fills the room it stirs the soul like nowhere else. There's just something magical about this place. I don't think it's just the canteen.'

Today he has string players coming in for the morning session followed by brass in the afternoon. The percussionists will be in at the weekend. There's a certain form to all this. He has met the arrangers and conductors beforehand, so when the musicians come in the time can be used as efficiently as possible. 'They start on the dot of eleven and they finish on the dot of two for lunch. Then there's a session from three to six, and at six they're out of the door even if you're in the middle of a song. I like it because it adds a discipline. There's a hierarchy as well. I talk to the string arranger, who talks to the conductor, who talks to the musicians. Rock and roll can be a bit loose sometimes.'

There are a dozen people in the control room: producers, engineers, arrangers, managers, mates. He finds that increasingly these days he's the only person actually looking in the direction of the speakers while listening back. Everybody else is staring at the glowing screen of some computer.

'A lot of music is made by committee nowadays. I'm an independent artist. The whole thing lives or dies by my decisions. In the major record labels you have twenty people listening to a tune and twenty opinions. That's the thing that's crept into the music business over the last twenty years – music being made by committee. I was at an awards ceremony with Ray Davies and eight people got up to receive some award for the record of the year. We were looking at each other and thinking, what do they all do? I can't be in a room with eight people. I'd kill seven of them.'

However, he concedes, there's no point fighting the digital audio work station. That's the industry standard, so that's the way he works. He's got a few items of vintage gear at his studio, just like the bulky items of hardware that can be found in every spare inch of Abbey Road, waiting to be thrown away when somebody gets up the nerve, but, he says, it's difficult to get the tape, and anyway they tend to keep breaking down. The thing he really likes about the studio process is being with people.

There are, he says, three parts to the life of a music-making man. 'There's the writing and demoing, which tends to be solitary. There's the preparing for playing live. In between there's the recording. This is what I regard as the real work. This is the kind of work we all love. It's making something from nothing. It's the most satisfying because it involves other people. It's only when other people come in and put their twist on it that it lives. My demos are great but they sound like me. In the studio, whatever you do turns into a collective effort.'

He's also a believer in a sense of place. He remembers first driving down Abbey Road when he was a mere roadie and seeing that the building at No. 3 was actually real. Then he started having hits and asked his management if he could afford a house down Abbey Road. They said no. Then he had lots of hits and then he could afford to buy a house just round the corner. The first time he came to this particular control room was in 1995 when he was taking part in that charity recording of 'Come Together', and there was Paul McCartney. 'You think you know Beatles songs but you only know them the way you play them. He was showing me the proper way. We were in here. I was sitting there with my guitar and trying to pay attention while all the time I couldn't help thinking there was one bead of sweat slowly running down to the end of my nose.'

There's a Forth Bridge element to the recording and re-recording of pop music these days. In the age of streaming an increasing proportion of our listening is directed towards the back catalogue rather than the new thing. The first challenge for acts putting out anything new is to wrest their fans' attention from the things they have already done. In addition, there's always a new format. Today in the Penthouse Suite they're doing a Dolby Atmos mix of Florence + the Machine's album, which was recorded in Studio Three back in 2011 – eleven years ago, which is a longer interval than the entire recording career of the Beatles.

For much of its history the narrative of Abbey Road could be retained in the memories of a small number of senior people. When Ken Townsend joined after the war he was still working with a few people who had been there from the beginning. Those who joined in the 1990s might have been working with Ken. As the studio approaches its centenary that link with the past is increasingly difficult to maintain. Thinking about its place in history is just part of the job of Mirek Stiles, who started in 1998 as an engineer and now, as Head of Audio Projects, is charged with developing hardware and software based on the studio's heritage. That has involved a lot of journeys through the past, which are rarely as straightforward as one might think.

In the fifties and sixties every recording session at Abbey Road would generate paperwork. EMI was a traditional company, and this is how traditional companies functioned. They had typists. They had carbon paper. The paperwork might include the so-called red forms via which the label bosses at Manchester Square would stipulate the songs to be recorded and the budget which had been assigned. Then there would be the session sheets, which were filled in by the engineer. These had a space in which they could add a child-like plan of where all the various instrumentalists and vocalists had been positioned. The leading performer would be named on the sheet, as would the producer supervising the session, but no record would be kept of who played guitar or second violin. This was strictly between them, the Musicians' Union and their accountants.

In the seventies and eighties sessions became longer and were less likely to be regimented, often because that was the way the band preferred it. They were working the way they wanted to work, rather than at the direction of a form from head office. Session sheets might still be filled in but they weren't always filed afterwards in the way they might have been in the past. An increasing number of the studios' clients were from outside the EMI umbrella and therefore it didn't seem to be the studios' business to impose any of their bureaucracy on them. As long as people got paid, the staff were increasingly relaxed about doing the paperwork. The old system of job bags and job numbers began to loosen.

From the nineties onwards, all the communication between record companies and studios became digital. This meant it grew exponentially and at a speed far in advance of any system's efforts to keep it organized. Anybody in the business of archives will tell you that it is far easier to keep track of paper than to keep track of digital information when you're at the mercy of the shifting sands of computer retrieval systems. They will also tell you that less than 1 per cent of the archival material you hold will attract more than 99 per cent of the interest from researchers. Hence the authors of that giant tome *Recording the Beatles* spent years going through every single piece of paper they could find about what that group did in the studio, but it's perfectly possible that what, for instance, Jeff Beck was doing in the studio at the same time has been lost to all but the imperfect memories of those who were there and happen still to be alive.

This paperwork may have been lost entirely or it may be sitting in one of the innumerable boxes at the EMI Archive Trust that are marked 'Abbey Road', the contents of which may be imperfectly sorted into years. Like people whose attempts to tidy the possessions in their home inevitably fall victim to the human tendency to linger over an old photograph or a swimming certificate, Abbey Road staff occasionally find the paper trail leading to a session they were unaware of ever having taken place in the studio and they get side-tracked into the kind of reverie which always awaits those who have a head full of music.

One such case happened recently when a researcher turned up a piece of paper indicating that on the evening of 21 May 1968 a session had taken place in Studio Two which had called for a twenty-three-piece ensemble at a total cost of £158. The session was overseen by John Burgess, who had in his time been responsible for recording Manfred Mann and Freddie and the Dreamers. We must assume that the composer of the music, Krzysztof Komeda, was on hand to direct the musicians who had been assembled at such significant expense. The singer, who had never made a record before, was the actress Mia Farrow. The song, 'Sleep Safe And Warm', was a lullaby which would be rendered eerie for all eternity by its use over the opening titles of the 1968 film *Rosemary's Baby*.

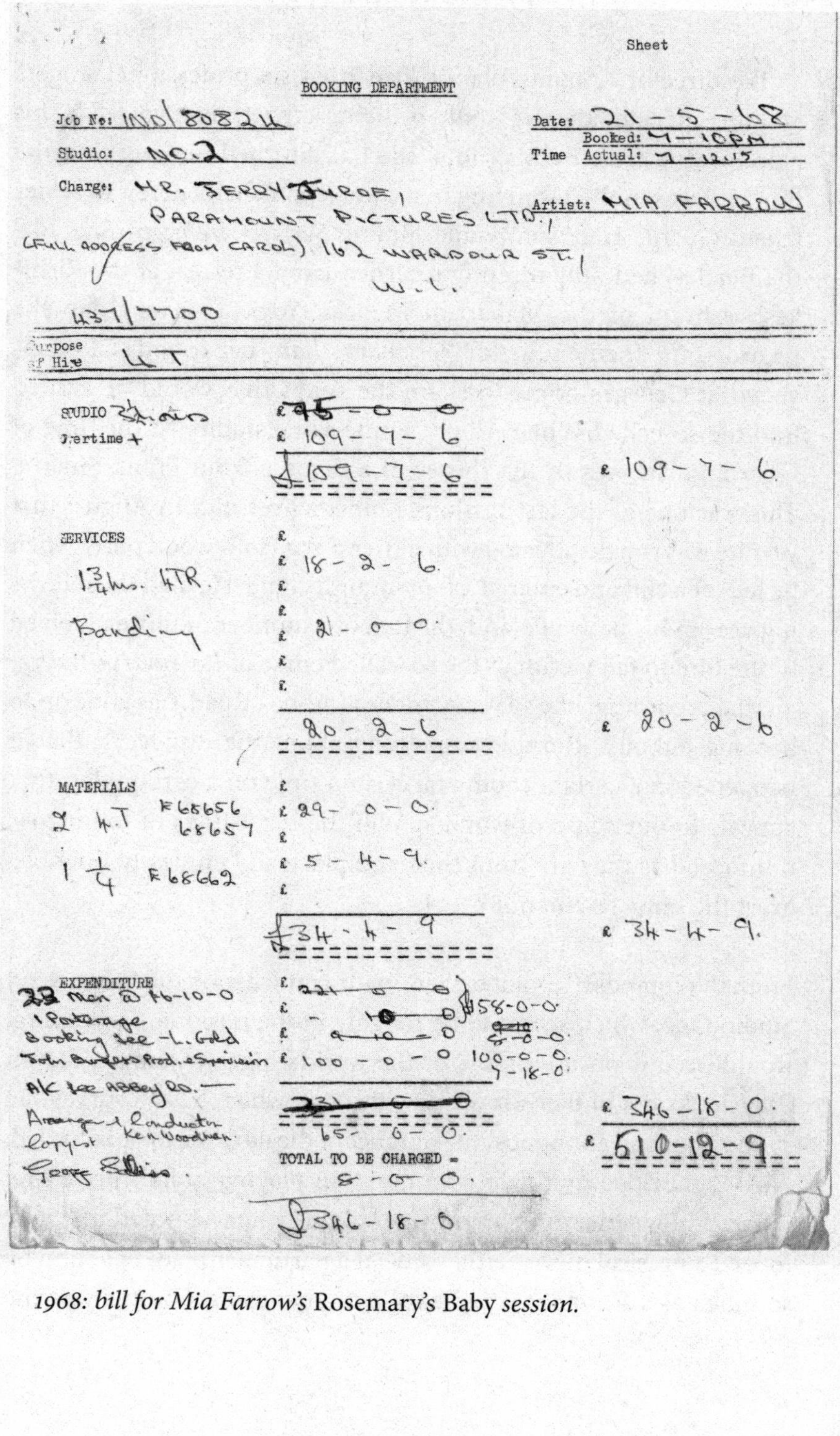

Sheet

BOOKING DEPARTMENT

Job No: 100/80824 | Date: 21-5-68

Studio: NO.2 | Time Booked: 4-10PM | Actual: 7-12.15

Charge: MR. JERRY BURGE, PARAMOUNT PICTURES LTD., (FULL ADDRESS FROM CAROL) 162 WARDOUR ST., W.1.

437/7700

Artist: MIA FARROW

Purpose of Hire: 4T

STUDIO 3½ hours £ ~~75-0-0~~
Overtime + £ 109-7-6
£109-7-6 | £ 109-7-6

SERVICES
1¾ hrs. 4TR. £ 18-2-6
Banding £ 2-0-0
20-2-6 | £ 20-2-6

MATERIALS
2 4.T E68656 68657 £ 29-0-0
1 ¼ E68662 £ 5-4-9
£34-4-9 | £ 34-4-9

EXPENDITURE
23 Men @ £6-10-0 £ ~~221-0-0~~
1 Porterage £ ~~10-0~~ } £58-0-0
Booking fee - L. Gold £ ~~9-10-0~~ 8-0-0
John Burgess Prod. & Supervision £ 100-0-0 100-0-0
AK fee ABBEY RD. — 7-18-0
Arranger & Conductor Ken Woodman
Copyist
Geoff Sellers
~~231-0-0~~
65-0-0 | £ 346-18-0
TOTAL TO BE CHARGED = 8-0-0 | £ 610-12-9
£346-18-0

1968: *bill for Mia Farrow's* Rosemary's Baby *session.*

The director Roman Polanski had tried six professional singers and then decided that he would be better off getting it voiced by his elfin leading lady. By May 1968 she had finished her work on the film and was in the UK living in a cottage in Esher, Surrey, near her friend George Harrison, while filming *Secret Ceremony*. She, like the Beatles, had only recently returned from a retreat at the Rishikesh ashram of the Maharishi Mahesh Yogi. The very day she recorded the theme tune for *Rosemary's Baby* her friends had convened at George's home to share the songs that would be turned into the so-called White Album in the same studio. At the time of recording she was in the throes of a divorce from Frank Sinatra. This was one of the last sessions Komeda ever did. In August that year he was rough-housing with a friend at a Hollywood party when he fell off a cliff and entered a four-month coma. He died the following year in his native Poland, the first of a number of those involved in the film to fall victim to the so-called curse of *Rosemary's Baby*.

That recording, like so many made at Abbey Road, has gone on to become famous. There is something about the discovery, that it happened in a certain room at a certain time on a certain day, that appeals to our sense of wonder. Will the recordings of tomorrow, unmoored as they are from time and place and endlessly fungible, exert the same fascination?

From the composer's point of view in the control room of Abbey Road Studio One, which seems to be roughly in the position the Admiral would occupy on the bridge of the world's biggest warship, Steven Price looks out of the vast window through which he can survey the studio floor and announces the number of the next cue to be recorded.

A Cambridge graduate who grew up playing guitar, Price first realized how powerful film music could be when he noted that if he moved a musical phrase either side of a particular piece of action by so much as a second it could have a dramatic effect on the way the viewer interpreted the story. He learned his trade as a music editor on the *Lord of the Rings* series at Abbey Road. This is a job which calls for the ability to keep track of the bewildering number of tiny cues that make up a film's score and then shepherd them all on the many gruelling stages through which a major motion picture must travel on its way to the screen. Now that he's the composer, having won an Oscar for *Gravity*, he gets to sit in the big chair. He works with his own music editor, one of the team alongside him in Studio One, each poring over their scores, agonizing about 'trems' and 'dims', turning over vast pages of manuscript paper as each bit is completed to their satisfaction and keeping an eye on what they have to do in the next half an hour as a huge orchestra works its way through the cues of music for a film called *Beast*.

'It's Idris Elba chased by lions' is Steven's cheerful summary.

Actually, it isn't yet. What we're seeing in the studio as the musicians play is a combination of footage featuring the aforesaid actor which has already been shot on the African savannah together with placeholder animations into which computer-generated images will eventually go. As the musicians play, on the screen above the control window there first appears Idris, then a lion, then a crash test dummy version of Idris, then a graphic lion, and at one point the lion gets on top of Idris and commences to gnaw his throat in a manner that is clearly going to be quite alarming in the cinema. In its present unfinished state, of course, everything is faintly ludicrous. Everything, that is, except the music, which in this context, live on the other side of that glass, picked up by the world's most sensitive microphones and conveyed into our presence through speakers which are not simply massive but also unbelievably strong on detail, is bigger than any live performance could ever be. This is live music on stilts.

Price, whose first proper job was at Abbey Road, has great affection for the place and Studio One in particular. His declared ambition when making this music is to 'make the sound go all over the room'. For this he relies on the input of engineer John Barrett, who in his eighteen years at the studio has worked with everyone from Jonny Greenwood to Frank Ocean. Film insurance being what it is, the musicians on the other side of the glass on this day are all wearing masks when they resume their places following a break. When Steven tells the conductor what cue they're going to play next there comes the sound of forty-two musicians turning the pages on their scores, a sound which, when relayed by all these high-quality microphones perfectly positioned to capture the notes produced by each player and sensitive enough to pick up a sheep clearing its throat on a distant mountainside, makes for an unforgettable, haunting susurration. It's via this that you can detect the preternatural liveness of the unique space beyond the glass and the peculiar magic of its three-second reverb time. Apparently Arturo Toscanini walked out in 1935 because he thought the sound was too dry, which meant his orchestra didn't sound exciting enough. He ought to come back now.

It's Friday evening. 'Now that the producer and director have gone home it's a bit of a Friday night mood,' Steven says. There's certainly food around but no drink. No relaxation. There's too much to get through. They'll be here all evening.

I leave them to it and wander out into Abbey Road. London is still not fully awake from its years of Covid. Tourism has yet to recover. Nevertheless it's a lovely evening, and as I make for the station the first teenagers of spring are gathering, waiting their turn on the zebra crossing.

Playlist

Fifty notable recordings made at Abbey Road.

Paul Robeson
'Rockin' Chair'
1931

Yehudi Menuhin and the London Symphony Orchestra (conducted by Sir Edward Elgar)
Elgar's Violin Concerto in B minor
1932

Ray Noble and his orchestra (with Al Bowlly)
'Midnight, The Stars And You'
1934

Pablo Casals
Six Suites for Cello Solo by J. S. Bach
1936

Noël Coward
'Could You Please Oblige Us With A Bren Gun?'
1941

Cliff Richard and the Shadows
'Move It!'
1958

Peter Sellers
Songs For Swingin' Sellers
1959

PLAYLIST

The Shadows
'Wonderful Land'
1962

Bernard Cribbins
'Right Said Fred'
1962

The Beatles
'Twist And Shout'
1963

The Hollies
'I'm Alive'
1965

Cilla Black
'Alfie'
1966

Matt Monro
'Born Free'
1966

Donovan
'Sunshine Superman'
1966

The Beatles
'Strawberry Fields Forever'/'Penny Lane'
1967

Jake Thackray
The Last Will and Testament of Jake Thackray
1967

Pink Floyd
'Interstellar Overdrive'
1967

The Zombies
'Time Of The Season'
1967

Jacqueline du Pré and Daniel Barenboim
Schumann Cello Concerto in A minor
1968

Procol Harum
A Salty Dog
1969

The Beatles
Abbey Road
1969

Fela Ransome-Kuti and the Africa '70
Afrodisiac
1971

PLAYLIST

Pink Floyd
The Dark Side Of The Moon
1973

Roy Harper and the Grimethorpe Colliery Band
'When An Old Cricketer Leaves The Crease'
1975

Pink Floyd
'Shine On You Crazy Diamond'
1975

Steve Harley and Cockney Rebel
'Make Me Smile (Come Up And See Me)'
1975

Be-Bop Deluxe
'Ships In The Night'
1976

Magazine
'The Light Pours Out Of Me'
1978

Kate Bush
'Babooshka'
1980

John Williams
'The Indiana Jones Theme'
1981

Dexys Midnight Runners
'Plan B'
1981

Kate Capshaw
'Anything Goes' (from *Indiana Jones and the Temple of Doom*)
1984

Rush
'Manhattan Project'
1985

Paul Simon and Ladysmith Black Mambazo
'Homeless'
1986

The Fall
Bend Sinister
1986

Basil Poledouris
RoboCop soundtrack
1987

PLAYLIST

Ryuichi Sakamoto
The Last Emperor soundtrack
1987

David Bowie
'Absolute Beginners'
1988

Nick Cave and Shane MacGowan
'What A Wonderful World '
1992

Radiohead
'Sulk'
1994

Travis
The Man Who
1999

Kanye West and Chris Martin
'Homecoming'
2007

Sigur Rós
'Ára Bátur'
2008

Lady Gaga
'Born This Way'
2011

Amy Winehouse and Tony Bennett
'Body And Soul'
2011

Adele
'Skyfall'
2012

Frank Ocean
'White Ferrari'
2016

Noel Gallagher's High-Flying Birds
'Go Let It Out'
2018

Brockhampton
'New Orleans'
2018

Taron Egerton
Rocketman soundtrack
2019

Bibliography

Andry, Peter, *Inside the Recording Studio* (Scarecrow Press, 2008)

Audissino, Emilio, *John Williams' Film Music* (University of Wisconsin, 2014)

Baade, Christina L., *Victory Through Harmony: The BBC and Popular Music in World War II* (Oxford University Press, 2012)

Bret, David, *The Real Gracie Fields* (Robson Books, 1998)

Burgess, Richard, *The History of Music Production* (Oxford University Press, 2014)

Butcher, Geoffrey, *Next to a Letter from Home: Major Glenn Miller's Wartime Band* (Transworld, 1987)

Chanan, Michael, *Repeated Takes: A Short History of Recording and Its Effects on Music* (Verso, 1995)

Cooke, Mervyn, *A History of Film Music* (Cambridge University Press, 2008)

Emerick, Geoff, *Here, There and Everywhere: My Life Recording the Beatles* (Gotham Books, 2007)

Fiegel, Eddi, *John Barry: A Sixties Theme from James Bond to Midnight Cowboy* (Pan Macmillan, 2001)

Forde, Eamonn, *The Final Days of EMI: Selling the Pig* (Omnibus, 2017)

Friedwald, Will, *A Biographical Guide to the Great Jazz and Pop Singers* (Random House, 2010)

BIBLIOGRAPHY

Gelatt, Roland, *The Fabulous Phonograph* (Littlehampton Book Services, 1956)

Giddins, Gary, *Bing Crosby: A Pocketful of Dreams* (Little, Brown, 2003)

Graves, Charles, *Champagne and Chandeliers: The Story of the Café de Paris* (Odhams, 1958)

Grubb, Suvi Raj, *Music Makers on Record* (Penguin, 1986)

Kaye, Lenny, *You Call It Madness: The Sensuous Song of the Croon* (Villard, 2004)

Legge, Walter, *On and Off the Record* (Faber & Faber, 1982)

Leigh, Spencer, *Halfway to Paradise* (Finbarr International, 1996)

Leonard, Geoff, *John Barry* (Sansom & Co., 1998)

Leyshon, Andrew, *Sites of Sound: Recording Studios and the Music Economy* (University of Nottingham, 2006)

Martin, George, *All You Need Is Ears* (Griffin, 1994)

Martland, Peter, *Since Records Began: EMI – The First 100 Years* (Batsford, 1997)

Mason, Nick, *Inside Out: A Personal History of Pink Floyd* (Weidenfeld & Nicolson, 2005)

Menuhin, Yehudi, *Unfinished Journey* (Futura, 1978)

Milner, Greg, *Perfecting Sound Forever* (Farrar, Straus and Giroux, 2010)

Moore, Jerrold Northrop, *A Voice in Time: The Gramophone of Fred Gaisberg* (Hamish Hamilton, 1976)

Morley, Sheridan, *A Talent to Amuse: A Life of Noël Coward* (Dean Street Press, 1969)

Read, Mike, *Cliff Richard: The Complete Chronicle* (Octopus, 1995)

Rust, Brian, *British Dance Bands on Record 1911 to 1945* (General Gramophone Publications Ltd, 1987)

Ryan, Kevin, and Kehew, Brian *Recording the Beatles* (Curvebender, 2006)

Scott, Ken, *Abbey Road to Ziggy Stardust* (Alfred Publishing Co., 2012)

Seabrook, John, *The Song Machine* (Random House, 2015)

Shankar, Ravi, *My Music, My Life* (Mandala, 2008)

Shipton, Alyn, *A New History of Jazz* (Continuum, 2001)

Sikov, Ed, *Mr Strangelove: A Biography of Peter Sellers* (Pan Macmillan, 2003)

Southall, Brian, *Abbey Road* (Omnibus, 2009)

Southall, Brian, *The Rise and Fall of EMI Records* (Omnibus, 2012)

Swann, Donald, *The Space Between Bars* (Hodder & Stoughton, 1972)

Thompson, Gordon, *Please Please Me: Sixties British Pop Inside Out* (Oxford University Press, 2008)

Thomson, Graeme, *Under the Ivy: The Life and Music of Kate Bush* (Omnibus, 2010)

Williams, John L., *Miss Shirley Bassey* (Quercus, 2010)

Wilson, Elizabeth, *Jacqueline du Pré* (Arcade, 2008)

Womack, Kenneth, *Sound Pictures: The Life of George Martin* (Orphans, 2016)

Sources

Lyrics on p.47: Noël Coward, 'I Went To A Marvellous Party' ('quite for no reason I'm here for the season') – performer Noël Coward, lyrics Noël Coward

Lyrics on p.52: George Formby, 'My Little Stick Of Blackpool Rock' ('it may be sticky but I never complain / it's nice to have a nibble every now and again') – performer George Formby, lyrics Harry Gifford and Fred Cliffe

Lyrics on p.77: Cliff Richard and the Drifters, 'Schoolboy Crush' ('At the candy shop, at the record house' / 'Or the drive-in show') – performer Cliff Richard and the Drifters, lyrics Aaron Schroeder and Sharon Silbert

Lyrics on p.123: the Beatles, 'Penny Lane' ('And the fireman rushes in') – performer the Beatles, lyrics John Winston Lennon and Paul James McCartney

Lyrics on p.217: Pink Floyd, 'Shine On You Crazy Diamond' ('When you were young, you shone like the sun') – performer Pink Floyd, lyrics David Jon Gilmour / George Roger Waters / Richard William Wright

Lyrics on p.262: Kate Bush, 'Moments Of Pleasure' ('spinning in the chair at Abbey Road') – performer Kate Bush, lyrics Kate Bush

Acknowledgements

From Abbey Road:

Thank you, David, for your passion and commitment to uncovering the tales and magic behind our walls with not only incredible detail, but great wit.

We would like to thank the Abbey Road Studios family past and present, in particular Isabel Garvey, Mark Robertson, Mirek Stiles, Cameron Colbeck, Jack Lintorn, Ken Townsend, Norman Smith, Hazel Yarwood, Sir George Martin, Alan Parsons OBE, Jeff Jarratt, Suvi Raj Grubb, Geoff Emerick, Peter Mew, Malcolm Addey, Peter Vince, Peter Bown, Geoff Pesche, John Barrett and Paul Pritchard.

The Abbey Road story comes to life through the countless artists, musicians, composers, engineers, producers and creatives who work within our walls. Our thanks go to everyone who has stepped inside the doors and shared the privilege of their music with us. For this book, our special thanks go to Paul McCartney, Steven Price, Noel Gallagher, Giles Martin, Adam Sharp, Bobby Elliott, Mary McCartney, Graham Hicks, Roy Harper, Hannah V, Steve Harley, Ringo Starr, Frank Ocean, Brockhampton, Fran Healy and Travis, Kat Killingley and Jill Furmanovsky.

We are grateful to everyone who has helped us research and

explore our archives over the decades, with special thanks to Jackie Bishop, Kate Calloway, Caryn Tomlinson, Joanna Hughes and Archie Ahern at the EMI Archive Trust and Naomi Larsson. At Universal Music, our thanks go to David Joseph, David Sharpe, Adam Barker, Dominic Jones and Guy Hayden. At Penguin Random House, our thanks to Bill Scott-Kerr, Eloisa Clegg, Graham Sim and Phil Lord.

We would also like to thank the team at Apple Corps for permission to include images of the Beatles at Abbey Road: Jeff Jones, Jonathan Clyde and Aaron Bremner. Additional thanks to Warner Music UK, Sony Music UK and Disney UK.

From the author:

I would like to thank my agent, Charlie Viney, and all the Abbey Road people past and present.

Picture Acknowledgements

Although every effort has been made to trace copyright holders and clear permission for the photographs in this book, the provenance of a number of them is uncertain. The author and publisher would welcome the opportunity to correct any mistakes.

First picture section

Page 1: [top] House purchase, estate agent particulars: courtesy EMI Archive Trust
Page 1: [bottom] House, 1931: courtesy EMI Archive Trust
Page 2: [top] Sir Edward Elgar and Yehudi Menuhin: courtesy EMI Archive Trust
Page 2: [bottom] Billy Cotton: courtesy EMI Archive Trust
Page 3: [top] Alan Blumlein: courtesy EMI Archive Trust
Page 3: [bottom] Igor Stravinsky: courtesy EMI Archive Trust
Page 4: [top] Jack Hylton: courtesy EMI Archive Trust
Page 4: [bottom] Edward Chick Fowler: courtesy EMI Archive Trust
Page 5: [top left] Gracie Fields: courtesy EMI Archive Trust
Page 5: [top right] Fats Waller: courtesy EMI Archive Trust
Page 5: [bottom] Glenn Miller and Dinah Shore: courtesy EMI Archive Trust
Page 6: Sir Thomas Beecham illustration: courtesy EMI Archive Trust
Page 7: [top left] *Song for Swingin' Sellers*: © Warner Music Group

Page 7: [top right] Peter Sellers and Irene Handl: © UMG Archive
Page 7: [bottom] Cliff Richard and the Shadows: © UMG Archive
Page 8: [top left] 'From Me To You' sessions: © UMG Archive
Page 8: [top right] Beatles in control room: © UMG Archive
Page 8: [bottom left] Paul McCartney, Norman Smith and George Martin: © Peter Tauber
Page 8: [bottom right] Geoff Emerick, John Ogdon and Sir John Barbirolli: © UMG Archive

Second picture section

Page 1: [top left] The Hollies in colour: © UMG Archive
Page 1: [top right] Ron Richards: © UMG Archive
Page 1: [middle] 'Strawberry Fields Forever'/'Penny Lane' record cover: © Vinyls/Alamy Stock Photo
Page 1: [bottom left] Ken Dodd: © UMG Archive
Page 2: [top] John Lennon, George Martin and Ken Townsend in AR studios, 1967: © Camera Press/Frank Hermann/Globe Photos 1967
Page 2: [middle] Jacqueline du Pré/Daniel Barenboim: © UMG Archive
Page 2: [bottom left] Morecambe and Wise: © UMG Archive
Page 2: [bottom right] John and Yoko: David Nutter/© Yoko Ono Lennon
Page 3: [top] Suvi Raj Grubb: © UMG Archive
Page 3: [middle] Pink Floyd at mixing desk, AR: © Andrew Whittuck/Redferns/Getty Images
Page 3: [bottom] *Dark Side of the Moon*: © Pink Floyd Music Ltd
Page 4: [top] 1979 redevelopment floor plan: © UMG Archive
Page 4: [bottom] John Williams supervising music for Star Wars: © Michael Humphreys
Page 5: [top] Kate Bush: © UMG Archive
Page 5: [middle left] Sale of the Century, overhead: © UMG Archive
Page 5: [middle right] Ken Townsend, Sale of the Century: © UMG Archive
Page 5: [bottom] 'Abbey Road Presents the Beatles', 1983: © UMG Archive
Page 6: [top] *Anthology* sessions: photo owned by Ringo Starr and used with permission

PICTURE ACKNOWLEDGEMENTS

Page 6: [middle] Spice Girls: © UMG Archive
Page 6: [bottom] Lara Croft: unknown
Page 7: [top] Travis: © Travis/Fran Healy
Page 7: [bottom] Amy Winehouse and Tony Bennett: © Kelsey Bennett/ courtesy of Sony Music Archives
Page 8: [top] Brockhampton: © Brockhampton/Ashlan Grey
Page 8: [bottom] Abbey Road zebra crossing, 8 August 2019: © Leon Neal/Getty Images

Chapter openers

Chapter 1: Fred Gaisberg and William Sinkler Darby: courtesy EMI Archive Trust
Chapter 2: Sir Edward Elgar opening ceremony: courtesy EMI Archive Trust
Chapter 3: Al Bowlly: © Pictorial Press Ltd/Alamy Stock Photo
Chapter 4: Noël Coward and Yvonne Printemps: courtesy EMI Archive Trust
Chapter 5: George Martin: © UMG Archive
Chapter 6: Cliff Richard and the Shadows live in Studio Two: © UMG Archive
Chapter 7: Hazel Yarwood: © UMG Archive
Chapter 8: Beatles on steps: © UMG Archive
Chapter 9: The Hollies: © UMG Archive
Chapter 10: *Sgt Pepper* sessions: © Apple Corps Ltd
Chapter 11: Pink Floyd: © Jill Furmanovsky via rockarchive.com
Chapter 12: Roy Harper with the Grimethorpe Colliery Band, 1975: © Adrian Boot
Chapter 13: Jacqueline du Pré: © UMG Archive
Chapter 14: Ken Dodd: © UMG Archive
Chapter 15: *Dark Side of the Moon* record cover: © Ben Molyneux/Alamy Stock Photo
Chapter 16: Steve Harley: © UMG Archive
Chapter 17: Ken Townsend: © UMG Archive

PICTURE ACKNOWLEDGEMENTS

Chapter 18: *Star Wars* sets down in God's aircraft hangar: © Michael Humphreys
Chapter 19: *Private Dancer* record cover: © Records/Alamy Stock Photo
Chapter 20: Paul Weller, Paul McCartney and Noel Gallagher: © Brian Rasic/Getty Images
Chapter 21: Shot of the studio from the street: © UMG Archive
Chapter 22: Kanye West at Abbey Road, 2005: © Andy Willsher/Redferns/Getty Images
Outro: Nile Rogers: © Jill Furmanovsky via rockarchive.com

Ephemera

Page 19: 1931 announcement: courtesy EMI Archive Trust
Page 94: Walter Legge memo: © UMG Archive
Page 133: Beatles handwritten recording confirmation, '66–'67: © UMG Archive
Page 150: Mellotron use, '68–'69: © UMG Archive
Page 153: Pink Floyd/Beatles/Dakotas diary, 22 March 1967: © UMG Archive
Page 155: Norman Smith memo, Pink Floyd broken mic: © UMG Archive
Page 167: Jeff Jarratt job offer: © UMG Archive
Page 181: Jacqueline du Pré diary, 24 April 1967 (Haydn C Major): © UMG Archive
Page 195: Ken Dodd/Beatles diary, 8 June 1967: © UMG Archive
Page 202: The Zombies session sheet, 10 July 1967: © UMG Archive
Page 246: Sale of the Century news story: © UMG Archive
Page 253: Ramon Lopez Studio One letter, 31 January 1980: © UMG Archive
Page 270: Flock of Seagulls penthouse confirmation: © UMG Archive
Page 345: Mia Farrow booking and payment sheet: © UMG Archive

Endpages

Two architectural drawings – house exterior and studios interior: courtesy EMI Archive Trust

Index

INDEX

INDEX

INDEX

INDEX

INDEX

INDEX

INDEX

INDEX

INDEX

INDEX

INDEX

INDEX

INDEX

About the author

David Hepworth is the author of the bestselling books *1971: Never A Dull Moment, A Fabulous Creation* and *Uncommon People*, was involved in the launch and editing of magazines such as *Q, Mojo, The Word* and *Smash Hits* and was one of the presenters of the BBC's telecast of Live Aid. He lives in London with more records than he could ever possibly get round to listening to. Some of these were made at Abbey Road.